EP 10/01/00 29.95

Blues Singers

BLUES SINGERS

*Biographies of
50 Legendary Artists
of the Early 20th Century*

by DAVID DICAIRE

McFarland & Company, Inc., Publishers
Jefferson, North Carolina, and London

Cover art by Stephen Shoemaker

Library of Congress Cataloguing-in-Publication Data

Dicaire, David, 1963–
  Blues singers : biographies of 50 legendary artists of the early
20th century / by David Dicaire.
      p.   cm.
  Includes discographies (p.   ), bibliographical references (p.   ),
and index.
    ISBN 0-7864-0606-2 (sewn softcover : 50# alkaline paper) ∞
    1. Blues musicians—United States—Biography.   I. Title.
ML400.D53   1999
781.643'092'273—dc21
[B]   99-16594
                                                                  CIP

British Library Cataloguing-in-Publication data are available

Manufactured in the United States of America

McFarland & Company, Inc., Publishers
  Box 611, Jefferson, North Carolina 28640
  www.mcfarlandpub.com

Contents

Introduction

Some of the most brilliant and influential names in American and international music of the twentieth century belong to the blues pantheon. Robert Johnson, Muddy Waters, T-Bone Walker, Bessie Smith, B. B. King, and John Lee Hooker are just a few of the innovators whose contributions have not only dictated the course of modern music but have also cast a long musical shadow that will reach far into the next millennium. Ironically, the two styles of American music that have borrowed most extensively from the blues—jazz and rock—have been accorded more respect.

The blues have never reached the prestigious position afforded to jazz or inspired the mass hysteria associated with rock and roll. Jazz has been performed in famous concert halls and the best nightclubs, and rockers, who began by entertaining in specifically designed rock venues, eventually graduated to the largest arenas in the land. In contrast, the blues were heard on the sly in roadhouses. The great names of jazz and rock and roll sound like royalty—Duke, Count, and the King—but blues musicians were nicknamed Muddy, Wolf, Gatemouth, and Hound Dog. Jazz was considered cool and hip, and rock was hailed as golden, but the blues were taboo and called the devil's music.

Yet the blues are part of the foundation of American music. Long before jazz exploded onto the scene and the big band sound swept the country, the blues had been born and had matured. Later, when the blues had a baby, it was christened rock and roll. If it were not for the motherly guidance of the blues, the childhood histories of jazz and rock would read like those of orphaned waifs.

To truly appreciate the blues, one must understand the past—and with the blues, the past goes very deep.

The birth of the blues can be traced back to the rhythms and chants

1

of African music that have existed since the dawn of humankind. When the ancestors of blues singers were seized and transported from their homeland to work as slaves on the plantations of the Southern states, they brought with them their music.

Stripped of their freedom and dignity, the slaves clung to their music as one of their only links to their distant homeland. From their very first days in America the slaves continued to create a distinct musical form. Unfortunately, since none of it was documented, an entire chapter of American music is lost to history.

On the plantations, the music underwent an important evolution. Once the music of ceremony and communication, the African chants and rhythms were now used to lighten the heavy workload and remind the slaves of their natural position in the universe. The invented lines that a lead slave would holler in the field, followed by the response calls from the workers in a line, were the first loosely structured forms of blues to be sung in America.

Another change to the ancestral music was in the types of instruments the slaves used to make sound. Unable to bring their traditional instruments along with them, and without access to the materials they had used to fashion their lost xylophones, ivory trumpets, reed flutes, and talking drums, the slaves were forced to improvise and test their knowledge and skill to craft crude instruments to accompany their singing.

Because they were forced to learn some English, the slaves also learned the rudiments of European folk music, which the first settlers had brought with them from the Old World. The slaves were able to assimilate the foreign concepts of European folk ballads with their own developing style of music to create a cohesive sound.

With black populations living in different regions, various strains of the blues emerged. Although unique forms of the blues were developed in many of the Southern states, the Mississippi Delta became the cradle of the blues.

The Mississippi Delta is the largest delta in the United States, stretching from Memphis, Tennessee, to Vicksburg, Mississippi, covering over 12,000 square miles. Two thirds of the physical landscape is above sea level, while the other third is marshland. The Delta is mainly a flat land of cotton and soybeans with a warm climate that creates an extended growing season.

The other natural ingredient in the recipe that makes up the Mississippi Delta is the mighty Mississippi River. The Mississippi is economically one of the three most important rivers in the world. But it is more than just a vital commercial waterway; it is also a symbol of movement, travel, and freedom—three crucial themes found in blues music. But the great Mississippi also has a dark side, an ability to lash out, causing prolonged misery and permanent scars to those who live by its banks.

The Mississippi River was only one potentially negative force in the lives of the black people living in the Delta and throughout the South. Poverty, disease, starvation, murder and illiteracy were common conditions—and continue to some extent to this day. The various elements of this brutal life were assembled into a musical form, creating the purest and deepest strains of the original Delta country-blues.

A hundred years later, the blues remain a potent musical force despite being amplified, urbanized, citified, intensified, and crossbred with jazz, rock, soul, country, and pop. No matter what cosmetic changes the blues have undergone, the roots of the music can never be altered or denied. The longevity and influence of the blues on American and international music dictate that the genre deserves respect.

After all, the blues are more than mojo moans. The blues go much deeper than a simple three-chord, twelve-bar progression with repetitive lyrics.

The blues are a subtle and methodical musical language requiring the precise use of refined techniques and a deep understanding of human nature. A good blues performer is able to capture every emotion in the human condition. No genre of music is even close to equaling the blues in style, range, and eminence.

Although the twentieth century saw hundreds of blues singers, this book is dedicated to the blues pioneers, innovators, superstars, and cult heroes who were instrumental in shaping the course of popular music from early on. All of the performers featured in this book were born before 1940. They were the first wave of blues singers to bring the secrets of the blues to the international stage. The fifty artists portrayed in this book are the outstanding musicians who lived for their art and often paid a terrible price for their mastery of the blues.

While the book concentrates on those born before the beginning of World War II, it is not my intention to discredit or slight the brilliant blues musicians born after 1940. The genre is alive today and owes its vibrancy to many modern-day blues practitioners. The blues exist at a grassroots level, where clubs are plentiful and festivals are common occurrences across the United States and around the world. The blues spirit is kept alive and strong by the road warriors who travel from one place to another, logging thousands of miles to spread the magical message ignited by the men and women featured in this volume.

In respect to the depth and breadth of blues styles, this book has been divided into five distinct categories. To give some feeling for how the styles developed, the musicians are presented in order of their birth.

The first section focuses on the Mississippi Delta bluesmen and features many of the country-blues pioneers including Charley Patton, Son House, Skip James, and Robert Johnson. The second section is titled "The Chicago Blues School" and features Muddy Waters, Big Bill Broonzy, Howlin' Wolf, Elmore James, Magic Sam, Otis Spann, and others who were instrumental in making Chicago the northern blues mecca that dictated the course of popular postwar music. The third section, "The Texas Blues Tradition," is dedicated to the rich force of the Texas bluesmen. The fourth section looks at women's vast contributions to the blues. The fifth section, "Blues Outside the Mississippi Delta," consists of blues singers born outside of the Delta and Texas who made an important impact on the music.

The most important common characteristic of the fifty artists profiled in this book is their commitment to the blues. Although other forms of music have received greater adulation, the blues truly represent the past, present, and future of American and international music. The blues are not a trend, wave, or fad; they are an original and enduring rich tradition that continues to prosper and grow in stature like the names who have carried the torch so proudly for so long.

PART ONE

The Mississippi Delta Bluesmen

The Mississippi Delta is the cradle of the blues and has produced more important contributors to the genre than any other region in the world. The earthy tones of the guitar-dominated music took shape in the late nineteenth century. By the beginning of the twentieth century, the Delta bluesmen were ready to make their mark on the world with their gritty, chilling guitar work and sandpaper vocals.

Charley Patton was the first country-blues great. He laid down the foundation that inspired a million imitators.

Eddie "Son" House traveled and recorded with Patton and carved his own reputation with his sharp, bottleneck slide technique.

Skip James, the leading exponent of the Bentonia style of Mississippi blues, delivered a completely different sound than Patton or House. With his uniquely expressive brand of blues, James added a new dimension to the rough, course Delta style.

Big Joe Williams, a fervent supporter of the Delta style throughout his career (which spanned over fifty years), never surrendered his art for commercial gains.

Robert Johnson, the shadowy figure whose sixty-year-old scratchy records continue to influence musicians even today, remains the greatest in blues history in the minds and hearts of many blues fans.

Robert Jr. Lockwood, the only bluesman to have ever received private guitar lessons from Robert Johnson, was never able to escape his mentor's shadow. Lockwood's star shined the brightest as part of the King Biscuit Live Radio Show when he sat in with Sonny Boy Williamson II.

Johnny Shines, a devoted country-blues artist, had an association with the enigmatic Robert Johnson that both helped and hurt his career.

John Lee Hooker, one of the greatest blues poets of the modern era, remains an enduring ambassador of the blues. His throbbing and intense rhythms have spawned a legion of imitators.

Albert King, armed with his crosscut saw guitar, was a premier stylist of the modern blues sound. Like Hooker, he also made a huge impact on the rock crowd.

B. B. King, the sultan of the single-note run, is arguably the biggest influence on modern guitarists. While there have been many great guitar stylists in the past hundred years, King occupies his own velvet throne.

The above ten men are featured in this book, but there are others who were also dedicated practitioners of the Delta-style blues. We must never forget the efforts of Willie Brown, Mississippi Fred McDowell, Bukka White, Arthur "Big Boy" Crudup, Tommy McClennan, Tommy Johnson, and Henry Stuckey. The Mississippi Delta bluesmen represent the apogee of original blues music.

CHARLEY PATTON (1891–1934)

Pony Blues

The Delta blues style—the driving rhythms, the slashing slide guitar, the earthy vocals, the extreme lyrics that reflect difficult times—can trace its origin to the late nineteenth century. Unfortunately, none of the pioneers who forged the primitive Delta blues style ever had the opportunity to record their music. Therefore, the burden of delivering the secrets of the Delta blues to the international stage fell squarely on the granite shoulders of the next generation. The first blues singer to record in the Delta style gave the world his "Pony Blues." His name was Charley Patton.

Charley Patton was born in April 1891 in Edwards, Mississippi. Although originally from the hill country, better economic prospects brought the Patton family to the Delta. It proved to be an important turn of events because it was on the Dockery plantation that Patton befriended Henry Sloan, one of the early Delta bluesmen who had never been lucky enough to record his own songs. Sloan became Patton's mentor and carefully tutored the budding musician.

By his early twenties, Patton was one of the better-known bluesmen in the Mississippi Delta as he roamed about in his native surroundings and beyond playing at local events. He traveled the dusty roads, sometimes by himself, sometimes with faithful companion Willie Brown. Despite acquiring a name for himself throughout the Delta and neighboring states, Patton was thirty-eight before he was given the chance to record any songs.

His first recording session occurred in 1929 after a chance meeting with white record store owner, Henry Spier, who had important musical connections to Paramount Records in Richmond, Indiana. Although unfamiliar with the recording studio, Patton cut fourteen sides for the label, including "Pony Blues," which became a minor hit in the South. The song later became a Delta staple and was part of every young guitarist's repertoire.

After the session, Patton returned to his life in the Delta. Because of his new stature in Delta blues circles, he experienced rough treatment from the elder bluesmen who had never been given the chance to record. But in the eyes of aspiring young singers, Patton was a hero, especially to one Robert Leroy Johnson.

Patton's second recording session took place in 1930, in Grifton, Wisconsin, once again for the Paramount label. On this occasion, Patton brought along Delta fiddler Henry "Son" Sims, whose fiddle work greatly enriched the thirteen sides the two cut in just a few days. With this second recording session under his belt Patton became a certified Delta country-blues star.

By his third recording session—in 1930, in Grifton, for his old label— Patton was more comfortable with the equipment of the recording studio and began to experiment. He brought along master slide guitarist Eddie "Son" House, traveling companion Willie Brown, and popular Delta pianist Louise Johnson. This small band created an entire wall of sound compared to the thin wail of a solo Patton with his acoustic guitar and left foot providing his rhythm section.

By 1934, Patton was the champion of the Delta blues. He was also a very sick man, but this did not stop him from participating in one last recording session, in New York City for the American Record Company. He made the trip with his wife, Bertha Lee, and cut thirteen sides for his new label, including "Oh Death." The song eerily foreshadowed the future events of his life.

Patton and his wife returned home to Indianola, Mississippi, where on April 28, 1934, he died of a heart ailment. He was only forty-three years old.

Charley Patton's contribution to the blues cannot be overstated. He was the first Delta country-blues star and established a style that was copied a thousand times over. He was an innovator whose showmanship and style stretched the parameters of the blues for his generation and all those that followed. After his death, Patton became a cult hero in the eyes of many young blues performers such as Muddy Waters, Robert Johnson, and Elmore James.

Patton was the first Delta bluesman to bring wide-scale attention to the style. He possessed a passionate and untrained guitar style that matched the power and grit of his gravely voice. He was not just a bluesman from the Delta, he *was* the Delta, raw and genuine. His sparse style reflected the stark landscape of the Delta region.

Despite his importance, apart from "Pony Blues," Patton never enjoyed much commercial success; however, his music remains a vibrant portrayal of the life of the common black man at the turn of the century. His biggest hit, the aforementioned "Pony Blues," dealt with the freedom of travel. It was dangerous for a black person to ramble about the South in the 1920s, but Patton risked his own safety to play the blues, which only emphasizes his determined love for his art. His song "High Sheriff Blues" dealt with the injustices of Southern law, something Patton experienced firsthand. His song "High Water Everywhere" sharply depicted the misery of the devastating floods, one of the many misfortunes that were common in the life of the black population. Patton's song "High Water Blues" shared the same theme as T-Bone Walker's "Trinity River Blues" and Bessie Smith's "Back Water Blues."

The realistic element of social commentary in Patton's music makes him one of the very first folk-protest singers, a title he shares with others, including Huddie "Leadbelly" Ledbetter, Mississippi John Hurt, Pete Seeger, and Woodie Guthrie. There are no official records, but because of their nomadic nature and coinciding birthdates there is a definite possibility that Patton and Leadbelly, the two great fathers of protest music, may have crossed paths at least once.

However, Patton was more than just a talented musician who excelled in different musical styles; he was also a showman extraordinaire. Charley Patton was a genuine clown with his guitar. He played the guitar in a number of unorthodox positions, tricks that T-Bone Walker and Jimi

Hendrix would later pick up on. Patton tapped his guitar, hit it, and kicked it up in the air with his foot, only to catch it with one hand and then whirl it over his head.

But Patton was no fool. He was a performing genius in the way he made his guitar a part of his act. He may have been the first bluesman to give his guitar a woman's name, a habit later copied by many other blues guitarists, notably B. B. King, who affectionately calls his Gibson beauty "Lucille."

Patton's legendary showmanship influenced a legion of future blues and rock singers, including Howlin' Wolf, James Brown, Jimi Hendrix, Chuck Berry, Little Richard, Jerry Lee Lewis, Jim Morrison, The Who, and many more. Furthermore, Patton's stage pyrotechnics planted the initial seeds of the "shock rock" theater that exploded in the 1970s with the exploits of the ghoulish Alice Cooper and the fire-breathing, blood-spitting, tongue-wagging masqueraders, Kiss.

But Patton's immense contributions to the blues is not just restricted to his musical abilities and stage persona. It was Patton who developed the blueprint for a bluesman's lifestyle which the rock and roll crowd would copy and expand later in the century. He followed the road of excess with reckless abandon in hopes of arriving at the palace of wisdom. He knew few boundaries. He was married at least ten times and fathered an unreported amount of offspring. He was jailed on at least a dozen different occasions for minor offenses, such as vagrancy. He was an incessant traveler roaming the Southern states to play his blues. He struggled between good and evil, a personal war he never won. He made quick decisions and often lived bitterly with the consequences.

But Patton's influence on other bluesmen is undeniable. Eddie "Son" House, Robert Johnson, Muddy Waters, Elmore James, Willie Brown, Johnny Shines, John Lee "Sonny Boy" Williamson, and Howlin' Wolf are just a few of the bluesmen who eagerly followed the path Patton blazed.

Although he exerted a large influence on a number of important bluesmen, perhaps he had the most effect on Robert Johnson, considered to be the greatest blues singer ever to have lived. Like Patton, Johnson possessed every quality an aspiring Delta bluesmen needed to become famous. But he was a more gifted musician than Patton and was able to bring the Delta blues style greater respect. Patton's influence on Johnson is incalculable.

Another dimension of Patton's legend is his running candidacy for the title as the first rock star. His harsh musical style, bohemian ways, pensive lyrics, stage antics, and career ambitions are characteristics that make up the biographies of hundreds of rock stars who definitely borrowed a page or two (and in some cases entire chapters) from Patton's book. One can only imagine how far he would have stretched the unwritten rules of rock if he had been born in the modern era.

In 1980, Patton was inducted into the Blues Foundation Hall of Fame. It is only fitting that he should be elected to the rock and roll hall of fame because the genre owes much to this pioneer. Although Patton may not have been the most gifted blues singer in history, no one can deny his legendary status. Patton was the first Delta country-blues star, a principal innovator, and a reputed cult hero. He remains the most vital link between the unrecorded Delta blues style of the nineteenth century and the recorded work of the twentieth century. He also gave the world his "Pony Blues" and sparked a fire that will burn for eternity.

Discography

Devil Sent the Rain Blues, Paramount 13040.
Charley Patton 1929–1934: The Remaining Titles, Wolf WES 103.
The Immortal Charley Patton, 2 discs, Origin Jazz, 1 and 2.
Charley Patton: The Complete Recorded Works, 3 discs, Pea Vine PCD 2255–2257.
Charley Patton: Founder of the Delta Blues, Yazoo L 1020.
King of the Delta Blues: The Music of Charlie Patton, Yazoo 2001.

EDDIE "SON" HOUSE (1902–1988)

Preachin' the Blues

There is a special relationship between gospel music and the blues—they are like cousins twice removed. Religion played an integral part in the lives of the black population, and it was no coincidence that nearly all of the great blues singers first sang in the choirs of their churches. However, despite a definite affinity between the two musical styles, each represents a very separate and different world. No other blues artist tried to combine both the religious and blues realms than the man famous for "Preachin' the Blues." His name was Eddie "Son" House.

Son House was born Eddie James, Jr., on March 21, 1902, in Riverton, Mississippi, near Clarksdale, the home of future blues singer John Lee Hooker. Like most black children of his generation, Son had few career choices. He could either be a sharecropper working long hours in the dusty fields for little pay, become a preacher and dedicate his life to spreading the good word of the Lord, or pursue the vagabond lifestyle of a bluesman.

House's career decision was facilitated when his parents separated and seven-year-old Eddie moved out of the Delta to live with his mother in Louisiana. Mrs. House, a women with strong religious principles, declared her home a "no blues zone," which killed one career elective. Perhaps because of his mother's strong religious convictions, Eddie was drawn by the powerful message of the church and even became a Baptist pastor before his twentieth birthday. Since he was obliged to obtain his musical fix from a source other than the blues, he was stirred by gospel, which was instrumental in shaping his crisp vision of the struggle between good and evil.

Upon his mother's death, House returned to the Mississippi Delta and worked as a fieldhand, fulfilling the first career choice. An ambitious young man with a streak of adventure in him, he moved to east St. Louis in the mid–1920s to work for a better wage in a steel plant. A year later he was back in the Delta. At this point in his life he decided to explore the third career choice: the life of an itinerant bluesman.

Although his mother had denied him access to blues music, House was no stranger to the primitive jungle rhythms of the most popular music in the South. Born to be a bluesman, House quickly became adept at the guitar. For the next few years he gained valuable experience playing fish fries and other events, as a solo artist or accompanied by other Delta bluesmen.

The decision to become a bluesman created some conflict with House's moral philosophy. Once a Baptist pastor who swore off the temptations of loose women and alcohol, House reverted completely and embraced the debauchery commonly associated with the blues. However, there was a price to pay for living one's life on the edge, as he was soon to find out.

In 1928, House murdered a man. While the facts of the incident were unclear, his act earned him a stint at Parchman Farm, a Mississippi penitentiary with a tough reputation. House faced the prospect of a long prison sentence, which placed his blues career in severe jeopardy. However, he was miraculously freed some time later and resumed the life of a traveling bluesman. House had been spared an unkind fate.

In an attempt to put his past troubles behind him, House resettled in Lula, Mississippi, in 1930. Here he formed a partnership with country-blues star Charley Patton and Patton's frequent traveling companion, Willie Brown. The trio performed all over the South and, in 1930, recorded for the Paramount label in Grifton, Wisconsin.

Son House was a definite asset in a recording studio. He had honed his guitar skills until he was undoubtedly the greatest slide guitarist of his day. He had a courageous voice and was keen to be in on any session, even if the pay was minimal, which it often was at the start of the Great Depression. House was reportedly paid thirty dollars for his session work, which in those days was a large sum of money to someone who had struggled financially his entire life.

The sessions were instrumental in House's blues career. Not only was he a featured guest on the sides Patton cut but he also recorded a few sides of his own, including his signature piece, "Preachin' the Blues," which depicted in vivid detail his internal emotional struggle between the forces of good and evil. He also recorded "Dry Spell Blues" and "My Black Mama" during that particular session.

House returned to the Delta, and it was around this time that he met an aspiring bluesman named Robert Johnson, who, like House, would unsuccessfully walk the same tightrope between good and evil. The extent of House's influence on Johnson is undetermined, but there is no doubt that the elder bluesman contributed to young Robert's bottleneck style. House became an infrequent traveling companion of Johnson's, more so after the death of his good friend Charley Patton. Upon Patton's death, House automatically inherited the top spot in the Delta blues hierarchy, if only for a short time before being dethroned by Robert Johnson.

With Johnson's mysterious death in 1938, House carried on the Delta blues tradition with his faithful traveling friend, Willie Brown. In 1941, House became one of the many country-blues artists to be recorded by the legendary Alan Lomax for the Library of Congress series. House made more recordings a few months later.

These sessions produced many House classics, including "Shetland Pony Blues," "Delta Blues," "Special Rider Blues," "Low Down Dirty Dog

Blues," "Depot Blues," "The Key of Minor," "Am I Right or Wrong?," "Country Farm Blues," "The Jinx Blues Part 1 and 2," and others.

Perhaps due to the death of his good friend Charley Patton or the series of disturbing events leading to the death of Robert Johnson, House moved out of the Delta in 1943 during the middle of World War II and went to live in Rochester, New York. He was accompanied by Willie Brown.

At this time, House turned his back on the music world. He earned his living working at menial jobs, including a long stint working for the railroad. His previous career as an important bluesman seemed forgotten by the public. While House was away from the blues scene, many changes occurred. The electric blues were created and perfected by such men as T-Bone Walker, Lonnie Johnson, B. B. King, and many others. The Chicago blues school with Muddy Waters at the helm was in session and rock and roll—which borrowed heavily from the country-blues that House had helped make famous—was born.

By the end of the 1950s folk-blues became all the rage. A feverish search for the old masters began. From the dusty blues highway emerged Son House, who was hailed as a mythical figure by the white audience primarily responsible for the renewed interest in folk-blues. The sudden and unexpected reappearance of House was the stuff of legends and read like a Hollywood movie script.

House's blues career, which had been dormant for two decades, became as vibrant as it had during his best days. In 1964 his popularity soared. He played the 1964 Newport Folk Festival to enthusiastic reviews. His country-blues style was the music to listen to despite the onslaught of the British invasion led by the Beatles.

House appeared at Carnegie Hall in 1965, a prestigious honor for any musician and one that had not been accorded to him during his peak years in the 1930s. His appearances at the Newport Folk Festival and Carnegie Hall led to a recording contract with CBS Records. House had not made any recordings in over twenty years, but he cut an album entitled *Father of the Folk Blues*, which received considerable attention and guaranteed more concert dates.

The official name of *Father of the Folk Blues* was later changed to *Death Letter* and featured the title song as well as "Perline," "Louise McGhee," "Empire State Express," "Grinning in Your Face," and "Levee Camp Moan."

House became a fixture on the major folk and blues festivals all over the United State and Europe in the latter part of the 1960s. The lost years of idleness were quickly made up for in a very brief span of time. For a few short years, House enjoyed the accolades that he had deserved all along. The height of his popularity culminated in 1969 with the documentary entitled *Son House*.

But House's good fortune was curtailed at the beginning of the 1970s. Due to his advanced age, he began to suffer from poor health. He still managed to appear at a handful of blues festivals, but by the mid–1970s his career was over. In 1976, he decided to make Detroit his new home, as it was one of the original northern meccas (along with Chicago) of the blues, and he remained a resident of the Motor City the duration of his life.

In a gesture of true justice, House was elected to the Blues Foundation Hall of Fame in 1980, the year of its inception. On October 19, Eddie "Son" House died. He was eighty-six years old and one of the last surviving original Delta bluesmen.

Son House was a blues star on two separate occasions in his long blues career: first in the Mississippi Delta during the 1930s and again upon his triumphant return to the music scene in the 1960s. Unfortunately, between those two peaks was a very long drought. However, despite the lull in his career, House deserves a place alongside other Delta blues contemporaries such as Charley Patton, Skip James, Robert Johnson, Willie Brown, and Big Joe Williams.

Despite his uncanny musical talent, House never sold a lot of records, which unfortunately restricted his popularity and, in the eyes of many blues historians, his overall contribution to the blues. Although it is true that House was never a great commercial success, his music contained a passion that has rarely been duplicated by other blues singers.

House had a furious guitar style that may have lacked proper technique, but never genuine emotion. While he may not have been an accomplished guitarist, he excelled on bottleneck slide, which became his true blues legacy. In the Mississippi Delta, all aspiring bluesmen broke the neck off a bottle and melted it until the jagged end was smooth and even. Then they slipped it on the little finger of their fretting hand and slid it up and down the strings. The haunting sound of broken glass sliding up and down the metal strings produced an extension of the bluesman's voice. With bottleneck, a guitarist could match whatever moanful and intense sounds his voice could produce. In a compiled list of the greatest slide guitarists of the twentieth century, Son House earned a definite name on the honor role with other master sliders Duane Allman, Robert Johnson, Muddy Waters, Elmore James, and Earl Hooker.

It is a fact that when a young Muddy Waters wanted to learn how to play slide guitar his first role model to copy was Robert Johnson. After Johnson's death, Waters began to study the style of Son House, who lived near the young Mississippian. Robert Johnson, Waters's first case study, learned his slide technique directly from House. Another slide guitarist who was greatly influenced by House was Elmore James, considered to be the greatest of the post–World War II slide guitarists until the arrival of Duane Allman.

Another dimension of House's contribution to the blues was his uneasy relationship with Robert Johnson. It is a well-known blues story of how House and Willie Brown were totally unimpressed with Johnson the first time they heard him play. But a few months later, they met up again at some juke joint and Johnson played like a man possessed, which fueled rumors of his supposed deal with the devil. There was a definite depth to their relationship that went beyond musical boundaries. Johnson represented something House knew was dangerous and figured was best to stay far away from. However, House was drawn to Johnson's genius, knowing full well that young Robert was a genuine blues talent.

While he remained unappreciated, if House had been a younger man when he was "discovered" in the 1960s, he would have made a serious impact on rock music. He played the guitar with the same furious emotion of Jimi Hendrix and Johnny Winter. House also lived the life of a rock star, as did his cohort Charley Patton. The temptations of women and alcohol were often too strong for House to resist. This struggle between good and evil was taken up by Johnson, whose personal battle was well documented in many of his songs.

Son House was part of a style in blues history that often does not receive the respect it deserves. Ever since the introduction of electric blues, the primitive sound of the acoustic Delta style has been restricted to the back pages of the blues history books. Of course, without the emergence of the Delta sound the contemporary blues would not exist in the form that it does today.

Although he never became a superstar, House delighted audiences with his hard-edged blues style. The spontaneity of his music is the essence of the blues. There is no doubt that the contribution of this blues pioneer should never be forgotten, but hailed as the work of a master who gained fame preachin' his blues.

Discography

Mississippi Delta, Folkways 2467.
The Real Delta Blues, Blue Goose 2016.
Son House and Robert Pete Williams, Live Roots 501.
Son House: The Complete Library of Congress Sessions 1941–42, Travellin Man TM 02.
Son House: The Legendary 1941–42 Recordings in Chronological Sequence, Arhoolie/Folklyric 9002.
Delta Blues: The Original Library of Congress Sessions from Field Recordings 1941–1942, Biograph BCD 118 ADD.
Father of the Delta Blues: The Complete 1965 Sessions, Columbia 48867.
Death Letter, Edsel EDCD 167.
Blind Lemon Jefferson/Son House, Biograph BLP 12040.
Blues from the Mississippi Delta: Son House and J. D. Short, FV 9035.

SKIP JAMES (1903–1969)

I'm so Glad

One of the saddest recurring stories in blues history is how many of the greatest stylists—men and women who had a profound influence on the course of popular music—remained neglected before they were "discovered" through the music of white blues bands. One of the goals of this book is to remind the domestic and foreign music world of the vast contributions made by the blues artists throughout this century. Unfortunately, many of these blues singers—including Skip James—are deceased. There is no doubt, however, that if Skip James could see that his contribution to the blues has not been overlooked he would be very glad.

Skip James was born Nehemiah James on June 9, 1902, in Bentonia, Mississippi. Because his father was a Baptist minister who played the guitar and organ, religion and music dominated Nehemiah's early life. When he was eight years old, Skip (a nickname he obtained from classmates) obtained his first real guitar and immediately began to teach himself how to play his prized instrument. His self-taught instructions were the start of his long quest to unlock the mysteries of the blues.

Skip's strongest musical education, however, came when he struck up a friendship with hometown blues hero Henry Stuckey. Stuckey took James under his wing and taught him not only the rudiments of the guitar but also the ways of a bluesman. The pair often performed at country events, where James gained invaluable experience.

By his teens James was a proficient musician, and he wandered his native Mississippi and other Southern states working in a mill by day and playing juke joints and rent house parties at night. James spent some time in Memphis playing in speakeasies, but he eventually returned to Jackson, Mississippi. He was determined to become a famous blues singer.

After serving a long apprenticeship by honing his skills on the road, James was ready to record. In 1930, Mississippi record store owner H. P. Spier, who had the foresight to record Charley Patton and Son House for posterity, added Skip James to his list of blues artists. James traveled to Grifton, Wisconsin, where in a few days he recorded a couple dozen sides for the Paramount label. Although there were some true gems in that collection, including "I'm so Glad," "Hard Times," "Farish Street Rag," "Hard Luck Children," "Cherry Ball Blues," "4 o'Clock Blues," "Yola my Blues," "Devil Got my Woman," and ".22-20 Blues," James never reaped any real financial rewards.

Like all other record companies, Paramount was hit hard by the Great Depression and only released a handful of the songs James had cut during his recording session. His records did not sell well, and his dream of fame and fortune slipped away. Totally frustrated by his lack of progress as a bluesman, James turned his back on the blues and returned to the religious world of his youth. Because of his rash decision, the blues community had lost one of its most highly individualistic stylists. He would not resurface until the great folk-blues revival thirty years later.

Although he bitterly swore that he was done with the blues, James was first and foremost a musician. Throughout the rest of the decade he earned a living by playing gospel music in his father's church in Dallas, Texas. He named his group the Dallas Texas Jubilee Singers and further proved that he had turned his back on the secular world for the sacred life by being ordained a Methodist minister in 1942. A year later he became a Baptist minister and toured the South preaching the word of the Lord.

He eventually returned to his native Mississippi in 1945. For the next twenty years he earned his living as a laborer in the mining and timber industries. Later he worked as a janitor, a tractor driver, and a plantation overseer. His days as a recording artist seemed lost in another dimension of time.

During his absence from the music world the blues underwent several drastic changes. The Mississippi country-blues, of which James had been a respected practitioner, were taken up North by Muddy Waters and others and amplified and citified. A few years later rock and roll arrived into the world kicking and screaming. With the rock and roll craze subsiding in the early 1960s for various reasons, the folk-blues sound became the great new rage.

By the early 1960s the hunt for old bluesmen was a full-time occupation for many blues historians and scholars. Forgotten blues singers of the 1920s and 1930s were the hottest property in the music business. After all, what greater source of folk-blues could there be than the originators? The search for Skip James ended when he was found in a Mississippi hospital by Stefan Grossman, a white blues intellectual. However, conflicting accounts claim that the combined efforts of John Fahey, Bill Barth, and Henry Vestine eventually located James. Skip James returned to the life he had left behind thirty years before. The whole experience read like a movie script for the old bluesman.

Suddenly, the opportunities that had been denied him during the first phase of his career were now abundant. He became an in-demand performer appearing at concert halls all over the country, including the Newport Folk Festival in Washington, D.C., in 1965. Seemingly overnight, a blues career that had lain dormant for three decades was resurrected with unmatched fervor. James played other festivals as a solo artist and sometimes teamed up with another "rediscovered" bluesman, Mississippi John Hurt. James was welcomed with open arms by an audience that had not even been born during the first phase of his career.

With renewed courage, James entered the recording studio. He recorded two albums in the mid–1960s, *Skip James Today* and *Devil Got my Woman*, both on the Vanguard label. The albums sold well, and he was once again doing what he loved best—playing music for the people. This time around he was able to make a living at it and received much-deserved respect.

Although he had recruited an entirely new legion of fans, James began to enjoy his greatest success after his song "I'm so Glad" was covered by the 1960s psychedelic, prototype heavy metal group, Cream.

Eric Clapton, a tireless champion of past blues masters, personally saw to it that James received the royalties that belonged to him. Cream's version of "I'm so Glad," which was far removed from the original effort by James, didn't stop Clapton from giving one of his early blues heroes a writing credit for the song.

Aware that the golden opportunities were found primarily on the East coast instead of the poverty-stricken Mississippi Delta, James moved to Philadelphia in 1966. He lived in the City of Brotherly Love for three years. On October 3, 1969, Skip James, one of the original Delta bluesmen, died of cancer. He was sixty-seven years old.

Although Skip James was never a great commercial success, and his recording catalog is rather slim in comparison to others in the genre, his contributions to the blues should not be ignored. James was a brilliant stylist, an inspirational country-blues musician who also invoked a strong influence on later generations of blues artists.

The career of Skip James can easily be divided into two distinct phases: The first occurred during the late 1920s and 1930s and brought him little fame or financial success. The second phase, in the 1960s, marked his triumphant return to the blues world and proved much more rewarding on a personal and artistic level.

As a stylist, James is easily separated from other Delta country-bluesmen because of his devotion to the Bentonia school of blues taught to him by his mentor, Henry Stuckey. The Bentonia school of blues featured an intricate fingerpicking scheme that James mastered to such an extent that he was nicknamed the "Fastest Fingerpicker in the World."

James was able to distinguish himself as the leading exponent of the Bentonia school of blues, as indicated by a second nickname he earned: "Mr. Genius." With his penchant for minor chords, strange tunings, and chilling falsetto vocals, James was able to create special worlds that reflected the moods of the Mississippi Delta landscape: eerie nights of dense fog, dark shadows, and screeching owls infected with full moon fever; somber, rainy days with strong winds whistling through bare trees; a warm spring night with the soothing sounds of chirping crickets and bullfrogs' mating moans; and lonely, cold days when large swarms of blackbirds swooped through the dark gray Mississippi skies like lost souls.

Despite his scant volume of recorded material, the unique, deep, earthy tones of James's special country-blues were a direct influence on future bluesmen. The Delta blues of Skip James were just one strain that the migrating bluesmen took up North to create the Chicago sound. His

Bentonia school of blues was an essential part of the bottomless blues well from which both the Chicago blues and rock and roll drew their inspiration.

The Skip James sound also helped shape the musical direction of other Delta bluesmen, including Robert Johnson. Johnson, who recorded his songs just a few years after Skip James, stole a page from the professor's textbook and incorporated it into his efforts. The haunting, falsetto phrasings that James used extensively to shape his individual sound are found scattered throughout the most panic-stricken vocals in some of Johnson's most powerful songs, such as "Hellhound on My Trail," "Me and the Devil Blues," and his classic, "Crossroads Blues."

Muddy Waters, Elmore James, John Lee Hooker, Johnny Shines, and Robert Jr. Lockwood are just a few of the other blues artists influenced by Skip James. The high-pitched screaming styles of Little Richard and early Beatles work can trace their roots back to Skip James. Many competent heavy metal vocalists with their exuberant caterwauls also owe a certain musical debt to Skip James.

Because of his importance as a bluesman, in 1992, Skip James was inducted into the Blues Foundation Hall of Fame. Although he might not have sold millions of records or played before stadium-sized crowds, there is no doubt that Skip James with his strong musical skills and deeply individualistic style made anyone who listened to his music very glad.

Discography

Greatest of the Delta Blues Singers, Melodeon 7321.
King of the Delta Blues Singers, Biograph 12029.
She's Lyin', Genes.
Complete Skip James 1931 Session, Yazoo 1072.
Skip James Today!, Vanguard VMD 79219.
Devil Got my Woman, Vanguard VMD 79273.

BIG JOE WILLIAMS (1903–1982)

Poor Joe's Blues

Many of the blues personalities discussed in this book were born in poverty and remained poor throughout their distinguished careers despite making important contributions to the blues. In the era before MTV, multimillion-dollar tours, and large advances, almost all blues singers lived a hand-to-mouth existence. Often, it was their genuine love of the blues that was the driving force behind their creative spark. One of the greatest ambassadors of Delta country-blues constantly lived on the edge of poverty, but still managed to give the world his Poor Joe Blues. His name was Big Joe Williams.

Joe Williams was born on October 16, 1903, in Crawford, Mississippi; the moniker "Big" came later. Williams was the son of hardworking sharecroppers and one of eleven children. He developed a love for the blues at an early age; because of the harsh economic conditions he was forced to make his own guitar out of a cigar box like many other young aspiring bluesmen of his generation. When he was fifteen he obtained his first manufactured guitar and immediately began to unravel the secrets of the blues universe.

Williams left home when he was a young man to seek his fortune, and he wandered throughout the South picking up valuable work experience and future material for his songs. He padded his résumé by taking jobs at levee and lumber camps. When he wasn't sweating in the sun earning his meager wages, Williams was playing his guitar at a small venue to pick up extra money.

In his early twenties, he became a member of the Birmingham Jug Band, which toured with the Rabbit Foot Minstrel Revue. In 1930—the same year that other Delta bluesmen like Charley Patton and Son House were recording their songs—Williams cut a few songs for the Okeh record label with the Birmingham Jug Band. Some of the songs to emerge from this session included "Whoopee Blues," "Tell Me Baby," and "The Dead Gone Train." Although they became concert favorites, none of these songs earned Big Joe any substantial money.

From his earliest days as a blues performer, Williams realized that a country-blues singer's career was established on the road. He earned a reputation as a fantastic roamer who constantly traveled from one small town to another, playing back-home places for very little money. "Have guitar, will travel" was Big Joe's personal motto. His traveling ways eventually led him to St. Louis in the early 1930s, where he hooked up with his cousin, J. D. Short.

J. D. Short was another Delta musician who was heavily influenced by Charley Patton. Short recorded a few sides for Paramount and Vocalion in the early 1930s, but never made a large splash in the blues scene. Big

Joe was given a chance to record for the Bluebird label, and it immediately paid off. His song "Baby, Please Don't Go" was recorded in 1935 and has been a favorite of blues and blues-rock acts for the past sixty years. Williams struck gold again in 1941 with his interpretation of "Crawling King Snake," a song that fellow Delta bluesman John Lee Hooker incorporated into his repertoire. The song later found its way onto The Doors' last studio album, *L.A. Woman*.

About this time, Williams and his friend Peetie Wheatstraw became entrepreneurs. They operated a nightclub in St. Louis. The place was a hot spot for local bluesmen and continued to prosper until Wheatstraw's death. Williams continued to play at the club until it closed in the mid–1950s.

Throughout the 1940s Williams kept making records. As part of the Bluebird roster of musicians, Big Joe participated in the recording sessions of others, including Wheatstraw, John Lee "Sonny Boy" Williamson, Charley Jordan, and Robert Nighthawk. While Williams was establishing his blues reputation in mid–1930s, a pair of future blues greats, the blues shouter Big Joe Turner and pianist extraordinaire Pete Johnson, were carving out a name for themselves in Kansas City clubs, planting the seeds that would eventually evolve into the second boogie-woogie craze.

Unlike other country-blues artists who disappeared during the late 1940s and for much of the 1950s, Williams continued to perform and record. He kept the country-blues tradition alive while Muddy Waters and his cohorts were busy creating the loud electric urban blues on Chicago's south side. Big Joe's dedication to the traditional Delta rural blues is a testimony to his fierce spirit and individuality.

Although Williams never laid down any serious roots throughout his career, he eventually settled in Chicago for a while in the early 1960s. His decision to move came after the death of his wife, which made Williams reflect on his current life. Big Joe used Chicago as a home base for a few short years before moving down South and eventually settling in Georgia.

With the folk music revival of the 1960s, Big Joe's patience paid off handsomely. Seemingly overnight, a host of new venues opened up for folk-blues singers like Williams; he became one of the most popular performers touring coffeehouses around the country. He also appeared in a number of folk and blues festivals along with Skip James, Son House, and Mississippi John Hurt. For the first time in his musical career, Big Joe was earning enough money to make a living without an outside job.

During the golden era of folk music in the 1960s, Williams met and often shared the same stage with Pete Seeger, Richie Havens, Arlo Guthrie, Sonny Terry, Brownie McGhee, and a young Bob Dylan. He earned the respect of the "folkies" with his working-man vocals and distinct guitar style of repeated riffs and insistent, throbbing intensity.

Always eager to be in on any gig, Big Joe jumped at the chance to play in Europe as part of the American Folk Blues Festival in 1968. He delighted audiences with his authentic, rich, Delta country-blues acoustic sound. While the financial rewards may not have been excessive, the international exposure added to his solid reputation as a genuinely exciting performer.

As a proud champion of his musical heritage, Big Joe was pleased to spread the magic of Delta-style blues throughout the world. In 1974, Big Joe brought his Delta-inspired music to Japan, breaking new ground as one of the first blues artists to tour in the Land of the Rising Sun. He gave the blues-deprived Japanese a delicious taste of genuine American regional down-home music.

His fondness for touring aside, Williams also kept his blues career alive with constant recordings for a variety of companies who favored his hard-edged country-blues. With the many repackaged albums, he was assured of having material available to the buying public.

In the 1970s, in an attempt to reach a wider audience Williams appeared in *The Devil's Music—A History of the Blues* and *Good Mornin', Blues*, documentaries that were the early forerunner of MTV-like videos. Big Joe Williams, a well seasoned performer, was aware of the visual advantages that a documentary provided over the limitations of a sound recording. One can only wonder at the videos that Big Joe Williams and some of the other early blues singers would have created if the technology had been available to them.

Williams continued to record and perform despite advancing age. He was one of the last surviving Delta country-blues artists. With his death on December 17, 1982, in Macon, Georgia, the blues world, particularly the Delta tradition, lost one of its most fervent artists.

Big Joe Williams was a dedicated bluesman who, despite a genuine guitar sound and unique vocal ability, never became a big star. His innovations on the guitar were interesting, and he was a competent songwriter. He will forever be known as the man who wrote "Baby, Please Don't Go," which has been covered by such diverse talents as Van Morrison (while a member of Them), AC/DC, and American guitar showman Ted Nugent both as a member of the Amboy Dukes and as a solo artist. The Motor City Madman's live version—found on his party album *Double Live Gonzo*—is a masterpiece and a tribute to the universal appeal of Big Joe's songwriting abilities.

Big Joe's intriguing guitar sound was the result of a combination of factors. Although he started out playing a regular six-string guitar, he kept adding strings until he made the nine-string guitar his instrument of choice, allowing him to explore an incredible range of musical possibilities.

Big Joe's guitar style was very unique. He was able to hit the bass strings with clarity while using the bottleneck slide to maximum effect. His hypnotic rhythms and use of minor tunings were also important elements of his unique style. Add to the mixture that Big Joe only knew about fifty chords, and it is amazing that he was able to produced the thundering wall of sound that became one of his musical trademarks.

Although none of his compositions ever equaled "Baby, Please Don't Go" in commercial popularity, some of the better-known songs featured in his repertoire included "Mink Coat Blues," "Sloppy Drunk Blues," "Throw a Boogie," "Yo Yo Blues," "Brother James," "49 Highways," "Stack O' Dollars," "Providence Help the Poor People," and "Worried Man Blues." Many of Big Joe's songs were a reflection of his experiences on the road.

He was a wayward spirit who drifted down lonesome roads, hopped railroad cars, and caught rides on the backs of moving wagons. The engine that always drove him from one town to the next was the sheer joy he received from playing the blues in front of a live audience. He logged hundreds of thousands of miles over the years to spread the beauty of the blues, a music that flowed through his veins. Big Joe made the traveling country-bluesman the unappreciated hero of the blues world and in his later years was one of the genre's greatest ambassadors.

Also, like Johnny Shines, Williams had a large influence on modern acoustic blues. Big Joe was a distinguished member and therefore held a direct connection to the first generation of Delta bluesmen including Charley Patton, Son House, Robert Johnson, Bukka White, and Willie Brown. In fact, Williams played and traveled with many of the aforementioned blues singers.

In 1992, Big Joe Williams was inducted into the Blues Foundation Hall of Fame, an honor that was long overdue. Throughout his career he remained loyal to the Delta country-blues and never changed his style.

Although he remained fixated on one musical style, Williams delighted fans everywhere he went with his special brand of "Poor Joe's" blues.

Discography

Nine String Guitar Blues, Delmark DD 627.
Blues on Highway 49, Delmark DD 604.
Shake Your Boogie, Arhoolie CD 315.
Big Joe Williams, Vol. 1 (1935–41), RST Blues Documents BDCD 6003.
Big Joe Williams, Vol. 2 (1945–49), RST Blues Documents BDCD 6004.
Piney Woods Blues, Delmark 602.
Back to the Country, Testament 2205.
Delta Blues—1951, Trumpet 702.
Early Recordings 1935–1941, Monlith 2047.
Big Joe Williams, Arhoolie 1002.
Big Joe Williams, Arhoolie 1053.
Blues Bash with Lightnin' Hopkins, Olympia 7115.
Big Joe Williams and Sonny Boy Williamson, Blue Classics BC 21.
Stavin' Chain Blues (with J. D. Short), Delmark DD 609.
Throw a Boogie Woogie (with Sonny Boy Williamson), RCE 9599-2-R.

ROBERT JOHNSON (1911–1938)

At the Crossroads

In the Mississippi Delta and communities throughout the South the folkish idea that the blues were the devil's music was a rigidly accepted truth. It was commonly believed that blues singers were shadowy individuals who moved under the cover of the moon and sang songs directly inspired by Satan. Blues singers were deemed shiftless, unstable, and dissolute characters who gathered at country crossroads on moonless nights to have their guitars fine-tuned by the dark force. In exchange for their souls the bluesmen were guaranteed a life of fame, easy money, and women. No other singer in blues history embodies this concept more than Robert Johnson.

Robert Leroy Johnson was born on May 8, 1911, in Hazlehurst or Robinsville, Mississippi. Like his true birth place, the details of Johnson's life are sketchy. It is known, however, that he was the illegitimate result of a love affair between Julia Dodds—who was married to Charles Dodds at the time—and Noah Johnson.

Robert's early years were brutally harsh because his stepfather was not thrilled by his wife's affair, and he was unduly cruel in his treatment of Robert. The rejection and unstable family life that was part of his childhood is a scar he carried into adulthood. His unfulfilled quest for love and acceptance resurfaced in the lyrics of many of his songs.

Young Robert was not enchanted with the life of a sharecropper, and because he had little chance at a formal education he turned his attention to music as his chosen career. Johnson learned how to play the harmonica before he took up the guitar. Much happier to sit and practice his guitar or harmonica all day than go out and break his back in the cotton fields, Robert's attitude only intensified the rift between him and his new stepfather, Willie Willis. As a result of this harsh family life, Robert escaped and went to the home of his biological father, Noah Johnson. Not long after, he proudly assumed his father's surname.

He was married at age sixteen, but tragedy struck when he lost his wife, Virginia Travis, in childbirth. Two years later, Johnson married Calleta "Callie" Craft, but later abandoned his bride for the life of the traveling blues musician. He roamed the Mississippi Delta and other parts of the South and began his dedication to mastering the blues. Like all other musicians, Robert was inspired by those who had unlocked the very mysteries he so desired to discover. The three greatest influences on him were the original country-blues minstrels, Charley Patton, Son House, and Willie Brown.

Charley Patton is regarded as the first of the great Delta blues singers. He was a credible bluesman and a solid entertainer; he also epitomized the lifestyle of the blues musician. He indulged in everything to excess: booze, cigarettes, and women. His influence on Johnson was extremely important.

Eddie "Son" House was Patton's opposite in some ways, but also his running buddy. He brought two very important aspects to blues music: The first was his painful vocal harmonizing, which sent chills down the spines of those who listen to it, even today. The second was his uncanny use of the bottleneck slide guitar technique. House flirted on and off with the lifestyle of a blues singer and seemed to be one of Johnson's few somewhat stable musical examples.

Of the three primary influences, Willie Brown was Johnson's most frequent traveling partner and is immortalized in the song "Crossroads Blues." Brown was a very capable slide guitarist and was well known in and around the Delta, but he never achieved the wider appeal of either Patton or House.

If Charley Patton is credited with establishing the blueprint for a bluesman's lifestyle, then Robert Johnson is responsible for breathing life into the plan. Johnson was a traveler, often alone, drifting down dusty highways, a shadowy figure lurking around the Mississippi Delta like a cat on an important adventure. He was a real ladies' man; a complete list of the women that Johnson courted is unobtainable, but many references can be found scattered through the cycle of songs he wrote and performed with painful brilliance. He drank and smoked excessively (one of only two known photographs of Johnson shows a cigarette dangling from his lips).

From his adventures he collected the raw material that formed the foundations of his songs. In 1936, he was finally able to record the pieces of life stories that he had perfected while on the road the past ten years. His first recording session occurred on November 23–27, 1936, in a San Antonio, Texas, hotel room. In a few short days he recorded "I Believe I'll Dust my Broom," "Sweet Home Chicago," "Terraplane Blues," "Crossroads Blues," "Come in my Kitchen," "Walkin' Blues," and other songs that would be copied over the next sixty years. The song "Terraplane Blues" later became a minor hit in the South.

Johnson's only other recording session took place between June 19 and 20, 1937, in a Dallas warehouse. From this second stint other classics added to the Johnson canon were "Travelling Riverside Blues," "Love in Vain," "Hellhound on my Trail," and "Me and the Devil Blues."

He took his blues back on the road and ended up in Greenwood, Mississippi, one summer night at a juke joint with the intent of playing there. Robert Johnson, the original backdoor man, had supposedly carried on a flirtatious relationship with the owner's wife. He was given strychnine-laced whiskey and died a few days later. The possessed young genius left us when he was only twenty-seven years old.

Robert Johnson was a brilliant, tortured musician whose intensity and passion for the blues has never been matched. He was an innovator of extreme significance, and his influence on all of blues music is immeasurable. Despite his vast contributions to the blues, Johnson's name is tainted among certain blues circles because of his supposed association with the devil.

A tale that has been repeated so many times that it has been accepted as truth describes a young Robert at the beginning of his career who was such a poor guitarist that the other bluesmen would not let him share the stage with them. At this time Johnson disappeared to learn his craft. When he met up with the others only a few months later they were stunned by what he was playing. How could anybody master the guitar in such a short time? Seemingly overnight, Johnson had gone from fledgling bluesman to guitar genius, which fueled rumors about a supposed deal at the crossroads with Papa Legba, the darkest spirit in voodooism.

It is utter nonsense to diminish Johnson's status as a bluesman based on the concept of a deal with the devil. The blues has been called devil's music by those living in the South, notably Baptist ministers, who warned their congregations of the evils of the most potent music. To this day, the blues musician is still somewhat taboo in the American South.

Robert Johnson was not the first musician rumored to be associated with the devil. More than a hundred years before anyone had heard of him, Niccolò Paganini, the virtuoso violinist, was believed to have struck a bargain with the devil. In plays and books, the devil has always been attached to stringed instruments. In Goethe's play *Faust*, the devil appears with bow and violin. In Charlie Daniels's song "The Devil Went Down to Georgia," the devil appears as a fiddler, who bargains with a young, talented fiddler boy. It is a tired concept that has worked its way into the mythology of many cultures.

While the legend of the crossroads makes for a good story, there are people who fundamentally believe it. Was the crossroads myth an old southern superstition spun by Baptist ministers to keep their flock in check, or was there some validity to it? Did Johnson know a good gimmick when he heard it and cleverly used the lurid pact with the devil story to his best advantage? Did Johnson ever *deny* the crossroads pact? Did he ever claim its authenticity? Because there are no records of his opinion on the subject, and it is impossible to ask him, we are left guessing at his true feelings about the rumors that surround his legend.

The only other source available to put the debate to rest are the songs Johnson gave to the world, but even these are controversial. Were the references to the devil found scattered throughout his songs an attempt to further confuse the issue of his supposed involvement with the dark forces? Or were the songs that evoked the devil's name a tribute to his own incredible vision of the struggle between good and evil?

The best three examples of Johnson's songs that imply a relationship with Satan are "Crossroads Blues," "Me and the Devil Blues," and "Hellhound on my Trail."

In "Crossroads Blues," perhaps his most famous song, Johnson writes and sings openly about the consequences of making a pact with the devil. The song is a chilling, eerie portrait of his vivid imagination. He convinces the listener that he *did* strike a bargain with the devil in exchange for his mastery of the blues. He also believes a genuine self-exorcism will help him escape his bargain. But in the last lines of the song Johnson sings with the honest, painful insecurity of someone who may be living on borrowed time.

In "Me and the Devil Blues," Johnson writes and sings openly about walking hand in hand with the devil. Perhaps he was making references to yielding to the many temptations that came his way that are also a large part of his legend.

But easily the most disturbing song is "Hellhound on my Trail." The panic-stricken chill of Johnson's voice conjures up the haunting image of the diabolic pursuit by Papa Legba, the fiendish creature, huge and black, with firey eyes and jagged, sharp teeth dripping with blood.

It is interesting to note that "Me and the Devil Blues" and "Hellhound on my Trail" were both recorded during his last recording session, shortly before his untimely death. Was Johnson crying out for help in these songs? Did he feel that his time was near? Could he feel the beast breathing down his neck?

Even after his death, the rumors persisted. The fact that very little is known about Johnson's life only strengthens the legend of the crossroads bargain. After his death it is rumored that his guitar vanished and that he was buried in an unmarked grave. Add to the confusion that Robert Johnson may not have died at all, but disappeared from the blues scene altogether, and the water grows muddier.

It is unfortunate that Johnson's contributions to the blues have been overshadowed by the legend of the crossroads. Whatever the clouded circumstances that shroud his life, there is no denying his musical importance. Robert Johnson is the most crucial blues musician who ever lived, and his contributions to the blues and modern music as a whole are simply immeasurable. His pungent guitar lines executed with the same passion as his vocal projection were the perfect vehicle to highlight his intense lyrics. His bottleneck slide guitar work was exceptional, producing a distinctly plaintive sound. Johnson was also very adept at using his thumb to steadily hit the bass strings.

He provided the world with a cycle of songs that formed the basis of rock and roll. His lyrics were a mixture of simplicity and brilliance exploring many themes of daily life—fleeting love affairs, a longing to be elsewhere, the sadness of parting. His songwriting revealed an extremely skilled and disciplined composer who often delivered lines of equal length and defined a strict order in the way a song should develop that is used almost without change in rock music. Many of his songs began with an instrumental introduction followed by several verses, interspersed with a solo, a last verse, and an ending that incorporated the beginning, giving the song a cyclical edge.

Johnson not only gave the world a collection of songs that are as vital and universal as many of the classical works from the great composers, he also brought to the guitar a new, fresh sound. He is credited with introducing the turnaround chord. He was able to rearrange Patton's boogie-woogie walking bass line into a much clearer sound that was adopted by the masters of Chicago's electric blues school.

Without Robert Johnson the face of popular music as we know it today would be drastically different. The changes he brought to the creation of the blues were innovative and have been copied by everyone who has ever dared to play the blues. His unique and driving style is the yardstick by which all other blues singers are measured. But perhaps more than any other blues musician, Robert Johnson lived and died for his art. The blues were in his blood and he devoted his entire short life to the musical genre. Fittingly, Johnson was inducted into the Blues Foundation Hall of Fame in 1980 and the Rock and Roll Hall of Fame in 1986.

While "Terraplane Blues" was a minor hit in the South, Johnson enjoyed very little commercial success. He was never a star during his lifetime, but his life took on mythical proportions after his death. How could someone who never recorded a national hit create so much excitement sixty years later?

The sheer fascination of the Robert Johnson story certainly provides part of the answer. Because the details of his life are so sketchy it creates intrigue. Some twenty years after his death a renowned scholar finally decided to provide the world with a complete (as much as possible) biography of Johnson. By then, the facts were even more scarce, which only added to the mystery. If the complete details of Robert Johnson's life were known on the same level as, say, Muddy Waters, our curiosity would probably cease to exist.

Johnson is also one of the few bluesmen who after his death left behind a small coterie of disciples, including Johnny Shines, Robert Jr. Lockwood, Muddy Waters, and Elmore James. These and other musicians touched by the Johnson mystique played many of his songs and retained the best phrases of his guitar vocabulary, passing it on to the next generation. His song catalog has been raided over the years by a variety of blues singers, including Eric Clapton, The Rolling Stones, Elmore James, The Allman Brothers, Led Zeppelin, Muddy Waters, Lynyrd Skynyrd, and countless others.

Perhaps a true measure of the power of Robert Johnson's cult status and importance as a bluesman lies in the fact that although he recorded only twenty-nine tracks during his lifetime—a scant contribution when compared to the large output of other blues singers such as John Lee Hooker, B. B. King, Lightnin' Hopkins, and Bessie Smith to name a few—Johnson remains a blues giant. In 1990, *The Complete Recordings of Robert Johnson* were made available in CD Format. The disc, which was expected to sell only a few thousand copies, instead sold an incredible half-million units and won a Grammy. The disc prompted the issuing of complete catalogs of other blues legends by various companies.

Nearly sixty years after his death, Robert Johnson continues to color and fuel popular music. His music, charisma, and mystique remains as fresh today as it did so long ago. The universal cult of Robert Johnson gathers no dust; it is ageless.

Perhaps on warm Southern nights when the wind passes through the Mississippi Delta, the musical shadow of Robert Johnson can be heard best. Is it the master of the blues moaning to the moon, or the strains of a desperate man on the run from the restless, evil spirit of the dark side?

Such is the legend of Robert Johnson.

Discography

The Complete Recordings of Robert Johnson, Columbia C2K 46222.
Robert Johnson King of the Delta Blues Singers, Columbia C30034.
King of the Delta Blues Singers, Columbia CL1654.
King of the Delta Blues Singers Volume II, Columbia C3003/CBS (UK) 64102.

ROBERT JR. LOCKWOOD (1915–   )

The Master's Apprentice

The blues are a special kind of magic that requires focused instruction. It is a long-standing tradition in the blues that those who hold the key to the magic pass the secrets down to the next generation in order to keep the blues spirit alive. When one young boy was first introduced to his mother's new boyfriend, he had no idea how much his life was about to change forever. For the new beau was no ordinary person; he was Robert Johnson, arguably the greatest blues musician to ever live. From that moment on, Robert Jr. Lockwood became the master's apprentice.

Robert Jr. Lockwood was born on March 27, 1915, in Marvel, Arkansas. His family later moved to Helena, Arkansas, a thriving blues community that was part of the intricate network of Southern blues hubs. Lockwood developed an early interest in music and was studying the organ before Robert Johnson arrived in his life. Upon meeting Johnson, Lockwood immediately switched to playing the guitar.

Lockwood's mother, Estelle, nicknamed Stella, found the slightly built Johnson to her liking, and soon they were living together. Lockwood was about thirteen years old when Johnson became an integral part of his life, and young Robert looked up to the elder bluesman as a father figure.

By the time he was fifteen, Lockwood was accomplished enough on the guitar so he could play at juke joints and house parties. Sometimes he traveled with Johnson, but most often Lockwood teamed up with the young harmonica player Rice Miller, who eventually adopted the *nom de blues* of Sonny Boy Williamson. They roamed the Delta together, sharing good times in much the same way that Johnny Shines and Robert Johnson would just a few years later. Lockwood also played with Jimmy Rogers, who went on to play in the Muddy Waters Band.

Lockwood difted for a few years throughout the South, just another bluesman trying to make a name for himself. He eventually made his way to Chicago to try his luck out there. Although he recorded for the Bluebird label, the Windy City did not suit his tastes. Besides, his old friend Sonny Boy had a much better offer for him back in Arkansas.

Williamson, by this time, was a successful disc jockey for radio station KFFA in Helena, Arkansas, on the "King Biscuit Time," which was very popular with audiences throughout the area. Williamson was hired to plug King Biscuit flour on his show and in return was able to announce to the radio listening audience the location of his next concert. A spot on Sonny Boy's show was the best advertising a bluesman could get in the Helena area, and Lockwood was able to secure some performances from his appearances on the well-known radio show.

Robert spent the entire decade of the 1940s in his native Arkansas, but he eventually returned to Chicago to resume the career he had begun ten years before. He immediately began performing in the blues clubs in a band ensemble, adding his distinct guitar touches to the nasty, electric blues sound that was going down. In 1953, Lockwood joined the impressive stable of blues stars on the Chess label. While with Chess, he had the opportunity to work with Otis Spann, Little Walter, Jimmy Rogers, and Sunnyland Slim. Lockwood eventually recorded some of his own songs as a solo artist for various independent labels. None of the recordings he made brought him any serious financial or critical rewards, however.

By the end of the 1950s Robert Jr. Lockwood was a frustrated man. He had poured all of his energy into building a blues career in Chicago, but had not made any major progress. Throughout his stay in the Windy City he had constantly been overshadowed by other artists, like Muddy Waters, Howlin' Wolf, Little Walter, Buddy Guy, Otis Rush, Freddie King, Magic Sam, Elmore James, and Willie Dixon.

Lockwood, who had traveled extensively throughout the country, chose Cleveland as his new home. The Lake Erie city was not well known as a blues center. For the first time in his career he formed his own band and assumed the role of leadership. Robert prospered in Cleveland, where he played a vital and active part in the city's burgeoning blues community.

Although he lived in Cleveland, Lockwood often returned to Chicago to record for a variety of labels, which enabled him to supply his fans with a continuous stream of new music. While the blues revival of the 1980s did not catapult Lockwood onto the international blues scene, it did unite him with Johnny Shines to record two albums: *Hangin' On* and *Mister Blues Is Here to Stay*.

The album *Dust my Broom* features songs by both of these blues artists. Shines contributed "Fish Tail," "Cool Drive," "Ain't Doin' no Good," and "Ramblin'." Lockwood's cuts include "Dust my Broom" and

"Party." The record is interesting because it features the traditional blues of Shines versus the more progressive sound of Lockwood. It would have been a true blues treat to hear these two Johnson disciples make a record with the master himself.

While not recording landmark albums with Shines, Lockwood continued to travel and perform throughout the country and various parts of the world. Some of the songs he recorded as a solo artist include "Black Spider Blues," "I'm Gonna Train my Baby," "Little Boy Blues," "Take a Walk with Me," and "I'm Gonna Dig Myself a Hole."

In 1989, Lockwood was inducted into the Blues Foundation Hall of Fame. At the ripe old age of seventy-five, he became a businessman by forming his own record company. Lockwood's album *What's the Score* was the label's initial title release.

Like Shines, Lockwood has long been associated with Robert Johnson, which has been both a blessing and a curse. The mysterious existence of Johnson has continued to intrigue generations of blues fans and the release of *The Complete Recordings of Robert Johnson* in 1990 sparked a new wave of interest in his life and music. Suddenly, Lockwood was cast into the spotlight and was able to turn some of the attention devoted to Johnson into performance dates and special interviews for his own benefit.

Lockwood has carried the Johnson flag with pride, despite the fact that his own musical contributions have often gone unnoticed. It is a fate that Shines has also suffered. Lockwood handled the attention thrown his way because of his association with the legendary Johnson in a professional and dignified manner. His ability to speak clearly and truthfully of past blues history has made Lockwood one of the most important ambassadors of the blues. He remains prominent in blues circles.

Although Robert Jr. Lockwood possesses a furious and unique individual guitar style and has earned the respect of the entire blues world, he has never seemed to live up to his full potential. Lockwood has always been on the verge of breaking away from the magnetic pull that kept him in the shadow of his famous stepfather, but never seemed to be able to make a complete break.

Considering his remarkable guitar work, it is intriguing that Lockwood was never able to totally disassociate himself from the aura surrounding the famous Robert Johnson. Inspired by his stepfather's precious teachings, Lockwood's guitar work contained more than just clichéd phrasing's from Johnson's guitar vocabulary. Lockwood used Johnson's guitar licks as the foundation of his own sound, and incorporated a jazz feeling as well as the clever use of unusual chord structures, giving his Delta acoustic style a special flavor. Lockwood also played a twelve-string acoustic guitar—a rarity in the blues and an honor he shares with the great folk-blues artist Leadbelly.

Another of Lockwood's major contribution to the blues is as a virtual studio hired gun. He participated in numerous sessions, becoming an important part in the development of the Chicago blues sound. Although he was never recognized for his lead guitar work, Lockwood became an accompanist of the highest order whose delicate guitar passages added special tones to the songs that established the rhythmic structure and spurred everyone's imagination to greater heights in the band ensemble.

Although his guitar skills are impressive, Lockwood's singing voice is not particularly outstanding, which was one of the reasons he never became a bigger star. Throughout his career, Lockwood has been relegated to a lesser role. When he performed on Sonny Boy Williamson's radio show there was no doubt that the great harmonica player was the true boss. In Chicago, Lockwood was a sideman for Chess, but was never offered to record his own songs. When he performed in the Chicago blues clubs he was an accompanist, never a bandleader.

Although he may have played a secondary role as a session man and on stage, as a practicing blues historian Lockwood occupies a prominent position. Lockwood is one of only a handful of bluesmen who can claim participation in a variety of blues eras. He was one of the genuine Mississippi blues singers who was a keen practitioner of the Delta style. He made enormous contributions to the rise of live radio shows as part of the King Biscuit Time with Sonny Boy Williamson. He was a behind-the-scenes character in the golden era of electric Chicago blues. He is also responsible for spreading the blues to different cities, particularly Cleveland.

Lockwood played with all the greats: Muddy Waters, Howlin' Wolf, Elmore James, Little Walter, Willie Dixon, Freddie King, Sonny Boy Williamson II, Johnny Shines, Buddy Guy, Otis Rush, Magic Sam, and, of course, the enigmatic Robert Johnson. From a purely historical point of view he is an invaluable link in the blues chain. He was also an outspoken champion of the Mississippi Delta blues tradition and has kept the flame burning brightly for many decades.

More than anyone else (including Johnny Shines), Robert Lockwood holds the key to unraveling the many mysteries that shroud the life and career of Robert Johnson. It may be true that Johnson showed Shines a few chords, heavily influenced Muddy Waters, and taught Elmore James some slide technique, but Lockwood remains the *only* bluesman that Johnson personally tutored. As the master's apprentice, Lockwood was able to unlock the secrets that allowed him to make the brooms dance with incredible fury.

Discography

The Baddest New Guitar, P-Vine PCD 2134.
Steady Rollin' Man, Delmark DD 630.
Contrast, Trix 3307.
Lockwood Does 12, Trix 3317.
Plays Robert on Robert, Black and Blues 33740.
What's the Score, Lockwood Records.
Mister Blues is Here to Stay (with Johnny Shines), Rounder 2026.
Hangin' On (with Johnny Shines), Rounder 2023.
Dust my Broom (with Johnny Shines), Flyright CD 10.

JOHNNY SHINES (1915–1992)

A Traveling Companion

In the dusty, poverty-stricken days of the Great Depression, basic survival was a struggle for many in the South, especially penniless bluesmen who traveled throughout the regions playing for what little money was thrown their way. Yet despite the severe hardships, it was a time of good friends, constant travel, brief and intense love affairs, and the blues. One of the greatest roamers during the Great Depression who kept the flame of traditional Delta blues alive was also the frequent traveling companion of the shadowy Robert Johnson. His name was Johnny Shines.

Shines was born on April 15, 1915, in Frayser, Tennessee. His family moved to Arkansas when he was just a little boy, and it was here that Johnny learned how to play guitar. From the moment he tasted the blues,

Shines was attracted to its dark, strange powers and just couldn't get enough of it. Once he became proficient enough to play in front of an audience he began to hobo all over the South working the juke joints and fish fries.

With the thousands of small blues venues spread throughout the South and the hundreds of blues musicians who played them, it was pure fate that Johnny Shines and Robert Johnson met. There was an instant camaraderie between the two traveling bluesmen, which was strange because Johnson was somewhat of a loner who preferred to slip down the quiet country roads on his own.

Johnson was a few years older than Shines and more experienced in the ways of a traveling bluesman. Nevertheless, both shared a love of women, alcohol, the blues, and travel. The pair roved all through the Mississippi region, scurrying through the woods under the stark moonlight like two crazy teenagers on a wild adventure. In fact, Shines *was* a teenager.

The pair walked for miles in the darkness through the creepy Delta landscape where unexpected shadows lurked around every corner. They had to worry about the strict presence of southern law enforcement, which raised concerned eyebrows at the sight of two young black blues (devil's music) singers slipping and sliding through the Mississippi night with reckless abandon.

Perhaps the highlight of their road experiences together occurred when they crossed the border into Windsor, Ontario, and performed on the Elder Moten Hour, a well-known gospel radio show. This was one of the last appearances the duo made together; soon after they dissolved their unofficial partnership and went their separate ways. Any chance at a possible reunion was shattered with the sudden death of Robert Johnson.

After Johnson's death, Shines disappeared from the blues scene for some time, but later resurfaced in Memphis. A man who had once been in the company of the elite, Shines was just another shabbily dressed street musician who played his battered acoustic guitar in parks and on street corners. Although Memphis was a thriving blues community, few opportunities existed for him there. In 1941, in hopes of giving his sluggish career new life, he moved to Chicago. At the time, the Windy City was earning a growing reputation as the Northern mecca of the blues.

Shines instantly found work in his new home playing the local blues clubs with a variety of artists, including Tampa Red, Big Maceo, Big Bill

Broonzy, Sonny Boy Williamson, Memphis Slim, Sunnyland Slim, and other denizens of Chicago's thriving blues family. Despite a lifetime of playing the blues, Shines had never recorded any of his own material. In Chicago, he was finally given the opportunity to put his songs on vinyl.

In 1946, he cut fourteen sides for the Okeh label; however, none of the songs were ever released. In 1950, he became one of the first bluesmen to record for Chess. But Chess Records, which would go on to record the legends of the electric urban blues, had little interest in the acoustic Delta style. In a further attempt to have his name known before the public, Shines recorded for the J.O.B. label, but the records didn't sell very well because of the trend toward the loud, amplified blues as practiced by the likes of Muddy Waters, Howlin' Wolf, Little Walter, Willie Dixon, Elmore James, and Sonny Boy Williamson II.

Shines also spent some time out on the West coast, where he performed and recorded with fellow Arkansas native Luther Allison. Easy-going Shines thoroughly enjoyed the laid-back California lifestyle. Unfortunately, the sunny California weather and the opportunities that came his way did nothing to enhance his sagging blues career.

Shines returned to Chicago to try his luck there, but as before his hopes were quashed by an unforgiving recording industry. By the end of the 1950s, Shines quit the music business, frustrated over the lack of progress of his stagnant career. A naturally talented individual, he was a perfect example of the lack of promotion that many record companies afforded blues artists. It has always been an unwritten belief among the executives who decide the type of music the public would like to hear that the blues don't sell well. Proper marketing techniques beget sales, but in the case of Johnny Shines it just never happened.

Shines was forced to find work in a factory, and he frequented the blues clubs on the weekends to keep in touch with the music. By the early 1960s a whole new world of opportunity had opened up for the original Delta bluesmen, which was one of the main factors that prompted Shines to resume his blues career. He was eager to begin a new phase of his musical life that would hopefully bring more artistic and financial credibility than his previous attempts.

Shines managed to secure a recording contract with the Vanguard label; when some of his songs were included in the compilation *Chicago/The Blues/Today* his blues career suddenly gained some momentum. He was able to continue recording, and more permanent offers came his way. The coffeehouse circuit and the blues and folk festivals were perfect venues for a Delta country-bluesman like Shines, considered to be a traditionalist. With his solid reputation as a blues performer and historical associations with Robert Johnson, Charley Patton, and Son House, Shines became a busy entertainer.

Always a rolling stone, Shines moved to Holt, Alabama, in 1969, back to his original roots in the South. He spent much of the next ten years touring more than he had before, including during his freewheeling days with Johnson.

Now that Shines was recognized as one of the torchbearers of the original Delta style, he accepted the awesome responsibility of spreading the blues around the world. He performed extensively in Europe and the Far East, playing his guitar-dominated acoustic country-blues with genuine emotion. His brilliant interpretations of the Delta blues enabled the original style to burn brightly amid the onslaught of amplified preferences.

In 1980, after a severe stroke, Shines was forced to cut down on his globetrotting. He still managed to perform a few occasional dates and continued to win over audiences with his special brand of country-blues. He also recorded for such labels as Rounder, Blind Pig, and Hightone. He even recorded a few times with his good friend Robert Jr. Lockwood.

In 1992, Johnny Shines became an honored member of the Blues Foundation Hall of Fame. On April 20 of that year in Tuscaloosa, Alabama, Shines passed away. He had celebrated his seventy-seventh birthday just five days before his death.

Johnny Shines was never a country-blues star of the same magnitude as Charley Patton. His fragmented career, the result of constant relocating, prevented him from every gaining any true momentum. Shines was no great innovator, and his influence on other blues singers was not truly profound. However, despite these obvious shortcomings, Johnny Shines dedicated his entire life to keeping the Delta country-blues flame alive. Although other styles of blues would have proven more profitable, Shines never sold out. He remained loyal to the music that lived in his heart. For him, the blues were a genuine art, not a money-making venture.

Because Shines never scored a number-one hit during his career, he enjoyed very little commercial success. His entire recording catalog is rather slim compared with some of the blues giants, but in retrospect it is much larger than that of his famous traveling partner, Robert Johnson. His contributions as a recording artist exist in his ability to produce country-blues after the style had seen its popularity fade in favor of electric blues.

Shines and his good friend Lockwood endured many of the same frustrations in their careers. Like Lockwood, Johnny's early association with Robert Johnson was both a blessing and a curse. His role as ambassador for the country-blues often involved stories that surrounded his friendship with Johnson. Because of the sketchy details of Johnson's life, Shines was often called to talk about Johnson, and similar to Lockwood, he always did so with great compassion and class. However, while everyone was inquiring about Robert Johnson they forgot about Johnny Shines, whose contribution to the blues was all too often ignored.

Although never a published author, Shines was a living blues historian whose insight into the development of the music was unmatched. Shines was a traveler—literally, but also historically. His life spanned the beginning of the century, when the blues first became popular, and stretched until the last blues revival that occurred in the 1980s, spearheaded by Stevie Ray Vaughan. Through it all, Shines witnessed all the changes in the blues and the personalities that created the music.

Although not a major influence like T-Bone Walker or Muddy Waters, Shines was an inspiration to the school of modern acoustic blues dedicated to keeping alive the spirit of the traditional country-blues. John Hammond, Keb Mo', Kelly Joe Phelps, Rory Block, John Cephas, Taj Mahal, and Bonnie Raitt at the beginning of her career represent just a partial list of the new breed of country-blues who can trace a direct line back to Johnny Shines.

Johnny Shines was an original country bluesman with Delta blood running in his veins. Although his musical contributions never matched those of other blues singers, his name, spirit, and music live on forever. Most important, throughout his long career he refused to change. Although the country-blues road was often a rough walk, Johnny Shines remained the ultimate traveling blues companion.

Discography

Standing at the Crossroads, Testament 2221.
Hey Ba-Ba-Re-Bop, Rounder 2020.
Robert Jr. Lockwood and Johnny Shines, Rounder 2023.
Mister Blues is Back to Stay, Rounder 2026.
Johnny Shines, Hightone HCD 8028.
Traditional Delta Blues, Biograph BCD 121.
Last Night Dream Blues, Horizon 63212.

Traditional Delta Blues, Biograph 121.
The Collection, CBS 44441.
Walking the Blues, Candid 79025.
Dust my Broom: Johnny Shines and Robert Lockwood, Flyright CD10.
Johnny Shines with Big Walter Horton, Testament 2217.
Back to the Country (with Snooky Pryor), Blind Pig BP74391.

JOHN LEE HOOKER (1917–   )

Boogie Child

The blues are composed of many different musical elements of which rhythm is one the most essential parts. Unfortunately, because plantation owners feared that slaves would communicate through the use of coded messages in order to rise up and attack their white masters, all types of percussion instruments were forbidden during slavery. In an effort to retain the magic of their ancestral music the slaves cleverly invented repetitive riffs whose intensity replaced the tones of the African drums. This new rhythm, a complex and subtle musical language, eventually evolved into boogie, the very foundation of the blues and later rock and roll. For the past fifty years the king of this boogie blues rhythm has been the incomparable boogie child, John Lee Hooker.

John Lee Hooker was born in Clarksdale, Mississippi, on August 22, 1917. His early years read like an historical portrait of the life of a black kid growing up in the South in the 1920s. He was no stranger to poverty or hard labor; he received a limited education and spent a good deal of his free time in church. Hooker would never have broken out of the endless cycle of hard work, little education, and awesome grip of the church if he hadn't caught blues fever. His musical education began most naturally with gospel. He enjoyed singing in the choir, but it wasn't long before Hooker discovered the blues, and his life was changed forever.

He was influenced by his stepfather, Will Moore, as well as old-time Mississippi guitarist Garfield Akers. But mostly, Hooker was self-taught. The music was a major attraction, but it was the life of a bluesman that enthralled young John Lee. He particularly liked a bluesman's restless spirit and as a result ran away from home to Memphis when he was only fourteen years old. To support himself, he worked at menial jobs around the city and played his guitar for passersby. The big adventure lasted only two months before he returned to the Delta and his former life. At age seventeen, his restless spirit was recharged; this time he left home for good to seek his fame and fortune.

He returned to Memphis, where he met a young B. B. King. The two future blues greats played a few house parties together. But John Lee grew tired of life in Memphis and drifted east to Cincinnati, arriving there when he was eighteen years old. He stayed in Ohio for three years trying to make it in the music business, but the doors of opportunity remained closed to him. Hooker left Cincinnati and decided to move to another industrial city.

In 1943, John Lee Hooker arrived in Detroit hoping to make a better life for himself by landing a prosperous job in the city's booming wartime car industry. His economic prospects brightened tremendously when he found work in a factory. But even more important was his association with two Detroit-area music businessmen, Bernie Besman and Elmer Barber, who possessed the connections that an aspiring blues singer like Hooker needed. While he waited for his big break, John Lee played in hundreds of clubs and house parties and made enormous contributions to the burgeoning Detroit blues scene.

In 1948, Hooker recorded his first two songs, "Boogie Chillen" and "Sally Mae." The classic "Boogie Chillen" was a smash hit, reaching number one on the R&B chart in 1949. He continued to record for Modern Records, providing the world with "Hobo Blues," derived from his traveling experiences. Other notable Hooker classics of this period include "I'm in the Mood" and "Crawling King Snake." The latter remained one of his signature songs and became a concert staple for dozens of blues-rock bands.

During the early 1950s he continued to write and record songs in his distinct percussive guitar style. Although he claimed authentic Mississippi Delta roots and had been inspired by the original country-blues minstrels Charley Patton and Son House, Hooker never bothered to learn how to play slide guitar. The omission of the bottleneck in his overall guitar sound separated him from the other Delta bluesmen of his generation. Instead, Hooker built his career on the rhythmic unison of his driving guitar style and his unique vocal phrasing. His use of chopped-off word endings carried a primitive, dramatic charge that was hammered home by a functional guitar technique.

In the mid–1950s, Hooker recorded for Chess Records, which brought him in contact with the Chicago blues school of Muddy Waters, Willie Dixon, Elmore James, Howlin' Wolf, and Little Walter. During his brief time on the Chess label, Hooker became one of the prime architects of the electric Chicago blues sound. His deep, Mississippi bullfrog voice; catchy, repetitive riffs; and street-poet lyrics all combined to create a sound that could never be genuinely duplicated, only imitated. His distinct blues vision added a new course to the electric Chicago blues school. He toured with Muddy Waters and other blues singers while sometimes donning the guise of solo performer.

In 1955, he signed with Vee-Jay Records in Chicago and became a fixture with the label until it folded due to financial difficulties. Hooker recorded for more than twenty different labels throughout his career, but he is most associated with Vee-Jay Records. During his time at Vee-Jay, Hooker recorded two classics, "Dimples" and "Boom Boom." The latter song was recorded by The Animals, one of the leading British invasion rhythm and blues bands of the mid–1960s.

Hooker was one of the first blues singers to break through the color barrier. He placed his song "Shake it Baby" on top of white charts, and it became a worldwide hit. "Let's Make it Baby" was on the B side. His crossover success proved that the blues were an international music, not limited to stringent racial boundaries.

Although he remained popular and his records always sold well overall, interest in the blues remained weak until the folk-blues revival in the early 1960s, which catapulted Hooker into the international spotlight. He was an original American folk-blues artist and one of the very best. And, unlike other "discovered" folk-blues singers Skip James, Johnny Shines, Big Joe Williams, Mississippi John Hurt, and Son House, Hooker was not attempting a comeback after twenty years out of the music business. He was a known commodity, which only increased his already substantial drawing power.

Hooker was intelligent enough to capitalize on this golden opportunity, and he became a regular fixture at jazz festivals and on the coffeehouse/folk club circuit. He appeared with a number of folk artists, including the legendary Bob Dylan at Gerde's Folk City in Greenwich Village in 1961. Dylan, whose first album consisted mainly of reworked blues numbers, was still a few years away from international fame. While the two were heading in different musical directions the unlikely pairing of Hooker and Dylan on the same bill was a clear indication of the complex diversity of the blues.

The 1960s were very good for Hooker. He performed regularly in his home country and toured England and continental Europe almost every year, always winning a warm reception and spreading his poetic blues to new audiences. Hooker's versatility on acoustic as well as electric guitar opened up more doors than if he had favored one rigid form. Not only was Hooker popular on the folk-blues circuit but he was also a smash hit on the rock tours. He was one of the few original bluesmen not too old to benefit financially from the debt owed to the originators by the rock generation.

The respect that Hooker earned came from a variety of different sources. He recorded with blues mate Muddy Waters and Otis Spann in a collaboration that pleased many blues fans. A trip to England brought Hooker in contact with John Mayall, the bluesiest of the Brits, and the two recorded an album together using Mayall's band, The Groundhogs.

In 1970, Hooker left Detroit, the city that had been his home since the early 1940s, and moved to Oakland, California. He continued to record and perform on the West coast. One of his more interesting projects was an album with the white blues band Canned Heat. The record *Hooker and Heat* was a big hit and demonstrated the respect accorded to Hooker for his vast contributions to postwar music. White blues bands like Canned Heat inspired John Lee Hooker to create throbbing rhythms, which furthered expanded the master's reputation.

Hooker was also a featured singer at the Palladium in New York in a concert entitled "Tribute to the Blues." Hooker shared the stage with Muddy Waters, Foghat, and Paul Butterfield among others. Hooker padded his already outstanding résumé as a guest performer on Bonnie Raitt's tour in the early 1970s. He also appeared in the movie the *Blues Brothers* in the late 1970s.

Hooker kept recording his own material, but by the late 1970s with interest in the blues at an all-time low, his recycled material was selling very poorly. But with the repackaging of his old songs and the constant cover versions of his many hits, Hooker retained a notable stature in blues-rock circles.

Although he continued to record and perform in the 1980s, he was mostly ignored by the new generation of music fans. His blues star did not shine harder during the blues boom that occurred during the decade with the release of *Texas Flood* by Stevie Ray Vaughan. It wasn't until 1989 that Hooker revived his career with the release of his album *The Healer* on the Chameleon label. The album featured fresh material and proved that the blues spirit still burned in Hooker with a fierce intensity. The album was also shaped by the talents of Bonnie Raitt, Carlos Santana, and George Thorogood. Fittingly, Hooker won a Grammy for *The Healer.*

With this newfound enthusiasm for his work, Hooker followed up with the album *Mr. Lucky,* which was another critical and financial success. He was supported on the album by some of the same cast as the previous recording as well as Johnny Winter and Keith Richards. Hooker continued to release new albums and in 1997, recorded "Don't Look Back" with the help of his old friend Van Morrison and the band Los Lobos.

Today, Hooker leads a quiet suburban life in Redwood City, California. He quit smoking and drinking back in the 1970s and takes daily walks to keep himself in good shape. He continues to perform, but because of fragile health most of the concerts are in California. Because of the infrequency of his live appearances, when he does perform in front of an audience it is a genuine blues event.

John Lee Hooker remains the king of boogie and continues to capture the hearts and souls of blues fans of all ages throughout the world. His status as a blues giant of the postwar era is solid, and he is undoubtedly one of the most popular bluesmen in history. He is a superstar, a torchbearer, and an unqualified influence on three generations of musicians.

Hooker is one of the most prolific recorded blues artists in history and, perhaps with the sole exception of Sam "Lightnin'" Hopkins, may be the most recorded blues singer ever. He has made over 200 recordings for a variety of labels including Modern, Regal, Gone, Staff, Sensation, Chess, Vee-Jay, Charly, GNP Crescendo, Chameleon, and Point Blank/Charisma. To avoid contract obligations Hooker cleverly used a variety of pseudonyms that were somehow derived from his name or his hypnotic style. The list is long, complex, and guaranteed to give discography scholars a major headache.

With the deaths of Muddy Waters in 1983 and Willie Dixon and Albert King in 1992, Hooker, along with B. B. King, remains the last of a vanishing breed of Delta bluesmen. With King playing more of a "citified" blues, Hooker remains the last true country-blues musician to carry the torch that was lit so long ago by Charley Patton, Son House, and the late, great Robert Johnson. His death will, unfortunately, bring an end to the reign of the Delta bluesmen who changed the face of popular music in the twentieth century.

John Lee Hooker is one of the most respected musicians on the international scene. In 1990, a large number of blues musicians, rock singers, and other well-wishers threw a party for him at Madison Square Garden, in New York. The seventy-three-year-old Hooker basked modestly in the spotlight. Such adoration has been bestowed on only a handful of twentieth-century musical figures.

Hooker has been an influence on three generations of guitarists. The driving riff of "La Grange" by ZZ Top is a slight alteration of Hooker's classic "Boogie Chillen." The group Canned Heat owes much of their boogie riff ideas to the creative genius of Hooker. The Doors, The Animals, and Bruce Springsteen are just a few of the rock-blues alumni that have paid homage to Hooker.

But there is more to the blues legend of John Lee Hooker. Although he may have trouble working up his rich, deep voice to sing over the loud instruments, Hooker still cuts a dashing and dangerous figure on stage. His choice of tasteful black hats, casual attire, and simple instrumentation is contrasted by his surly, hypnotic glare that sends shivers through his audience. It is evident that Hooker is not about to relinquish his title as one of the baddest bluesmen in history.

One of the most interesting aspects of Hooker's music is his unique knowledge of the guitar fret board. He has a firm command of the entire instrument, but almost his entire repertoire is concentrated in one area. His syncopated riffs and rough style that are firmly entrenched in the country roots are the basis of his original sound.

In 1980, Hooker was elected to the Blues Foundation Hall of Fame and ten years later to the Rock and Roll Hall of Fame. Despite the numerous changes in music during his lifetime, Hooker has never swayed away from his Delta roots. He has continued to play the amplified, hypnotic, repetetive riffs, accentuated by his deep, bruising voice and street-soaked lyrics delivered with a slurred Southern accent. It is this particular style that has earned him the title "Boogie Child."

Discography

The Ultimate Collection: 1949–1990, Rhino R2-70572.
John Lee Hooker Plays & Sings the Blues, Chess MCA CHD 9199.

The Healer, Chameleon 74808-2.

The Real Folk Blues, MCA-Chess CHD 9271.

Hooker 'n' Heat, EMI Liberty CDP 7-97896-2.

Mr. Lucky, Point Blank-Charisma 91724-2.

The Best of John Lee Hooker, MCA-Chess MCAD 10539.

That's my Story, Riverside OBCCD 538-2.

Graveyard Blues, Specialty 7018.

Folk Blues, Crown 5295.

Original Folk Blues, Kent 525.

Boom Boom, Point Blank-Charisma 86553.

House of the Blues, Chess 9258.

Don't Turn Me from Your Door, Atlantic 82365.

The Hook, Chameleon D@-74794.

Don't Look Back, Point Blank/Virgin.

Johnny Lee Hooker at Newport, Vee Jay 1078.

On Vee Jay 1955–58, Vee Jay 713.

John Lee Hooker: The Greatest Hits, Kent KST 559.

Detroit Special, Atlantic SD 7228.

Boogie Chillum, Fantasy 24700.

The Best of John Lee Hooker, Vee Jay VJS 2-1049.

John Lee Hooker Gold, Vee Jay VJS 2-1004.

John Lee Hooker: The Blues, Crown CLP 5157.

The Country Blues of John Lee Hooker, Riverside 12-838.

More Real Folk Blues and the Missing Album, MCA-Chess CHD 9329.

Sings the Blues, Crown 5232.

John Lee Hooker 40th Anniversary Album, DCC CC D25 042.

John Lee Hooker—Alone, Specialty SPS 2125.

ALBERT KING (1923–1992)

Born Under a Blues Sign

Why do some youngsters aspire to be blues singers? Do individuals choose the blues or do the blues choose the individuals? Why are certain people targeted to carry the blues flag? Is it in the stars? Great blues singers have been born under every sign of the zodiac, so there is no justification in assuming one constellation has an inspirational advantage over another. However, because of his status as one of the greatest postwar blues guitarists, it is safe to assume that Albert King was born under a "blues" sign.

Albert King was born in Indianola, Mississippi, on April 25, 1923. His early life in the Delta is one seen many times before. He received a limited education and was introduced to hard labor as a young boy, performing all the duties of a normal sharecropper, including milking cows, picking cotton, working the plow behind a mule, and other assorted chores. After his father died, Albert's mother moved the family to Osceola, Arkansas.

King's first musical experiences, like so many of his contemporaries, was gospel, which he heard in church. Early indications of a future musical career were realized when he joined a family gospel group. Eventually, King discovered the blues. Like most children of his era, he was too poor to afford a real guitar, so he built one. Once he had saved enough money he bought a manufactured guitar and immediately began to diligently unravel the mysteries of blues guitar that intrigued him so much. By his teens, King was good enough to play in a blues group called the In the Groove Boys, performing the occasional local gig around his home of Osceola.

Although he burned to be recognized as a blues singer, Albert was well aware that success was a fleeting adventure, at best, and he needed a steady job to pay the bills. So, King—a large, intimidating man—found work in the construction business operating a bulldozer. This restricted pursuing his musical career to nights and weekends.

In the late 1940s he moved to Little Rock, where he continued working in construction while chasing his musical dreams in his limited spare time. Despite many initial disappointments, King persevered. He spent the entire decade of the 1950s earning his living on the construction site, paying his dues and making little progress with his blues career. In 1962, in an attempt to improve his fortunes, King moved to Gary, Indiana. He also traveled frequently to Chicago, where he moonlighted playing in Jimmy Reed's band, first as a drummer, then as rhythm guitarist, until he was promoted to a frontline position.

King was able to record for the Parrot label, and he cut "Bad Luck Blues" and "Be on Your Merry Way." Neither song turned out to be the big hit that would have enabled him to quit his day job and concentrate on his blues career. He became frustrated with Parrot Records and life in general in Gary, so in the mid–1960s he moved to Love Joy, Illinois, directly across from the city of St. Louis. He formed a band that consisted of musicians from the St. Louis area and gained recognition through the Midwest. He also managed to make a few records for the Bobbin label, including "I'm a Lonely Man" and one of his biggest hits, "Don't Throw Your Love on Me so Strong," which provided Albert with a quick stab at fame.

Yet it wasn't until 1966, after years of moving around and searching for the winning combination that King began to gain the recognition that he deserved. He signed a recording contract with Stax/Volt. Backed by the soul strains of Booker T. and the MGs, King hit pay dirt with "Laundromat Blues," "Born Under a Bad Sign," "Crosscut Saw," "I'll Play the Blues for You," "Blues at Sunrise," "Travelin' to California," "Ooh-A Baby," "Blues Power," and "Let's Have a Natural Ball." He also delivered a smashing version of "Kansas City," joining the long list of musicians, including the Beatles, who had recorded this classic.

After years of frustration, King's career was finally gaining positive momentum. His hard-rocking sound was quickly accepted by the rock crowd, and he enjoyed considerable crossover success—a rare triumph reserved for only a handful of bluesmen. King appeared at the Fillmore West on the same bill as Jimi Hendrix and John Mayall who were thrilled to have the giant bluesmen performing on the same stage with them. He was accepted wholeheartedly by the rock fraternity in the same manner as Freddie King, B. B. King, John Lee Hooker, Buddy Guy, and Muddy Waters.

As the blues boom of the 1960s subsided, King's career declined with it. He still played to enthusiastic crowds, but his star did not shine as brightly as it had in the previous decade. By the mid–1970s, King's career continued on a steady hum. He played numerous rock and blues venues and recorded for various labels like Tomato and Fantasy. Although he made solid records during this period, including the dynamic *I Wanna Get Funky*, the solid *Truckload of Lovin'*, and the self-titled *Albert*, none had the powerful impact of his earlier efforts with Stax.

King patiently plugged away without changing his dominant style, waiting for the next blues boom to hit. In the early 1980s his patience paid off with the arrival of Stevie Ray Vaughan and his lightning Texas blues. Vaughan considered Albert King to be no less than one of the immortal gods of the electric guitar, and he did much indirectly to revitalize his hero's career.

King recorded an album in 1983 (his first in five years) on Fantasy Records called *San Francisco '83*, which featured the track "Floodin' in California." King continued to record and appear in concert throughout the 1980s. He played numerous blues festivals and was firmly established as one of the most important bluesmen of the times.

In 1992, on the eve of a major European tour, Albert King, the behemoth bluesman with the thick rock sound and incredible string-bending technique, died of a heart attack just four days before Christmas. He was 69 years old.

Although it took Albert King more than forty years to become a blues star, once he had reached that exalted plateau he remained there for the rest of his life. He recorded a truckload of songs that not only became blues classics but worked their way into the repertoire of many of the major rock-blues acts, including Jimi Hendrix, Eric Clapton, Stevie Ray Vaughan, Jeff Beck, Led Zeppelin, John Mayall, George Thorogood, and a host of others.

King's somber and unpretentious style made him a supreme innovator of blues music and a powerful influence on many guitarists. One of his prime students was another left-handed guitarist—Jimi Hendrix. The two first met in 1964 in Nashville, Tennessee. Hendrix, who was three years away from achieving international fame, was in awe of the six-foot-four-inch King. They formed a strong bond despite a twenty-year age difference. Hendrix, always eager to learn from another guitarist, watched King play, took good notes, and incorporated some of King's technique into his own style. One of the most important lessons the elder bluesman taught the impressionable young Hendrix was to tune down in order to make the strings easier to bend. Both were monster note benders, and it was an important lesson for the flashy, studious Hendrix.

In 1968, King and Hendrix performed together. At the time, they hadn't seen each other in five years, and it was a joyful reunion. Although he was impressed with Hendrix, the old bluesman conceded nothing. King was one of the few guitarists who did not feel intimidated by the guitar wizardry of Hendrix and gave the young Seattle ax hero a solid run for his money. After Hendrix's death, King sometimes played a Gibson flying V as a tribute to Hendrix, who had also used the uniquely shaped instrument.

Stevie Ray Vaughan, the most exciting guitarist since Hendrix to blast out of a stack of Marshall amplifiers, owed much of his sound to the teachings of Albert King. Before Vaughan's tragic death, Stevie Ray and

Albert played together, and the Texas bluesman was as much in awe of the formidable King as Hendrix had been twenty years earlier.

The king of British blues guitar is without a doubt Eric Clapton. During his career, he has constantly brought to the attention of the international music world the vital contributions of the old blues masters. During his Cream days, Clapton recorded "Born Under a Bad Sign." It spread the musical gospel of Albert King to an even wider audience.

One of the guitar techniques that King feverishly swore by was the use of his bare fingers—a classic trademark of the country-bluesmen—instead of a flat pick or a plectrum. This technique influenced another noted rock guitarist, Mark Knopfler. Knopfler's laid-back style is the heart of the Dire Straits sound, and he learned much from Albert King. He added his own licks to create a very distinct style.

Given his unique approach to the guitar, it is amazing that King became such a major influence on so many contemporary guitar players. Although Hendrix and King were both left-handed, Hendrix would often restring the guitar properly, but King maintained the low strings close to the ground with the high strings aimed for the sky. King's slower style with shorter riffs is a direct result of this handicap.

King used a unique tuning—a full three notes down—creating a fresh, new sound. He preferred minor scales to major scales. His solos were in some way related to those of another Albert, Albert Collins. King's solos were not note-infested rages but masterpieces for their use of space. He combined space and time with the delicacy and precision of the great masters often in a slow 12/8 beat.

Albert played in a rural style that was close to rock as it later evolved, but his voice was soft and husky. He was known for his hard blues-rock sound, but King recorded "Please Love Me" and "Blues Power" in a slow, lazy ballad style that demonstrated his gentle country-blues side.

In the galaxy of revered blues guitarists, King's star shines brightly along with another guitar player, Freddie King. With the masterful use of all his individual techniques, Albert, like Freddie, was able to create his own unique sound that is instantly recognizable. They were both able to develop a distinct style that separated them from other blues guitarists.

Throughout his career, King recorded many interesting albums, including an entire blues package featuring many of Elvis Presley's greatest hits, including "All Shook Up," "Hound Dog," "Jailhouse Rock," and "Love Me Tender." The record, pure Albert, featured short breaks, a few brief solos, and his strong voice. His *Live Wire/Blues Power* album, recorded at the Fillmore in 1968, was a major hit with rock audiences. His boxed set collection is a must-have for all rabid blues and rock fans.

In 1983, Albert King was inducted into the Blues Foundation Hall of Fame. It was a well-deserved honor because Albert King lived and died for the blues. The blues fired deep emotions inside him that he released through the genius of his guitar playing. Albert King gave the international music world a bountiful bouquet of beautiful blues, and his efforts continue to inspire all students of the guitar. Undoubtedly, Albert King was truly born under a blues sign.

Discography

Masterworks, Atlantic AD 2-4002.
I Wanna Get Funky, Stax 8336.
Live Wire/Blues Power, Stax 4128.
Let's Have a Natural Ball, Modern Blues Recordings 723.
I'm in a Phone Booth, Baby, Fantasy 9633.
Wednesday Night in San Francisco, Stax MPS 8556.
Thursday Night in San Francisco, Stax MPS 8557.
Born Under a Bad Sign, Atlantic-Stax 7723.
The Ultimate Collection, Rhino 71268.
Blues for Elvis, Stax 8504.
I'll Play the Blues for You, Stax 8513.
San Francisco '83, Fantasy 9627.
Years Gone By, Stax 8522.
King of the Blues Guitar, Atlantic 8213-2.
Tomato Years, Rhino/Tomato.
Blues at Sunrise: Live at Montreux, Stax 8546.
Laundromat Blues, Edsel 130.

B. B. KING (1925–   )

The Little Blues Boy

What do Lonnie Johnson, Blind Lemon Jefferson, Charlie Christian, Django Reinhardt, T-Bone Walker, and Bukka White all have in common? Were they all guitar players who were born in the Mississippi

Delta? Although it is true that they were all guitarists, only Bukka White was from the Delta region. Johnson was from Louisiana, Jefferson and Walker were from Texas, Christian was from Oklahoma, and Reinhardt was originally from Belgium. The one characteristic that the six afore-mentioned names share is their profound influence on the little blues boy who assimilated the styles of his heroes into a smooth sound of his own in his quest to become the most dominant blues singer of the postwar era. Today, that little blues boy is better known to the world as B. B. King.

B. B. King was born Riley B. King in Indianola, Mississippi, on September 16, 1925. Like many other black children of the era, his early childhood was one of misfortune and hardship. His parents separated when he was a youngster, and Riley moved with his mother from the Delta to the Kilmicheal Hills area of Mississippi. At the tender age of eight, he lost his mother; a short time later his grandmother died.

To ensure his basic survival, Riley worked as a hired hand on a farm, where he picked cotton, milked cows, and worked the plow behind a mule. Though not faced with abject poverty, Riley's life was still very harsh. He received little in the way of a formal education, and his future seemed rather bleak. Music was the key that enabled him to escape a certain long life of hard labor.

Music was all around him. There was the gospel he heard in church, which stirred deep emotions inside him. He grew up listening to the recordings of Lonnie Johnson and Blind Lemon Jefferson, two favorite blues artists of an aunt who owned an extensive record collection. But one of his biggest musical influences was his cousin Bukka White, a genuine bluesman whose biggest hit was "Shake 'em on Down." With his fancy clothes, generosity, and tall tales, White made a burning and lasting impression on young Riley.

King eventually joined a gospel group and played the blues on the street corner when he wasn't singing with his choir group. He was paying his dues in hopes of someday becoming a successful blues musician. However, the way was not paved with gold.

He was married at age eighteen, and his responsibilities prevented him from making any real musical progress. Then, in 1944, he was drafted into the army. King had graduated to tractor driver on the plantation and was deemed too important to be sacrificed in Europe. He was spared from active duty after he completed basic training. At twenty-one years old, he returned to his wife and job on the plantation.

Life as a hired hand was stifling. Riley was a young man who craved adventure and excitement. In a desperate effort to break out of the restrictive boundaries, King struck out on his own and made his way to Memphis, Tennessee, where Bukka White lived and played. While he only had one significant hit, White was still a noted bluesman in his own right. King stayed in Memphis for a few months, then returned to Indianola. A short time later, King moved away from Indianola permanently, determined to make his fortune as a blues singer.

King arrived in West Memphis, Arkansas, with his guitar, very little money, and a dream. West Memphis was Sonny Boy Williamson II territory, and King bravely sought out the dangerous bluesman to audition for his radio show on station KWEM. King impressed Williamson enough that he was allowed to sing his song at the end of the show.

It was through Williamson that King scored a gig at the 16th Street Grill in West Memphis. From that point on, King moved quickly. He found a job as a disc jockey at station WDIA in Memphis selling Pepticon, a health medicine guaranteed to cure all ills. Not only did the job allow him to announce his next concert date but it also led to his famous moniker. He was called various names including "The Boy from Beale Street," "The Beale Street Blues Boy," and eventually just shortened the version to B. B., which simply stood for "Blues Boy." It was also in Memphis while working as a disc jockey that he began to attract the attention of record companies.

In 1949, the prolific recording career of B. B. King began. He cut four songs: "Miss Martha King," "When Your Baby Packs up and Goes," "Got the Blues," and "Take a Swing with Me" for Bullit Records. Although the songs were good and featured the skillful arrangement of horns, Bullit Records went out of business shortly afterward.

Visions of stardom danced before his eyes, but the dream was short-lived. Soon, King was in a funk, and his career was making very little progress. Then, through a chance meeting with Ike Turner, King was sought out by Modern Records in Los Angeles. Turner was a talent scout for Modern, and he liked what he heard and suggested that King would be a wise investment.

After years of paying his dues, King scored with "Three o'Clock Blues," which reached number one on the Billboard charts and stayed there for nearly a dozen weeks. The song catapulted King into better times. He was booked into the most prestigious black venues in the country, including the Regal in Chicago and the Apollo Theatre in New York. Though King was finally making headway with his musical career, his personal life was crumbling. His marriage to his first wife, Martha, came to an end.

King resumed his flourishing blues career and recorded extensively throughout the 1950s, often at Sun Studios under the auspicious guidance of producer Sam Philips. A very short list of some of the classics he recorded in this period includes: "Woke up this Morning," "You Know I Love You," "Ten Long Years," "Sweet Little Angel," "Troubles, Troubles, Troubles," "Everyday I Have the Blues," and "Sneakin' Around." It was also around this time that King began to earn a reputation as a road warrior. He logged hundreds of thousands of miles each year performing one-night shows throughout the country.

In 1958, RPM was discontinued and King switched to Kent Records. In 1960, he scored three best-selling songs — "Sweet Sixteen," "Got a Right to Love my Baby," and "Partin' Time" — and added "Someday" and "Peace of Mind" in 1961. Despite the success, he was still seeking ways to expand his popularity base.

Because of a disagreement with Kent, King moved to ABC Records in the early 1960s. But this did not stop Kent from releasing prior recordings, and they continued to do so through much of the 1960s. The move did little to hurt King's career; if anything, it strengthened his reputation, which by that time was steadily increasing among blues circles.

While the "British invasion" and the Motown sound dominated the musical scene in the early 1960s, King continued to plug away. While his career progressed, it seemed that he was being overlooked in favor of soul and rhythm and blues artists like Sam Cooke, Ray Charles, Otis Redding, Wilson Pickett, and others.

At the beginning of the 1970s, King scored a number one hit with "The Thrill Is Gone." It was the first song that earned him important crossover appeal. After twenty years of constant touring and numerous recordings, his hard work was finally starting to pay off. One of the reasons why King was enjoying such grand success was that rockers who knew a good thing when they heard it were singing his praises. Mike Bloomfield, Johnny Winter, Eric Clapton, and Jimi Hendrix all admitted to being heavily influenced by B. B. King.

The 1970s were King's golden days. At the beginning of the decade he could barely see the light at the end of the tunnel; by 1979, he was acknowledged as the greatest living bluesman. King acquired a management team that booked him in many different venues that only widened his burgeoning appeal. King performed in jails, on colleges campuses all over the United States, and on television when he made a guest appearance on shows like *Sanford and Son*.

Awards and honors also started to come his way. He received two honorary doctorates from Toulagoo College in Mississippi and one in music from Yale University. He won a Grammy for the "The Thrill Is Gone," six consecutive Downbeat awards for best rock/pop/blues group, was nominated five years in a row as best blues guitarist of the year by the magazine *Guitar Player* and was elected to the Ebony Hall of Fame in 1974. Most important, throughout many parts of the world his name was synonymous with the blues.

King picked up in the 1980s where he left off in the 1970s. He won three more Grammy awards, was inducted into the Rock Walk of Fame in 1989 as well as the Amsterdam Walk of Fame in the same year—the only blues singer ever to accomplish that feat. He also won four W. C. Handy awards.

One of the albums that King recorded in the 1980s was *Midnight Believer* including the songs "When It all Comes Down I'll Still Be Around" and "Never Make a Move too Soon," which became hits. Another of his albums included *There Must Be a Better World Somewhere*, which won a Grammy as well as the record *Blues 'n' Jazz* for best traditional blues album. The *Blues 'n' Jazz* album was recorded with a number of noted jazz musicians, including Woody Shaw, Don Wilkerson, Fred Ford, Arnett Cobb, Lloyd Glenn, Major Holley and James Bolden.

King appeared on the sitcom *The Cosby Show* and the soap opera *General Hospital*. By the middle of the decade, B. B. King was a household name. He had done as much for the blues as any other musician in the past hundred years.

He has continued to record and perform, but has cut down on his touring the last few years because of health and advancing age. He still remains the "Chairman of the Board" and is considered the greatest living bluesman (his only serious rival is John Lee Hooker). A recent television commercial selling hamburgers for the Wendy's food chain exposed him to a new generation of the record-buying public.

B. B. King is a superstar. He is the most important modern postwar guitar player and has sold over 100 million albums worldwide. He is one of the few bluesmen whose name is recognizable in many corners of the globe. He has given the blues international respect and is one of the most prestigious musicians of the twentieth century.

B. B. King is also one of the most important innovators of the blues.

He has been able to channel the blues lessons of Lonnie Johnson, T-Bone Walker, Blind Lemon Jefferson, and the jazz improvisations of Charlie Christian and Django Reinhardt into his own playing, which has in turn influenced a host of modern guitarists. Buddy Guy, Magic Sam, Otis Rush, Hubert Sumlin, Magic Slim, Son Seals, and Lonnie Brooks are just a handful of the blues musicians who patterned their guitar styles from King's musical vocabulary.

Of the many guitarists who had a deep influence on King's growth as a musician, none holds a higher spot than T-Bone Walker. Walker was a Texas bluesman whose jazz-based harmony and natural fluidity on electric guitar became an integral part of the King style. It was T-Bone's definitive touch on the electric guitar that King greatly admired. T-Bone was also one of the first bluesmen to go electric, which inspired King to plug in. But Walker influenced King in other ways as well. T-Bone was a sharp dresser and gave the blues a touch of class and distinction—two qualities King has passed on to the world.

Another building block in the B. B. King music foundation was his cousin Bukka White. Although White and King were altogether different kinds of blues musicians, the impression that the older, more experienced bluesman had on his young cousin was extremely important. White's ability to entertain and hold a crowd's attention without any gimmicks but his blues voice and his guitar skills taught King a valuable lesson he never forgot.

King, an eclectic bluesman, also loved the hard brass sounds of the swing bands led by Duke Ellington and Count Basie, which found its way into the King style. The jazz guitars of Charlie Christian, Django Reinhardt, Les Paul, and Oscar and Johnny Moore formed part of the bedrock of the mature King sound. Other jazz influences included Cootie Williams, whose note bending King tried valiantly to reproduce.

B. B. King's guitar style is a blend of rural blues, jazz, and pop elements. He retained a sense of the traditional blues rhythms that he heard when a youngster, but incorporated trills and vibrato. His dazzling fast breaks of flowing torrents of notes are one of his major trademarks. King's expert use of "swamping" his sound separates him from his country roots and the urban jazz guitarists who had such an influence on him. Add his dramatic voice tailored for the blues and his keen understanding of showmanship and it is not hard to understand why B. B. King is considered by many to be the greatest blues singer in the world.

Although not the first guitar virtuoso, King was the inspiration for many future rockers, including Jimi Hendrix, Stevie Ray Vaughan, Billy Gibbons, Mike Bloomfield, Robert Cray, Buddy Guy, Otis Rush, Magic Sam, Freddie King, Jimmy Vaughan, Jimmy Page, Jeff Beck, Eric Clapton, Kenny Wayne Shepherd, and so many others that a complete list is impossibly long.

There are many sides to B. B. King. He has been a superb bandleader who bought a bus in the 1950s, renovated it to comfortably outfit his group, and proceeded to travel the country spreading the blues. B. B. King is the ultimate road warrior and has performed in more places in the United States than any other single blues singer in history. He has also taken his show to Japan, China, Russia, Brazil, and dozens of other places around the world.

King was one of the first bluesmen to skillfully use the media as a tool to increase his popularity. He has appeared on stage with Elvis, Jerry Lee Lewis, Bonnie Raitt, Stevie Wonder, Eric Clapton, Etta James, Stevie Ray Vaughan, John Lee Hooker, Willie Dixon, Albert King, the Rolling Stones, the Marshall Tucker Band, and countless others. He also performed with U2, even making a video with them. The song "When Love Comes to Town" was on the group's *Rattle and Hum* album, a giant best-seller that exposed King to the new rock generation.

He has written music scores for films like *Into the Night*, in which he appeared with his "new" bandmates, talented actor Jeff Goldblum, the lovely Michelle Pfeiffer, and funny men Steve Martin and Eddie Murphy. Because of his eagerness to spread his wings and get involved in a variety of different projects, King has been able to gain greater recognition than many other blues singers.

B. B. King is one of the greatest ambassadors of the blues. He has always worn his blues badge proudly and spoken eloquently of the music that runs through his veins. Perhaps more than any other modern musician, B. B. King has proven that music is international and that there are no boundaries of race, language, or nationality.

A world traveler, King has lived in different parts of Mississippi, Memphis, New York, California, and Las Vegas, where he currently resides. Of course, because of his heavy touring schedule, King has spent very little time in any of the cities he temporarily called home.

B. B. King is a private man. The father of fifteen children, he has never shirked any of his responsibilities, which is perhaps the essential ingredient that makes him such a special person. From the beginning, when he was a little boy, King has been a steady worker, a man who saw the task ahead of him and plowed straight through, never wallowing in self-pity or bitterness.

In 1980, King was inducted into the Blues Foundation Hall of Fame. In 1987, in a gala event attended by Jimmy Page, Carlos Santana, Jeff Beck, Steve Cropper, Robbie Robertson, The Edge, Keith Richards, and John Fogerty, King was inducted into the Rock and Roll Hall of Fame. B. B. King has come a long way from his days when he first picked up a guitar as a boy and marveled at the secrets it held. His songs have been and will continue to be an audio bible for generations to come.

Discography

B. B. King, Modern RLP 498.
B. B. King Story, Blue Horizon.
B. B. King Story, vol. 2, Blue Horizon.
Blues on Top of Blues, Blues 6011.
Blues for Me, United 7708.
Blues of B. B. King, vol. 1, Flair/Virgin 86230.
Blues of B. B. King, vol. 2, Flair/Virgin 86231.
Blues is King, MCA 31368.
Blues is King, Blues 6001.
Blues is King, ABC 704.
Best of B. B. King, ABC 767.
Back in the Alley, ABC 787.
B. B. King Live, Kent 565.
B. B. King on Stage, Kent 515.
B. B. King L.A. Midnight, ABC 743.
B. B. King Friends, ABC 825.
B. B. King 1949–50, Kent 9011.
B. B. King Better than Ever, Kent 561.
Boss of the Blues, Kent 529.
The Blues, United 7732.
Blues in My Heart, Crown 5309.
B. B. King/Bobby Blue Bland Together Live, MCA.
B. B. King/Bobby Blue Bland Live Again, MCA.
Blues 'n' Jazz, MCA 27119.
Blues Summit, MCA.
Completely Well, ABC 868.
Confessin' the Blues, ABC 528.

Don't Answer the Door, Bluesway 6001.

Doing my Thing Lord, Kent 5663.

Do the Boogie, Ace 916.

Electric B. B. King—His Best, ABC 794.

Easy Listening Blues, United Records 7705.

From the Beginning, Kent 533.

Guess Who, ABC 759.

Greatest Hits, Galaxy 8208.

Great B. B. King, United 7728.

His Best the Electric B. B. King, Bluesway 6022.

Heart to Heart, MCA.

Heart and Soul, MCA.

Heart Full of Blues, United 7703.

How Blue Can You Get Classic Live Performances 1964–1994, MCA.

Indianola Mississippi Seeds, ABC 713.

Incredible Soul of B. B. King, Kent 539

In London, ABC 730.

I Love You So, United 7711.

The Jungle, Kent 521.

King Size, ABC 977.

King of the Blues, MCA 10677.

King of the Blues, United 7730.

Love Me Tender, MCA.

Lucille, Bluesway 6016.

Lucille, BGO BGOLP 36.

Live at the Apollo, GRP 9637.

Live at the Regal, ABC 509.

Live & Well, Bluesway 6031.

Lucille Talks Back, ABC 898.

Live in Cook County, MCA 27005.

Live at San Quentin, MCA.

Let Me Love You, Kent 513.

Live in London, MCA.

Midnight Believer, MCA.

Mr. Blues, ABC 456.

Now Appearing at Ole Miss, MCA 2-8016.

The Rarest King, Blues Boy 301.

Rock Me Baby, Kent 512.

Singing the Blues, United 7726.

Singin' the Blues, Capitol 86296.
Soul of B. B. King, United 7714.
Six Silver Strings, MCA.
Sweet Sixteen, Kent 568.
Spotlight on Lucille, FLAIR 2-91693.
There Is Always One More Time, MCA.
There Must Be a Better World Somewhere, MCA.
Torn into B. B. King, Stateside SCO54-90296.
To Know You Is to Love You, ABC Records 794.
Take a Swing with Me, Polydor UK 2431.004.

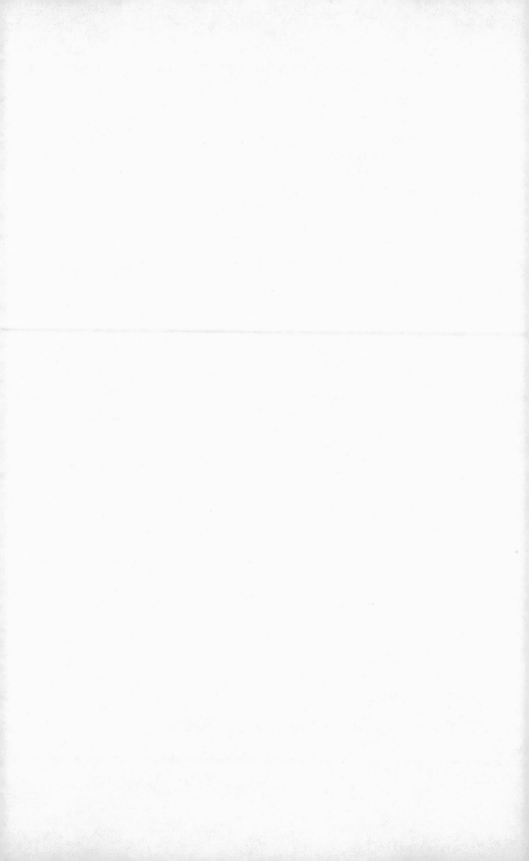

PART TWO

The Chicago Blues School

In the 1920s things began to change in the old South. Because of technological advancements in agriculture, unemployment was rampant. Waves of blacks migrated north in search of better economic prospects. They brought with them their regional guitar-dominated down-home blues. Though the industrial cities of Detroit, Cleveland, Milwaukee, and Gary, Indiana, boasted large black populations, it was Chicago that became the northern blues mecca.

The first semester of the Chicago blues school era is best known as the "Bluebird Period" because all of the artists who put the city on the blues map—including Big Bill Broonzy, Tampa Red, John Lee "Sonny Boy" Williamson, Big Maceo, Robert Nighthawk, Leroy Carr, Scrapper Blackwell and Jazz Gillum—recorded for the Bluebird label. Though the Chicago blues class of the mid–1930s to late 1940s was overshadowed by the efforts of the next crop of students, the group who recorded around the time of World War II had their day in the sun. The three artists in this section featured from that period, Big Bill Broonzy, Tampa Red, and Sonny Boy Williamson, all made important contributions to the blues.

The electric Chicago blues, the golden age, lasted from 1948 to 1965 and can be divided into two different "semesters." The Chess years began in 1948 with the release of two singles, "I Can't Be Satisfied" and "I Feel Like Going Home" by a transplanted Delta bluesman named Muddy Waters. By the end of the 1950s, Muddy Waters and his colleagues Willie Dixon, Howlin' Wolf, Elmore James, Sonny Boy Williamson II, Little Walter, and Otis Spann had become an institution. Their gritty, rude, amplified, Delta-based blues would spawn thousands of imitators and reach every corner of the globe.

The second "semester" began in the late 1950s with the emergence of three prized students: Otis Rush, Buddy Guy, and Magic Sam. They learned their lessons well from the preceding generations, and Rush, Guy, and Sam ushered in the modern blues era.

The Chicago blues school became the curriculum for countless future blues and rock musicians who later turned the world on to the music of the old bluesmen from the deep South. The combination of circumstances that were necessary in the creation of the Chicago blues are unlikely ever to occur again. Some of the international musical giants of the last 100 years are found in this category. The musical contributions of the innovators, superstars, and cult heroes who are part of this category will continue to be heard in the music of future generations. Today, Chicago remains as the northern mecca of the blues.

BIG BILL BROONZY (1893–1958)

Key to the Highway

Throughout the history of the blues the names of certain artists have been eternally linked to one specific song. Big Joe Williams will always be known as the man who penned "Baby, Please Don't Go." Other examples include Charley Patton with his "Pony Blues," Blind Lemon Jefferson with "Matchbox Blues," and Blind Willie McTell with "Statesboro Blues." Although he wrote hundreds of songs, the creator of "Key to the Highway" will forever be associated with that stone classic. His name was Big Bill Broonzy.

William Lee Conley Broonzy was born in Scott, Mississippi, in 1893, the son of hard-working sharecroppers and one of seven children. He was a young boy when his family moved to Arkansas in search of better economic prospects. He developed an early interest in the country-blues that was encouraged by an uncle. Broonzy's first instrument was the violin; at age eleven he made his first one out of a cigar box. Later he acquired a real fiddle, and by his middle teens, was competent enough to earn spare change at country events around the Little Rock area.

In his early twenties Broonzy enlisted in the army and returned to Arkansas after his discharge. But he became increasingly disenchanted with the stifling life of a sharecropper and decided to make his way to Chicago to pursue a career as a blues singer. Originally a fiddle player, it was on his arrival in the Windy City that Broonzy began to learn the rudiments of guitar under the careful tutelage of Papa Charlie Jackson, one of the big names on the Chicago blues scene at the time.

Despite his ambition, there was no overnight success for Broonzy. After some discouraging, dues-paying months spent diligently developing his laid-back country-blues guitar style, he slowly began to climb up the city's blues hierarchy. By the mid–1930s, he was one of the biggest names in Chicago and appeared on the same bill at various times with Tampa Red, Jazz Gillum, Black Bob Alexander, Papa Charlie Jackson, and Memphis Minnie.

Broonzy's immense popularity was a result of his enthusiastic live act and the good records he was making. He began his recording career in 1928 and produced many classic blues songs, such as "Mississippi River Blues," "Stove Pipe Stomp," "Long Tall Mama," and "Starvation Blues." The themes of these songs were hardship and suffering, women, and good times—in all, a typical bluesman's assortment. Later on, Broonzy recorded "Southern Fried Blues," "When I Been Drinking," "Just a Dream," "Bull Cow Blues," "Night Time Is the Right Time," "Truckin' Little Woman," "All by Myself," "Big Bill Blues," and his signature tune, "Key to the Highway."

Broonzy was not only making good records but he was also playing on the recordings of other noted blues artists, such as Georgia Tom Dorsey, Sonny Boy Williamson I, and his brother-in-law, Washboard Sam. Broonzy was a valuable asset in the recording studio, and all the sessions that he sat in on benefited from his powerful voice and flowing guitar style.

In 1938, John Hammond, the legendary producer for Columbia, was scouring the South for Robert Johnson to appear in his "From Spirituals to Swing" concerts. Hammond had heard "Terraplane Blues" and realized Johnson's genius. When Hammond discovered that Johnson was dead, he hired Broonzy instead. This unexpected break proved to be vital to Broonzy's career because it established his name beyond the borders of Chicago and the Little Rock, Arkansas, area.

Broonzy's performance at Carnegie Hall was a memorable event. He won the audience over with his warm, soothing voice and skilled guitar work. Broonzy made such an impact that Hammond booked him to appear the following year. The "Spiritual to Swing" concerts confirmed that Broonzy was among the brightest blues stars in the world.

However, despite his widespread success, Broonzy never made enough money from his music to be able to quit his menial jobs. For years he owned a farm in Arkansas and worked it during the busy growing seasons. He also served a stint as janitor at Iowa State College. At various times in his career he was also employed as a part-time preacher and even worked as a coal miner. Despite his busy schedule Broonzy somehow found time to head back to Chicago to record and perform.

By the late 1940s and early 1950s a new electric sound invaded the clubs on Chicago's South Side. The Muddy Waters Band, the leaders of this hard, energized urban music, soon overshadowed the softer, acoustic style of Broonzy and his fellow musicians. Big Bill had become the unofficial father of Chicago blues in the mid–1930s and late 1940s, but was forced to find a different venue.

In 1951, Broonzy became the first Chicago bluesman to tour Europe. In his European performances he played traditional down-home blues and gospel-influenced numbers to an audience aching for the artistry of a genuine American bluesman. Broonzy's European tour was so successful that he returned in 1953, expanding his international reputation as one of the premiere bluesmen of the day. On his second tour of duty, Broonzy was accompanied by pianist Blind John Davis.

Broonzy, who was regarded more as a folk-bluesman with an urban dimension (rather than an electric warrior like Elmore James), was still very much in demand as a performer back in his home country at choice venues. In the mid–1950s he went into the recording studio with folk singer Pete Seeger and later teamed up with famed blues duo Sonny Terry and Brownie McGhee. The result was the album *Blues with Big Bill Broonzy, Sonny Terry, Brownie McGhee.* The album also included an exclusive interview with Broonzy.

In 1955, Broonzy became one of the first bluesmen to write a book; it was entitled *Big Bill's Blues,* co-written with Yannick Bruynoghe. It was not only the story of Big Bill's life but also of the blues. From a historical aspect *Big Bill's Blues* was a groundbreaking effort because candid stories of blues singers were rare. The book became the predecessor of a number of autobiographical blues books, including Willie Dixon's *I Am the Blues* and B. B. King's *Blues All Around Me.*

In 1957, Big Bill Broonzy discovered he had throat cancer. Despite his illness, he pressed on, but it was obvious that the career of one of the greatest bluesmen had come to a tragic end. On August 15, 1958, the incredible talent that was Big Bill Broonzy was silenced forever. Broonzy's death was a severe blow to the blues community. He was sixty-five years old.

Broonzy was a blues star of stellar magnitude. He was a pacesetting musician whose performing and recording career were of equal importance. He was a blues force on American soil as well as internationally. Broonzy, like Lonnie Johnson, was a pioneer in bridging the primitive, rural acoustic blues and the more sophisticated urban blues sound of the 1930s and 1940s.

Broonzy was the father of prewar Chicago blues. He laid down the foundation for future blues artists arriving from the deep South, including Muddy Waters, Willie Dixon, Howlin' Wolf, John Lee Hooker, B. B. King, and Elmore James. He opened the door for the wave of later migration, and he also assisted many of them in organizing their careers. It was Broonzy who took a young Muddy Waters under his wing and helped the Delta bluesman—destined to replace Broonzy as the principal man in Chicago blues—get his start in the Windy City.

Broonzy was one of the first blues musicians to popularize the three-piece band. There was Broonzy on guitar and vocals, a rhythm section composed of a bass or piano player, and a drummer. This power trio format was later adopted by such rock acts as Buddy Holly and the Crickets, the Jimi Hendrix Experience, Cream, Genesis, ZZ Top, and Stevie Ray Vaughan and Double Trouble.

Broonzy's flexibility as a musician and singer was the true cornerstone of his success and appeal. He played a wide range of styles, including rag, hokum, spirituals, folk, jazz, and country-blues. He was comfortable in a band ensemble or as a solo artist, always proud of carrying the torch that had been passed down to him from his ancestors. The emotional intensity he expressed in his songs has been copied by hundreds of blues and rock singers in the last forty years, but rarely duplicated.

Broonzy was an integral part of the Bluebird sound made famous by producer Lester Melrose and played on numerous sessions of many noted blues artists of the era who recorded for the famous label, including Tampa Red and Sonny Boy Williamson I. Broonzy himself was a prolific songwriter, the author of some 300 songs. Of the many gems he wrote and recorded none brought him more fame than "Key to the Highway."

The theme of the song juxtaposes the glory and the loneliness of a bluesman's traveling life complicated by a fleeting love affair. This motif was very popular and found its way into many of the songs recorded by

Robert Johnson. This theme was later utilized extensively by the rock-blues groups, especially southern-fried boogie bands like the Allman Brothers and Lynyrd Skynyrd. Broonzy's ability in combining chauvinistic-flavored lyrics, jazz improvisations, boogie-woogie bass patterns, and a reverence for the old South into one package makes him one of the forefathers of Southern rock.

Yet, the "key" to the highway has a multitude of different meanings. It suggests a mode of transportation, such as an automobile, bus, or freight car, the latter a favorite among wandering bluesmen. The "key" is the secret formula that enables the obsessed bluesman to unlock the secrets of the sacred music, which allows him to capture the soul of his audience. The "key" may also be a symbol of the musician's choice instrument, which he utilizes as a the powerful weapon to express every emotion of the human spectrum.

In 1980, Big Bill Broonzy was inducted into the Blues Foundation Hall of Fame. His expressive vocal style and incredible speed on the guitar always left his audiences wanting more. He proved that the blues was not a limited musical idiom but one of great versatility that could be used to express any human emotion. There was a genuine honesty in his lyrics that gave his blues a special appeal and strengthened the bond with his audience. He was a true gentleman, a credit to the genre, an ambassador of the art he practiced with pride. Throughout his illustrious career, Broonzy used the key to the highway to spread the message of the blues around the globe.

Discography

The Big Bill Broonzy Story, vols. 1–5, Verve MG SV 3000-1/5.
The Young Bill Broonzy (1928–1935), Yazoo L 1011.
Big Bill Broonzy, Columbia 30-153.
Big Bill Broonzy, Vocalion 04706.
Big Bill Broonzy, Vanguard VRS 5523-4.
Big Bill's Blues, Columbia LP WL 111 o.p.
Big Bill's Blues, Epic EE 22017 o.p.
Big Bill's Blues, Portrait RK 44089.
The Blues, Scepter S 329 o.p.
Sings Country, Blues Disc D112 o.p.
Sings Country Blues, Folkways 2326.
Sings Country Blues, Folkways 31005.

Good Time Tonight, Columbia CK 46219.
Do that Guitar Thing, Yazoo (1035)
Big Bill Broonzy Sings Folk Songs, Smithsonian Folkways SF 40023.
Big Bill Broonzy 1934–1947, Story of Blues 3504.
Trouble in Mind, Fontana.

Big Bill Broonzy also performs on the following recordings:

Big Bill Broonzy and Washboard Sam, MCA-Chess CHD 9251.
Big Bill Broonzy/Sonny Boy Williamson, RCA Victor
Jazz Gillum, vol. 1, RCA Victor.
Washboard Sam, Blues Classics.
Pete Seeger & Big Bill Broonzy in Concert, Verve.
Blues with Big Bill Broonzy, Sonny Terry, Brownie McGhee.
Georgia Tom Dorsey, Georgia Tom, Riverside.
Washboard Sam, Feeling Lowdown, RCA.
Blues Classics by Sonny Boy Williamson, RCA Victor.
Sonny Boy Williamson, vol. 1, RCA Victor.

=====

TAMPA RED (1904–1981)

The Guitar Wizard

The guitar has been the most vital musical instrument of the twentieth century. Its refinement from the unsophisticated primitive models of yesteryear to the precise instruments of today is a reflection of the rapid technological advancements that have occurred in the past century. While the instrument has undergone several changes since the turn of the century, so has the development of the pioneers and innovators who chose the guitar as the key to fame and fortune. Although there have been a multitude of guitarists who have created classic blues moments with their individual styles, there has been only one blues guitarist who earned the magical title of "guitar wizard." His name was Tampa Red.

Tampa Red was born Hudson Whittaker in 1904 in Smithville,

Georgia. His family relocated to Tampa, Florida, when Hudson was a young boy. In the Sunshine State Whittaker first discovered the blues listening to one of the pioneers of the East Coast/Piedmont style, Blind Blake, who was born approximately ten years before the turn of the century and played inspired rag-blues with his impressive complex finger-picking style. Blind Blake had a minor hit with "West Coast Blues" in the 1920s before he disappeared from the blues scene.

Whittaker took up the guitar at an early age and loved to play to the rhythms of the tides among the palm trees and warm tropical breezes off the Gulf of Mexico. He played street corners for change and developed into a first-rate soloist and slide guitar player. He traveled throughout the Virginia-Piedmont region playing juke joints and house rent parties, gaining invaluable experience as a performer.

In the mid–1920s Whittaker left Florida and eventually made his way to Chicago. Although there were ample opportunities on the East coast, he felt that Chicago offered more promise. It was a naive young man with visions of fame and fortune dancing in his head who arrived in the big city; however, all was not immediately golden for him. He struggled for a few years playing the same venues—street corners and house parties—that he had back home. Although somewhat discouraged, Tampa Red was not about to give up on his dream of becoming an important blues singer.

During his first few weeks in the Windy City he acquired his nickname, Tampa Red. The first part of his moniker obviously came from the fact that he had lived in Tampa, while the other half was a reflection of his hair color.

In 1928, four years after he had arrived in the Windy City, he took a giant step forward in improving his fortunes when he teamed up with Georgia Tom Dorsey. The duo cut the hit single "It's Tight Like That" for the Paramount label and overnight they were credited with inventing the hokum style based on pure blues muscle, catchy melodies, and comical lyrics. In a sense, the hokum blues were an earlier forerunner of the novelty songs that were so popular thirty years later in the 1960s, such as "Alley Oop," "Li'l Red Ridin' Hood," and "Woolly Bully." The pair even went as far as calling themselves the Hokum Boys. The party came to an abrupt end in 1930 when Dorsey quit the blues in favor of gospel music.

Tampa Red continued as a solo artist, cutting a few sides for the Bluebird label. But he had tasted success as part of a duo, and his search for a partner was an exercise in frustration until he met the piano player Big Maceo Merriweather.

Big Maceo was born Major Merriweather on March 31, 1905, in Atlanta, Georgia. A self-taught piano player, Big Maceo was part of the large migration of blacks to the Northern cities—he moved to Detroit with his family in his late teens. In the Motor City he played at house parties and clubs, but realized that the real opportunities existed in Chicago. He arrived there in 1941 and soon befriended Tampa Red. During his time in Chicago, Big Maceo occupied the piano throne.

The partnership between Tampa Red and Big Maceo was the foundation on which the early Chicago blues school was built. Big Bill Broonzy, Memphis Slim, and Sunnyland Slim were also hanging around, playing the clubs and making great blues records. The period of the late 1930s and the 1940s was an important chapter in the history of the blues, but has often been overlooked because of other musical styles of the era and by what Muddy Waters and his friends did a decade later. However, if it were not for the groundbreaking work of Tampa Red, Big Maceo, and the other early Chicago bluesmen, Muddy Waters and his generation would not have had such a smooth road.

For Tampa Red, Big Maceo, Big Bill Broonzy, and others, the late 1930s and 1940s were their own personal golden age. Tampa Red was the hub of the blues activity in Chicago at that time. His apartment became the meeting place, like Chess Records became the place to go during the 1950s for Muddy Waters and his friends.

During his salad days, Tampa Red recorded for the Bluebird label under the direct supervision of Lester Melrose, an important figure in blues history. Melrose was born in Illinois in 1891 and became involved in the music business in the 1920s. He had a keen eye for talent, and under his tutelage many of the most famous blues stars of the 1940s gained their fame. Melrose boasted an impressive roster of stars, including Tampa Red, Big Bill Broonzy, John Lee "Sonny Boy" Williamson, Washboard Sam, Lonnie Johnson, Arthur "Big Boy" Crudup, Big Joe Williams, and Tommy McClennan.

The records made by these blues singers all possessed a similar quality because of the methods Melrose used. The same instruments were used in every recording session. Though the philosophy was a winning formula and made Tampa Red and his label mates stars, a certain staleness and predictability came to characterize the Bluebird material. Melrose has since been criticized for his rigid production techniques, but other companies, such as Chess, Motown, and Stax/Volt, followed a similar blueprint later in the century.

The era that Tampa Red starred in was over before it really began. Big Maceo was cut down in his prime by a debilitating stroke in 1946; two years later Sonny Boy Williamson I was murdered walking home from a club date. Big Maceo's death in 1953 at the age of forty-seven had a profound effect on his longtime partner, Tampa Red. Although Tampa Red continued his career without his dear friend, his sound was being phased out by the loud, brash, electric blues of Muddy Waters, Willie Dixon, Little Walter, Sonny Boy Williamson, Elmore James, and Howlin' Wolf.

Although Tampa Red continued to record and perform, by the mid–1960s his career was essentially over. There was always an audience for his rag-influenced blues and his undeniable unique talent, but his severe drinking problem spelled the end for Tampa Red. He retired from the blues scene in the late 1960s and continued to live in Chicago. On March 19, 1981, Tampa Red died. He was seventy-seven years old.

Tampa Red was an important star in Chicago in the 1930s and 1940s. Although the blues school that he ruled for a decade has since been overshadowed by the accomplishments of other groups, his era was important in its own right. It is unfortunate that Tampa Red gained his fame during a time when the blues were suffering a temporary lull in their popularity, as the musical spotlight of the 1940s belonged to the big bands of jazz. Despite living in the shadow of more popular music, Tampa Red added his own chapter in the Guitar Hall of Fame.

Tampa Red was a guitar hero long before the term was even coined. He was in some ways the Magic Sam of his day. His searing guitar licks encompassed his flashy single-string solos, and his clean bottleneck slide technique influenced Big Bill Broonzy, Robert Nighthawk, B. B. King, and a large number of other bluesmen of the postwar era. Very few guitarists in the history of the blues or rock have been able to play dazzling rhythm and lead guitar as well as sizzling bottleneck slide. Tampa Red had no equals in his time and never received full credit for his overall ingenious ability.

Although notable blues guitar heroes existed before he arrived on the scene, Tampa Red along with T-Bone Walker, Lonnie Johnson, and Chuck Berry paved the way for the future invasion of the guitar virtuosos of the 1960s, such as Eric Clapton, Jeff Beck, Jimmy Page, Duane Allman, and, the greatest of them all, Jimi Hendrix.

Tampa Red was arguably one of the top three guitar warriors of the premodern era. Prior to the emergence of the individual superstar lead guitarists, players were considered to be members of a band ensemble. While the individual styles of such guitar lords as Robert Johnson, Blind Lemon Jefferson, T-Bone Walker, Charlie Christian, and Lonnie Johnson did not go unnoticed, there simply did not exist the same kind of cult fascination that occurred with Hendrix and others later on in the century.

Not only was Tampa Red one of the great ax warriors but he was also the premier ambassador of the East Coast blues sound in the same way that Lonnie Johnson was the brightest torch bearer of the urban country-blues, Blind Lemon Jefferson the premier guitar stylist of the Texas tradition, and Robert Johnson the champion of the lowdown Mississippi Delta sound. Each musician brought innovations to the development of guitar playing that made the modern sound possible. Tampa Red was instrumental in bridging the gap between the ragtime piedmont blues and the Chicago sound. Tampa Red, like Muddy Waters, brought his down-home blues to the big city and built a successful career.

Although he recorded numerous songs, Tampa Red had only one big hit in his career—the ditty he and Georgia Tom Dorsey invented, "It's Tight Like That." The blues songs that Tampa Red gave the world are classic tracks and remain pertinent even today. "Worried Life Blues," "Chicago Breakdown," "Texas Stomp" "Detroit Jump," "It Hurts Me Too," "Don't You Lie to Me," "Denver Blues," and "Western Bound Blues" never became hits, but served as the blueprint for rock and roll.

A further list of songs includes "King Fish Blues," "Grievin' and Worryin' Blues," "Witchin' Hour Blues," "My Gal Is Gone," "When the One You Love Is Gone," "Delta Woman Blues," "Deceitful Friend Blues," "Travel On," "Why Should I Leave?" "Anna Lou Blues," "It's a Low Down Shame," "So Far So Good," "My First Love Blues," "I Can't Get Along with You," and "When Things Go Wrong with You." His early catalog was part of the songbook that many of the future blues stars of the 1950s began their careers by jamming on in the darkness of the South Side blues clubs.

Tampa Red was a friendly man whose love of the blues has been well documented. He was a generous soul who often took young musicians new to Chicago under his wing. He helped out a young Muddy Waters when the latter first arrived from the Delta. He was also a large influence on Ray Charles. More than anything else, he was a charismatic man who made the blues fun with his spunky feel and remarkable talent.

Tampa Red was inducted into the Blues Foundation Hall of Fame in 1981. As a new generation of blues singers emerge from various areas of the country and throughout the world they continue to pay tribute to the pioneers who made the necessary sacrifices to lay down the foundation for their future. While some eras will be remembered more than others, one should never forget the early days of Chicago blues when men like Big Bill Broonzy, Big Maceo, Sunnyland Slim, and especially the Guitar Wizard were creating magic.

Discography

The Guitar Wizard 1935–53, Blues Classics 25.
Tampa Red, Vol. 2, 1929–30, Blues Documents 2086.
Bottleneck Guitar, 1928–1937, Yazoo 1039.
Don't Tampa with the Blues, Prestige-Bluesville OBCCD 516-2.
Tampa Red, 1928–1940, Story of Blues 3505.
Tampa Red, Bluebird B 34-0711.
Tampa Red, Bluebird B 9024.
Tampa Red, Bluesville 1030.
Tampa Red: The Guitar Wizard, RCA/Bluebird AXM 2-5501.
It's Tight Like That, Blues Document 2001.
Bawdy Blues, Bluesville 544.

JOHN LEE "SONNY BOY" WILLIAMSON (1914–1948)

The Bluebird Blues

The first generation of Chicago bluesmen were an interesting assortment of characters. Tampa Red, Big Maceo, Big Bill Broonzy, Sunnyland Slim, and Memphis Minnie were just some of the singers who sparked the migration of blacks from the rural South up north to the Windy City. Another of the big names on the Chicago blues scene in the 1940s was the creator of the bluebird blues, a style based on his harmonica talents. His name was John Lee "Sonny Boy" Williamson.

John Lee Williamson was born on March 30, 1914, in Jackson, Tennessee. Like Little Walter and other great harmonica players, he was self-taught. He made an interesting choice of instruments, considering the lowly status of the mouth harp. But John Lee was better than the average typical harmonica player—he could draw incredible sounds from the instrument that were new and fresh. He was not just in love with the art of creating music, he was also enchanted with the lifestyle of a bluesman. By his late teens he was already roaming the South playing juke joints, parties, and fish fries.

Although he was a boy among men, Williamson was accepted by his older peers, like Sleepy John Estes, Yank Rachell, Big Joe Williams, and Robert Nighthawk. He proved their equal in every way. Because of his exuberance and youth he was nicknamed "Sonny Boy" by the older bluesmen. Although life on the road could prove exciting, Williamson tired of calling a small, strange, and different town home every night and decided to plant some roots in Chicago, joining the first generation of citified Southern bluesmen.

Williamson quickly prospered in Chicago for two basic reasons. First, he was the best harmonica player of his day, and second, he provided an exciting new dimension to the blues and was sought out by the other bluesmen on the scene. In 1937, Williamson secured a recording contract with Bluebird Records.

Armed with years of experience as a performing artist, Williamson delighted audiences as well as his fellow musicians with his intriguing musical skills. He was able to gain a whole new respect for the harmonica because of his ability to create fresh sounds. No one had heard anybody play the instrument with the same expertise as John Lee.

Williamson was also an important recording artist in his own right. His songs, "Good Morning Little School Girl," "Sugar Mama Blues," "Early in the Morning," "Check Up on My Baby," and "Bluebird Blues" helped establish his reputation as one of the mainstays on the Chicago blues scene in the late 1930s and early 1940s.

The eleven years that Williamson spent as one of the prime blues forces in Chicago were good. There existed a group of musicians dedicated to the purity and beauty of the blues. There was a fraternity among Tampa Red, Big Maceo, Jazz Gillum, Memphis Minnie, Big Bill Broonzy, Washboard Sam, Arthur "Big Boy" Crudup, and John Lee. The music he created with his fellow musicians is classic material and holds a special place in blues history. Perhaps if the era had lasted longer, maybe it would have garnered the true respect is deserves.

During this period, John Lee recorded a wealthy catalog of memorable songs, including: "Up the Country Blues," "Katie Mae Blues," "I Have Got to Go," "Desperate Woman," "Sonny Boy's Jump," "Win the War Blues," "Super Mama Blues," "I'm Tired of Truckin' My Blues Away," "Black Gal Blues," "Doggin' My Love Around," "I'm Not Pleasing You," "Tell Me Baby," "I'm Gonna Catch You Soon," "Elevator Woman," "Apple Tree Swing," "No Friend Blues," "Half a Pint Southern Dream," and "Better Cut That Out." Obviously, John Lee was one of the more prolific bluesmen of the late 1930s and 1940s.

The harmonica touch of Williamson can be heard not only on his own songs but also on the recordings of others, including Tampa Red, Big Bill Broonzy, Big Maceo, Memphis Minnie, and others of the so-called Bluebird period. The tight circle of Chicago blues singers of that era produced a remarkable body of blues poetry. Unfortunately, it seemed over before it had started.

While the explosion of the electric blues sound was one of the main reasons why the blues singers of the 1940s were soon forgotten and dropped by the wayside, there is another reason. On June 1, 1948, while walking home after a performance in Chicago, John Lee Williamson was killed. He was only thirty-four years old. His death brought about the end of the first chapter of Chicago blues.

John Lee "Sonny Boy" Williamson was a star during the late 1930s and much of the 1940s until his tragic death. During his decade-long run as the best harmonica on the scene he enjoyed a large amount of personal success as well as being a prime mover in the grand achievements of others. He was one of the most important members of the Chicago blues scene during his heyday. He was the best known and most inventive harmonica player of his era, and he was a favorite among the other blues musicians at the time. He became one of the best-selling blues artists on the Bluebird label.

Despite his obvious reign as harmonica champion for a decade, Williamson's major contribution to the blues was as an innovator. To understand fully what he did for the harmonica once must trace the history of the instrument from the turn of the century to 1948, the year of his tragic death.

By the late nineteenth century the standard instruments used in the blues had been established. The guitar occupied the dominant role in the blues, with the piano a close second and the violin and other string instruments third; various percussion devices were less popular. At the bottom of the musical heap—used mainly to add light touches and tones—was the neglected harmonica.

But, John Lee Williamson changed all that. Although there had been some very good harp players, such as Noah Lewis, Will Shade, and Hammie Nixon, before John Lee, none was able to elevate the harmonica beyond its lowly level. Along came Williamson, who played the most inspired blues on the harmonica. He forced the other musicians to reconsider their prejudiced opinion by showing them with his incredible passion that the instrument could be a force in blues music. He achieved this respect for the harmonica with sheer musical brilliance, impeccable timing, and clear, audible tones that sounded like words instead of simple down-home notes.

Williamson showed the blues world that the harmonica possessed the potential of creating magic, not just supplying minor riffs. He proved that it could lay down the rhythmic foundation of the song and provide great solo breaks that caused shivers to run down the listeners' spines. With his inventive playing, Williamson could take a song to dimensions that neither the guitar, piano, various stringed instruments, or percussion instruments were able to do. Williamson proved that the harmonica was capable of mimicking and evoking any emotion in the human experience.

But Williamson had another weapon in his arsenal, which he used to great advantage even though it could have been a weak spot in his armor. Williamson was born with a "slow tongue," which made it unable for him to correctly master the phonetics of the English language. But he cleverly hid his speech impediment by sounding like a singing harmonica. It not only gave him a unique vocal slurring style but also strengthened his accomplishments on the harmonica. He was able to interchange his "lazy" vocals with his bright harmonica notes to create a completely smooth sound.

Because he was the pioneer of the harmonica, Williamson exerted a precious influence on future players such as Little Walter, James Cotton, Junior Wells, Big Walter Horton, and Rice Miller, who also adopted the moniker "Sonny Boy." Rice Miller was not only an outstanding harmonica player on his own but he also realized the value of self-marketing. What better way to gain notoriety than to steal a name that was already established in blues circles? Although Miller enjoyed greater success and brought more fame to the nickname Sonny Boy, the title truly belonged to John Lee.

Though the harmonica has not been a major force in rock, those who have added the instrument to round out their sound can trace their roots back to the imaginative pioneering ways of Williamson. Paul Butterfield, a Chicago-born harmonica player who learned the blues on the city's South Side, was indirectly influenced by Williamson. Butterfield perfected his craft while listening and playing with Howlin' Wolf, Junior Wells, and Sonny Boy Williamson II. Other rock groups who have made the harmonica an important part of their act include the J. Geils Band, Led Zeppelin (especially in the early days), the Doors, the Lovin' Spoonful, and the early blues days of the Rolling Stones.

John Lee's signature song, "Good Morning Little Schoolgirl," was later covered by Texas Tornado bluesman Johnny Winter, who delivered a rocking version far removed from John Lee's initial effort. Williamson's song "Sugar Mama Blues," inspired John Lee Hooker to write "Sugar Mama." The great slide guitarist Elmore James had a hit with "Early in the Morning," adding his distinctive bottleneck sound. A collaboration on the song between Elmore James and John Lee would have been dynamite, but unfortunately never came about.

In 1980, John "Sonny Boy" Williamson was inducted in the Blues Foundation Hall of Fame, as the most important pre–War World II harmonica player. He was eventually overshadowed by Rice Miller, who had a longer, and more prosperous career. But because he broke new ground for all harmonica players who followed him, the original Sonny Boy should never be forgotten as the man who gave the world his "Bluebird Blues" and single-handedly gave the harmonica respect in the blues world.

Discography

Sonny Boy Williamson, Vol. 1 (1937–1938), Document DOCD 5055.
Sonny Boy Williamson, Vol. 2 (1938–1939), Document DOCD 5056.
Sonny Boy Williamson, Vol. 3 (1939–1941), Document DOCD 5057.
Sonny Boy Williamson, Vol. 4 (1941–1945), Document DOCD 5058.
Sonny Boy Williamson, Vol. 5 (1945–1947), Document DOCD 5059.
Sonny Boy Williamson I, Blues Classics BC.
Sonny Boy Williamson I, Bluesbird B 8580.
Original Rhythm and Blues Hits, RCA Camden CAL 740.
Sonny Boy Williamson I, Rare Sonny Boy, 1937–1947, RCA NL 90027.
Throw a Boogie-Woogie (With Big Joe Williams) RCA Heritage 9599-2.

MUDDY WATERS (1915–1983)

Catfish Blues

In every generation a few persons nobly dream of being known before the world. With raw determination, leadership, and boundless confidence these driven individuals eventually reach their destiny or spend their entire lives in search of it. In the late 1940s, the blues were at a crossroads. Although blues records sold well, the music had lost its fire and magic. The old style of the country-blues was quickly becoming outdated because of a lack of direction. The blues world needed a leader, somebody able to fuse the old, the present, and the new into something bold and exciting. Amid the chaos one man rose above his contemporaries to become the guiding light of the modern blues school. His name was Muddy Waters.

Muddy Waters was born McKinley Morganfield in Rolling Forks, Mississippi, on April 4, 1915. Like B. B. King and Bessie Smith, Waters lost his mother at a young age. His father took him to Clarksdale, Mississippi, to live with his paternal grandmother. Blues folklore insists that because little McKinley loved to splash around in a local muddy pond his grandmother gave him the name Muddy Waters. This was a blues name with dignity and authority; a true reflection of his deep Mississippi Delta blues roots. Years later, the name Muddy Waters became synonymous with the blues.

While he became the king of Chicago blues in his adult life, Muddy's early years were not easy ones. Waters was very well acquainted with the hard labor that was part of a rural farmer's life in the Mississippi Delta. He learned how to work a plow behind the mule, pick cotton, milk cows, and perform the other menial tasks of a sharecropper. Educational opportunities were slim, and the young Waters faced a lifetime of hard labor and low pay. Unlike the sports stars of a later generation who were offered attractive scholarships, for Muddy, the only ticket out of the Delta and a certain life of poverty was music.

As a young boy, Muddy Waters was fascinated by the blues. The magical music stirred deep emotions inside him; like the sorcerer's apprentice, he desperately wanted to make the brooms dance. Muddy's first choice of instruments was the harmonica, but later he bought a guitar from a friend. Once he had saved enough money he purchased a manufactured model and began to learn how to play slide guitar.

Like other blossoming bluesmen, Muddy knew he needed a "copy" and chose the immortal Robert Johnson. After Johnson's untimely death, Waters turned to Eddie "Son" House who lived just across from Muddy on another plantation. He spent long hours studying House; after much practice Muddy became a master slide guitar player like his mentor.

In 1941, Alan Lomax "discovered" Muddy Waters on the Stovall Plantation in Mississippi, where the aspiring bluesman was a member of the Son Sims Four. Lomax, who was searching for the great Robert Johnson to record for the Library of Congress, was forced to settle for the unknown Waters after learning of Johnson's demise. Muddy knew the value of a record and was eager to record for Lomax. But it was not overnight success for Waters, and he continued to pay his dues by playing at country events and in the streets of Clarksdale. The kind passersby who put a few coins in his tin cup had absolutely no way of knowing that they were listening to a future blues legend.

Muddy Waters became an excellent guitar player and dazzled everyone with his bountiful skills. But he was more than just a competent instrumentalist. He possessed a powerful singing voice, which gave him a definitive edge over many other blues guitarists. Although he was a genuine blues talent his musical opportunities were limited in the Mississippi Delta. By 1942, Muddy was twenty-seven years old and had been performing the blues for over thirteen years. He wanted a change and fully understood that if he was ever to realize his ambition of becoming a genuine blues force he would have to move to the big city. In 1943, Muddy Waters arrived in Chicago with a few dollars in his pocket and raw determination to be known before the world.

Though he had established a name for himself back in the Delta, in Chicago he was just another musician seeking his fame and fortune. Waters landed a job at a paper factory and played at parties that the workers gave. Through word of mouth he got a job at a small club called The Flame. He became a sideman for piano players Sunnyland Slim and Eddie Boyd until he formed his own small band. While he had made enormous progress in his musical career since arriving in Chicago, Muddy was keenly aware that in order to join the big players on the scene (which included Memphis Minnie, Big Maceo, Big Bill Broonzy, Tampa Red, and Sonny Boy Williamson), he had to make records. Through Sunnyland Slim,

Waters auditioned for Chess Records and finally was given the opportunity to record his own music.

The first important recordings of the postwar blues era can be traced back to 1948 when Muddy recorded "I Can't Be Satisfied" and "Feel Like Goin' Home." The label the songs were released on, Aristocrat Records, was owned by two brothers of Polish descent, Leonard and Phil Chess. Even though the Chess brothers had doubts that the songs Muddy recorded had any commercial appeal, they nevertheless pressed the record. To their utter astonishment, it sold out in just a few short hours. Unknowingly to the Chess brothers or even Muddy, the golden age of electric Chicago blues had begun.

The blues force that was Muddy Waters was like a juggernaut once it got started. Waters gave the blues the emotional punch and fire that it had been lacking since the days of Robert Johnson. Muddy's interpretation of the blues was quite simple. He pitted strict rhythm against deep-felt tone, and the interactive dynamics were the foundation that the Chicago blues were built on. Muddy also experimented extensively with the relatively new electric sound, retaining the harsh edges of power that made his guitar roar like an angry lion.

Muddy also possessed the uncanny ability to recruit the best musicians for his band and by 1951 all the pieces were in place. He had Jimmy Rogers on rhythm guitar, Fred Below on drums, Willie Dixon on bass, Little Walter on harmonica, and Otis Spann on piano (see list at end of chapter). While personnel changed over the years, there was no better assemblage of blues musicians from 1951 to 1960 than the Muddy Waters Band.

During this period Waters recorded many definitive modern blues classics, including "Long Distance Call" "Hootchie Cootchie Man," "I Just Want to Make Love to You," "Rollin' and Tumbling," "Got My Mojo Working," "Louisiana Blues," "Rolling Blues," "Trouble No More," "I Want You to Love Me," "I'm Ready," "Mannish Boy," "Gypsy Women," "Little Annie Mae," and "Honey Bee."

By 1953, ten years after he had made the trek up north with little more than his shirt on his back, Muddy Waters was the boss of Chicago. The crowds demanded a brash, citified brand of blues; Muddy and his band did not fail to deliver. With every performance at Sylvio's or the 700 Club and every new single released by Chess Records, Waters was expanding his sphere of influence.

But despite his prominence in Chicago, he was scarcely known in other parts of the United States. The blues, considered "race" music, were treated by the establishment like the plague. Also, the "new" music, rock and roll, overshadowed the efforts of the Chicago blues school which was insulting considering how much the first generations of rockers had borrowed from the blues. But Muddy, his bandmates and the rest of the blues singers who had come to Chicago were biding their time.

In 1958, there were two significant events that occurred in the career of Muddy Waters that directly shaped the future course of popular music for the remainder of the century. Interestingly, the two events are closely tied together.

The first was the release of his debut album, *The Best of Muddy Waters* a collection of his hit singles that became an audio-bible to many young musicians who would someday proudly carry the blues torch. Many of the dedicated blues-rock warriors of the next decade would emerge from England, so the availability of that record overseas was of great importance.

Fittingly, the second actually took place across the Atlantic. Though he was not the first American bluesman to tour England, Muddy Waters may have made the biggest impact. Many of the fervent blues fans in England received their education secondhand from imported records. Because they knew little of the actual inspiration for the blues, English blues fans had a decidedly strong notion of an American bluesman. Years before, Big Bill Broonzy had arrived in England and played slow, mournful, acoustic numbers which conformed to the British image of what a rural American bluesman should sound like.

But Muddy Waters had no intention of sounding like a recently freed slave from the plantation. He arrived with his nasty, citified Chicago blues band in their striped suits and greased pompadours and shook the very foundations of the British Isles. The raw energy and emotion displayed by Muddy and the rest of the band won over a legion of fans. Muddy had taken another gigantic step toward his vision of being known around the world.

By 1960, the amplified Chicago blues had gained respect in different corners of the world, but still had not received their proper due. The performance of the Muddy Waters Band at the Newport Folk Festival perfectly demonstrated why the Chicago blues were so powerful and why Waters was the dean of the electric Delta sound. The Muddy Waters Band turned the Newport Folk Festival into a rollicking blues fest.

For the rest of the decade, Muddy was portrayed more as a folk artist than as the wizard of the electric blues, mostly by Chess Records, to cash in on the folk-blues fever that was sweeping the country. But his electric days were not forgotten by British blues scholars like the Rolling Stones, the Yardbirds, the Animals, Cyril Davies, Alexis Korner, and John Mayall, who were trying to capture the electric magic of the Muddy Waters sound.

Muddy Waters was fully accepted by the rock and roll crowd as high priest of the blues. He appeared at numerous rock festivals, including the Sky River Rock Festival on Labor Day Weekend in Sultan, Washington, in 1968. In the late 1960s and early 1970s he recorded with some of the rock set who considered him their supreme idol. The albums *They Call Me Muddy Waters* and *The London Muddy Waters Sessions* both won Grammies and included guest appearances by Steve Winwood, Rory Gallagher, and Mitch Mitchell.

One of the most productive relationships that Waters made with a member of the rock generation was with Johnny Winter, the albino bluesman. Winter had a special veneration for Muddy and produced the Grammy award–winning album *Hard Again* in 1977. It was Muddy's first album for the CBS/Blue Sky label since his departure from Chess Records. The 1978 release *I'm Ready* was also well received by fans and critics. Waters and Winter also performed together frequently in the 1970s to appreciative audiences.

During the 1970s, Muddy continued to spread the word of the blues touring all over the world. Waters even performed for President Jimmy Carter and appeared in The Band's farewell concert film *The Last Waltz*, where he stole the show with a dynamic version of "Mannish Boy."

By the dawn of the 1980s, Muddy Waters had achieved his boyhood ambition of being known around the world. There was nothing that he hadn't accomplished in his long and distinguished career. In 1980 he was inducted into the Foundation Hall of Fame. In 1987, Waters was inducted into the Rock and Roll Hall of Fame, an honor he sadly did not live to see.

On April 30, 1983, in the suburban section of Westmount, Illinois, McKinley Morganfield, better known to the world as Muddy Waters, died peacefully in his sleep of natural causes. It was an international day of mourning.

Muddy Waters was more than just a superstar of the blues—he was an institution. He was the dean of the modern electric blues sound and ruled his empire for five decades. He was an innovator of the highest order, and his influence on the course of popular music of the last fifty years is incomparable. Perhaps only Elvis and Chuck Berry had the same kind of impact on later generations of rockers.

Muddy Waters was the supreme student of the Chicago blues school, which included Howlin' Wolf, Willie Dixon, Little Walter, Elmore James, Jimmy Rogers, Buddy Guy, Otis Rush, Magic Sam, Koko Taylor, Etta James, and Sonny Boy Williamson II. Though each one made a special contribution to the blues, none had the same potency. It was Muddy who put the city on the musical map forever.

Not only is Muddy Waters a strong candidate as the greatest blues singer in history but he also laid down the foundation of the rock and roll format that would be copied by hundreds of bands. He became one of the most compelling slide guitarists and ranks with the best of the bottleneck technique players, including Son House, Robert Johnson, Elmore James, Duane Allman, Earl Hooker, and Robert Nighthawk.

He was also an excellent bandmaster, and many of the biggest names in modern blues were members of the Muddy Waters Band at one time or another (see list at end of chapter). Some of the band members enjoyed considerable personal success, but they will forever be remembered as members of the famed Muddy Waters Band.

His direct influence on Jimi Hendrix, Eric Clapton, Johnny Winter, Rory Gallagher, Stevie Ray Vaughan, Buddy Guy, Otis Rush, Magic Sam, Freddie King, Albert King, Albert Collins, Luther Allison, Bob Dylan, Chuck Berry, Jeff Beck, Robert Cray, John Mayall, and Johnny Winter is incalcuable. The Rolling Stones took their name from a Muddy Waters song ("Mannish Boy"). The debt to Waters stated in hundreds of interviews by legions of rock and blues musicians only enhances his regal stature.

On a scale of world music leaders, Muddy Waters holds the same position in the blues as Bob Marley does in reggae. From a blues perspective, he was to his and other generations a Beethoven, a Mozart, a Bach, a Schubert, a Chopin. As a twentieth-century artist, Waters belongs in the elite company of Duke Ellington, Count Basie, Leonard Bernstein, Louis Armstrong, Bessie Smith, Robert Johnson, T-Bone Walker, B. B. King, the Beatles, Bob Dylan, Billie Holiday, and Hank Williams, Sr.

Muddy Waters was the most important link between the country-blues of the Mississippi Delta and the sophisticated urban sound. He was the welder who fused the two distinct styles together to create the modern electric blues. It was Muddy Waters with his mojo who gave back to the blues the strength and vitality that the genre had been lacking in previous years.

Throughout his career, Muddy Waters was a tireless defender of the blues faith. A simple man with little formal education who never claimed to be the most polished orator, he spoke from his heart and did not hide his feelings behind empty words. Through perseverance, undaunted conviction, and incredible stamina acquired in the harsh years as a boy growing up in the Mississippi Delta, Muddy Waters fulfilled his self-proclaimed vow to be known before the world. From the moment he became a star Waters was the biggest catfish in the giant blues pond and retained his prominence because of his superior talent and unmatched feel for the blues. He has never been nor will he ever be replaced.

The Muddy Waters Band Members
1951–1960[*]

Guitar	Harmonica	Bass	Drums	Piano
Jimmy Rogers, 1950–1955	Little Walter, 1951–1954	Ernest Crawford, 1948–1954	Leroy Foster, 1948–1950	Sunnyland Slim, 1948–1952
Pat Hare, 1955–1960[1]	Junior Wells, 1952–1953	Willie Dixon, 1955–1960	Elgin Evans, 1950–1954	Otis Spann, 1953–1960
	George "Harmonica" Smith, 1953–1954		Fred Below, 1954–1957	
	Henry Strong, 1954–1955[2]		Francis Clay, 1957–1960	
	James Cotton, 1955–1966			

[*]*These blues musicians were part of the Muddy Waters lineup from about 1951–1960. This list does not include the numerous musicians who got up on stage and jammed with Muddy or may have contributed on one of his recording sessions. While the band continued past 1960, the band's effectiveness was during the aforementioned period.*

Otis Spann, Willis Dixon, Jimmy Rogers, James Cotton and Junior Wells all eventually left the Muddy Waters band to form their own groups. However, some of them still played with Muddy on different occasions.

[1]*Pat Hare was fired after the Newport Jazz Festival in 1960 because of his serious drinking problem.*

[2]*Henry Strong was stabbed to death by his girlfriend in 1955.*

Discography

Fathers and Sons, MCA/Chess 2-92522.
I'm Ready, CBS PZ 34928.
Complete Muddy Waters, Charly 3.
The Best of Muddy Waters, Chess 1427.
McKinley Morganfield AKA Muddy Waters, Chess 60006.
Can't Get No Grindin', Chess CH 50023.
Down on Stovall's Plantation, Testament 2210.
Muddy Waters, Chess @A CMB 203.
Muddy Waters Louisiana Blues, Chess 1441.
The Chess Box, Chess/MCA CHD 3-80002.
Hard Again, Blue Sky 34449.
Muddy Mississippi Waters—Live, Blue Sky 35712.
King Bee, Blue Sky 37064.
Rare & Unissued, Chess 9180.
Blues Sky, Epic 46172.
Muddy Waters at Newport, Chess 31269.
One More Nite, Chess Records
The Complete Plantation Recordings, MCA-Chess CHD-9344.
Muddy Waters: The Chess Box, MCA-Chess 31268.
The Best of Muddy Waters, MCA-Chess 31268.
Rolling Stone, MCA-Chess 9101.
Muddy Waters Sings Big Bill Broonzy, MCA-Chess 5907.
Folksinger, MCA-Chess 9261.
The Real Folk Blues, MCA-Chess 9274.
More Real Folk Blues, MCA-Chess 9278.
Trouble No More, MCA-Chess 9291.
The London Muddy Waters Sessions, MCA-Chess 9298.
They Call Me Muddy Waters, MCA-Chess 9299.
Muddy and the Wolf, MCA-Chess 9100.

WILLIE DIXON (1915–1992)

The Background Man

The heyday of the Chess label, 1950–1965, was the golden era of modern blues. The songs that emerged from the company's recording studio during this period influenced an entire generation of musicians throughout the world who grew up listening to such genuine classics as "Little Red Rooster," "Hootchie Cootchie Man," "Evil," "Spoonful," "Back Door Man," "My Baby," "I Ain't Superstitious," and "I Just Want to Make Love to You," to name only a few. While the unmistakable voices of Muddy Waters, Howlin' Wolf, and Little Walter turned these songs into blues gold, the source of the material flowed from the same imaginative pen of the genius who, because he remained in the shadows, was best known as the "background man." His name was Willie Dixon.

Willie Dixon was born July 1, 1915, in Vicksburg, Mississippi, on the very edge of the Delta. By the time he was eight years old he was working as hard as a grown man. He shares this trait with blues brothers B. B. King, Muddy Waters, and Howlin' Wolf. However, unlike many Delta bluesmen, it was not musical opportunities that brought the young Dixon to Chicago, but the sweet dreams of a glorious life as a heavyweight boxer. When his professional boxing hopes were cut short—despite sparring with the legendary Joe Louis—Dixon turned his full attention to becoming a musician.

But long before his dreams of becoming the heavyweight champion of the world were dashed, Dixon had held a keen interest in music. Like many other black children, Dixon's musical education began in the church, where he sang in the choir as a young boy. He later appeared on a radio station with his gospel group, the Union Jubilee Singers. Because he received very little formal education, the influence of his mother's religious poetry was instrumental in shaping his future career as a songwriter. His mother taught him the magic of words, which later enabled him to create a remarkable catalog of treasured blues gems.

Once he began to concentrate on a musical career, Dixon formed his own band, The Five Breezes, who played in and around the Chicago area.

With the advent of World War II a new crisis developed in his life. Not wanting to go to war he spent time in prison as a conscientious objector. Once out of prison he continued to pursue his musical ambitions.

Willie Dixon was an enterprising young man. While playing with his own group, the Big Three, he was also moonlighting with Muddy Waters and other denizens of the Chicago blues scene in various clubs around town. The Big Three consisted of Dixon on bass, Leonard "Baby Doc" Caston, and Bernardo Dennis and recorded for different labels. While they were a slick musical trio, the Big Three never enjoyed much commercial success, and the band eventually ceased operations. Dixon was not unemployed very long—he went to work for the Chess brothers, owners of the Chess studios, on a full-time basis.

From this point on Dixon began to establish his primary role in the rise of electric Chicago blues. Dixon was the musical brains behind the great success of Chess Records. He was the background man who performed numerous roles including those of songwriter, arranger, session musician (bass player), recording artist, and talent scout.

Dixon was a member of the famous Muddy Waters Band. Not only did he help produce many of the songs that catapulted Waters to superstar status but he also wrote them. The songs "Hootchie Cootchie Man" and "I Just Want to Make Love to You" that are linked to Waters were actually penned by Dixon. His sophisticated, urban, humorous lyrics plus his talents as a musician and arranger gave Waters an incredible edge over other bluesman.

Dixon also helped Howlin' Wolf increase his blues stature. The Wolf, in his inimitable style, turned the Dixon compositions "Evil," "Spoonful," "I Ain't Superstitious," "Little Red Rooster," and "Back Door Man" into eternal classics. Little Walter's "My Baby" was another huge hit written by Dixon. The down-home Delta grit of "Bring it on Home," featuring the sorrowful harmonica touch of Sonny Boy Williamson II (Rice Miller), only enhanced Dixon's credibility as a songwriter.

Throughout much of the 1950s Dixon could be found in the Chess studios creating magic. He played an instrumental role in shaping the course of popular music—a role that often went unnoticed because he maintained a separate recording career that never matched that of other artists on the label.

However, Dixon was a superb bandleader. His group, the Chicago Blues All-Stars, was a talented lineup that backed him up on his many tours and recording sessions in the 1960s, 1970s, and 1980s. Despite the fact that his own records never did as well as those of other bluesman, there is no discredit to Dixon in any way. His contribution to other artists generously makes up for his lack of personal commercial success.

At the end of 1957, Dixon left Chess to work at the newly established Cobra Records, where he helped to establish and further the careers of Magic Sam, Otis Rush, and Buddy Guy. Once again his talents as arranger, producer, and musician shaped the sound of popular music, as the three young guitarists were blues fixtures in the late 1950s and early 1960s. On the demise of Cobra two years later, Dixon returned to work for Chess Records.

The 1960s were a productive decade for Dixon. Aside from his remarkable work for Chess, he also toured with Europe as part of a Folk Blues Festival package. The blues fans overseas were able to witness firsthand the man who was responsible for the songs that had been part of the blues education of so many. Long before many of the blues scholars began to play the music of their heroes, they had spent hours secluded in their rooms trying to absorb the genius of the American bluesmen.

While the popularity of the blues fell sharply in the 1970s, Dixon continued to tour and record. He cut albums for the Ovation, Columbia, and Yambo labels. With the Chicago Blues All-Stars, Dixon toured regularly, appearing in blues festivals throughout the country and around the world. Like he had always done, he went about his business carrying the blues flag with great distinction.

At the beginning of the 1980s, Dixon showed no signs of slowing down. He was responsible for the formation of the Blues Heaven Foundation, funded by money he earned from his classic songs. The foundation, was set up to keep the blues flame burning strongly by providing funding at the educational level, including special programs for music students. On occasion, the foundation also aided down and out bluesmen.

Dixon remained active on other fronts as well. He wrote the musical score for the film *The Color of Money*, starring Tom Cruise and Paul Newman. He earned production credits for soundtrack work in the movie *La Bamba*. Dixon was one of the few bluesman who had his story published. The title of the book, *I Am the Blues*, says it all. He also released one of the finest albums of his career, *Hidden Charms*, in 1988 on the Bug/Capitol label.

In 1990, Dixon's health problems forced him in semiretirement. On January 29, 1992, Willie Dixon, the gentle giant of the bass guitar, died of a heart ailment in Burbank, California. He was seventy-six years old.

Willie Dixon was a blues star of great importance. Although his success as a recording artist never reached the levels of some of his contemporaries, his accomplishments in other areas more than compensate for this slight chink in his musical armor. There is no doubt that Willie Dixon with his multitalented abilities as composer, session man, arranger, bass player, and talent scout was the ultimate blues warrior.

Dixon is probably the single most important songwriter in the history of the blues. No other bluesman can be credited with as many classics. Just a short list of his songs includes "Hootchie Cootchie Man," "I Just Want to Make Love to You," "Evil," "Spoonful," "I Ain't Superstitious," "Little Red Rooster," "Back Door Man," "My Babe," "Bring it on Home," "Wang Dang Doodle," "The Seventh Son," "You Can't Judge a Book by its Cover," "I Want You," "You Shook Me," and "I Can't Quit You Baby."

Many of his songs were later covered by British and American blues bands. "Little Red Rooster," "Back Door Man," and "Close to You" were done by the Doors. The Rolling Stones cut a version of "Little Red Rooster" that sounded like they were from the American South instead of Great Britain. Cream turned "Spoonful" into something very special. The Allman Brothers boosted their blues credentials with a solid version of "Hootchie Cootchie Man." Led Zeppelin covered "I Can't Quit You Baby" and "You Shook Me." The Jeff Beck Group also recorded a version of "You Shook Me" as well as "I Ain't Superstitious." Canadian-born Frank Marino of Mahogany Rush did an excerpt of "Back Door Man" on the band's live album *Mahagony Rush Live.* Foghat cut a studio and a live version of "I Just Want to Make Love to You." Jimi Hendrix, who never included a Dixon number on any of his studio albums, often played Dixon songs live in a way that only the Seattle guitar master could. Willie Dixon's songs were played live by many other bands that had the blues fever and countless garage bands jamming hard in hopes of becoming future rock stars.

As an arranger and session man, Dixon had a hand in the careers of Muddy Waters, Howlin' Wolf, Elmore James, Little Walter, Buddy Guy, Otis Rush, Magic Sam, Koko Taylor, Bo Diddley, and a young St. Louis hairdresser-turned-musician named Chuck Berry. Dixon is an important link between the blues and rock and roll. Many of Berry's classic rock and roll recordings featured Dixon on bass.

Willie Dixon was arguably as instrumental in the creation of the Chicago blues school as anyone else, including Muddy Waters. Though he didn't become the authoritative figure that Waters did, in many ways

Dixon was the supreme architect because he played so many different roles. Without the genius of Willie Dixon, Waters and many other blues singers who recorded for the Chess label would not have drawn the same amount of recognition.

Willie Dixon didn't bother to learn guitar, piano, or harmonica. His choice of musical instruments was the bass guitar; in the hierarchy of bluesmen, Dixon is the undisputed the bossman of the bass. While he set the bass line on fire with his thick, quick, skilled fingers, Dixon never received the same credit as Muddy Waters did with his slide guitar work or Little Walter for his role as the Mississippi Saxophone. Though Dixon is not regarded as an innovator of the bass guitar, his influence on rock's great bass players—Jack Bruce, Roger Glover, John Paul Jones, Berry Oakley, and Bill Wyman—is extremely important. In a world full of guitar players, Dixon adopted the bass and gave the instrument much-needed respect.

As a talent scout, it was Dixon who discovered Koko Taylor and signed her to Chess Records. Taylor's classic "Wang Dang Doodle" is yet another Dixon composition. To Dixon's credit, Koko Taylor became one of the most important female singers in the history of the blues. She continues to delight audiences even today with her powerful voice and energetic performances.

Despite the serious impact he made on the blues and rock music, Dixon never received all the credit he was due. There are several reasons for this. For one thing, Dixon never scored many hits, although other artists enjoyed wonderful success with his compositions. Also, Dixon was always lurking in the background running Chess studios. His quiet role did not put him in the forefront like a Muddy Waters, Howlin' Wolf, Little Walter, Elmore James, Chuck Berry, or other famous names on the Chess label.

Because of his major contributions to the blues in so many different areas, Dixon was inducted into the Blues Foundation Hall of Fame in 1980. He quietly assumed a lesser role than many of his more famous contemporaries, but Dixon's vast contributions to the blues cannot be overstated. In the history of the blues, Willie Dixon, the intelligent, humorous, good-natured background man, occupies a very special place.

Discography

Willie Dixon: The Big Three, Columbia CK 46216.

Willie Dixon: The Chess Box, MCA-Chess CHD2-16500.
Hidden Charms, Capitol C1 90595.
I Am the Blues, Mobile Fidelity MFCD 872.
Willie Dixon and His Chicago Blues Band, Spivey 1016.
Catalyst Ovation, OVQD 1433.
Memphis Slim and Willie Dixon: Blues Every Which Way, Verve V 3007.
I Feel Like Steppin' Out, Dr. Horse 804.
The Big Trio, CBS 46216.

═══════════

HOWLIN' WOLF (1910–1976)

Growlin' the Blues

The blues are about emotion. Happiness, anger, fear, disappoint-
ment, sadness—the entire spectrum of human experiences is expressed in
the blues. The intense passion displayed by performers is the essential
ingredient that has given the blues its supreme creative edge. Every other
musical style has tried to steal this lightning bolt from the blues in an
attempt to capture the same magic. One of the most imitated bluesman
who exhibited this feverish passion was known as the Growlin' Bluesman.
His name was Howlin' Wolf.

Howlin' Wolf was born Chester Arthur Burnett on June 10, 1910, in
West Point, Mississippi. Although he was named after the twenty-first
president of the United States, a career in politics was not a future possibility for young Chester. The son of hard-working farmers, Burnett was
expected to take over from them once he was old enough. Though he
did farm until he was almost forty, fate had different plans for him.

As a young boy growing up in the Mississippi Delta he frequented
many plantation picnics where he heard and saw Charley Patton and
Willie Brown. Burnett paid close attention to Patton, who became the
first Delta country-blues star. Not only did he learn how to play guitar
by watching Patton but he also picked up valuable entertainment tips. He
became a good guitar player, though he was never truly proficient on the
instrument.

Burnett learned to play the harmonica from one of the greats, Sonny Boy Williamson II, who was still known by his birth name, Rice Miller, when Chester first met him. Miller, who was dating Burnett's older sister, would give young Chester some harmonica tips in order to get rid of the little pest. Though he blew a mean harmonica, Burnett never mastered the instrument as well as his famous tutor.

Charley Patton possessed a remarkable blues voice, which intrigued Burnett, but the latter drew his inspiration from a rather curious source: the singing brakeman, Jimmy Rodgers. The emotional intensity that Rodgers displayed stirred certain emotions in Burnett, and he was quick to incorporate the finer points of Rodgers' vocal style into his own.

By his early teens, Howlin' Wolf had combined all of these influences into his own inimitable style and was traveling the Delta and other Southern regions honing his blues skills. By this time he had been tagged with the unlikely nickname Howlin' Wolf, which he earned because of the loud wail he could produce.

For someone who supposedly moaned and howled like a wolf, Burnett traveled with some very elite company, including Charley Patton, Willie Brown, Sonny Boy Williamson II, Tommy Johnson, Robert Jr. Lockwood, and the enigmatic Robert Johnson. Sometimes, Sonny Boy Williamson II, Howlin' Wolf, and Robert Johnson roamed the Delta together, playing juke joints and house parties. As a live musical trio, the Wolf, Sonny Boy Williamson II, and Robert Johnson must have been absolute dynamite!

Despite his musical affiliations, Howlin' Wolf continued to work with his father on the family farm. A careful man, he was eager to pursue his musical ambitions, but was deeply tied to the land. None of the bluesmen he knew were even moderately rich, and many lived a hand-to-mouth existence. The life of a farmer would not make him a millionaire, but the land provided a sense of security for Wolf, a family man who wasn't ready to throw it all away for the insecure life of a starving bluesman.

Wolf's decision about his future was put aside for a few years when he went to serve in the army during World War II. He returned to Mississippi and his father's farm in 1945. While he had been away, he had done a lot of thinking and realized that he had to give music a chance. He was intelligent and knew that if he failed as a bluesmen he could always return to the life of an honest, hard-working farmer.

When he was thirty-six years old, Howlin' Wolf struck out on his own, leaving his father's farm to work his own plot of land in Penton,

Mississippi. After two growing seasons, he moved to West Memphis, Arkansas. Burnett, who had important responsibilities, was willing to begin a new career at age thirty-eight—a testimony to the giant blues-man's spirit and determination.

Once in West Memphis, Wolf did not waste any time. He quickly put together a band of hot young musicians, including Willie Johnson and Willie Steele, eager to prove themselves. Burnett also took a job as a disc jockey at station KWEM, spinning the platters that mattered and promoting different products. He wisely promoted his band, announcing his next performance in the West Memphis area during his show. Since West Memphis was the backside of Memphis, Tennessee, it was a wide open town. Many of the venues Howlin' Wolf played at were speakeasies and whorehouses. Burnett, who stood six feet eight inches tall and weighed close to 300 pounds, could easily take care of himself in a tough situa-tion. In these dark venues Burnett was able to perfect his electrifying stage persona of Howlin' Wolf.

The band he formed in 1948 played the hard, rocking blues that would dominate the Chicago blues scene in the next decade. In addition to Johnson and Steele, Wolf's band featured two harmonica players, James Cotton and Junior Parker, who went on to later fame. With the Wolf as the ultimate frontman, the group's live performances were simply elec-trifying.

In 1951, at the age of forty-one, Howlin' Wolf began his recording career. Although he is best known for his Chess sessions, the Wolf's first recording occurred in Memphis under the skillful direction of Sam Philips. It was Ike Turner, working as a part-time talent scout for Sam Philips, who had found the Wolf wailing away in West Memphis and had quickly informed the boss of Sun Records. Wolf cut two songs, "Moanin' at Mid-night" and "How Many More Years?" Although the sides were cut at the Sun Studios, the songs were released on the Chess label. When the fight for the rights to the songs was over, Howlin' Wolf was heading to Chicago to record for Chess Records. At this point in time the transformation that had begun in West Memphis was completed. He was no longer Chester Arthur Burnett; he was Howlin' Wolf.

The Wolf took Chicago by storm and began to frequent the hottest night spots, like the Big Squeeze and Sylvio's. He recorded some of his greatest hits, such as "How Many More Years?" "Sitting on Top of the World," "Evil," and the Willie Dixon composition "Little Red Rooster" during this period.

There is no denying Howlin' Wolf's importance in the creation of the Chicago blues sound. Honors go to Muddy Waters and Elmore James for their guitar skills; to Willie Dixon for his background role, bass, and songwriting abilities; to Little Walter and Sonny Boy Williamson II for their inspired harmonica riffs; but it was the Wolf who was able to combine all of these elements into one nifty, nasty, complete package. In the golden years of the 1950s, Howlin' Wolf had few rivals on the Chicago blues scene; perhaps only Muddy Waters and Little Walter enjoyed the same amount of commercial success.

The competition between Howlin' Wolf and Muddy Waters went beyond normal boundaries. Both men were fiercely proud and feuded for years over recording studio time and the marvelous songs that flowed from the prolific pen of songwriter Willie Dixon. The rivalry between the two blues greats lasted all of their lives.

One of the Wolf's uncanny abilities was to locate young talent. He had spotted James Cotton and Junior Parker. His band in the 1950s consisted of Willie Johnson on guitar, Willie Steele on drums, and William Johnson on piano. Later, he recruited Hubert Sumlin, who never received the credit he was due for his role in shaping the Chicago blues electric guitar sound.

As the golden age of the Chicago blues came to end, Howlin' Wolf continued to work the clubs on the south side and record with Chess. But beginning in 1960, he began to expand his boundaries. He traveled overseas and throughout his native country, delivering the blues in his legendary fashion. Though he had made Chicago his permanent home, Wolf never severed his ties with his friends in West Memphis and returned periodically to play some of his old haunts.

While Wolf was busy retaining his old roots, he also began to develop new ones, particularly with the emerging rock and roll crowd. The British blues scholars who were captivated by the brash, electric Chicago blues style saw Howlin' Wolf as nothing less than a living legend. Encouraged by his new recognition, he recorded an album with Eric Clapton, Stevie Winwood, Bill Wyman, and Charlie Watts entitled *The London Howlin' Wolf Sessions*. The privilege of working with such a blues star as Howlin' Wolf was a career highlight for the awestruck British blues musicians.

In 1973, Howlin' Wolf began to experience various health problems, but continued to record his new album entitled *The Back Door Wolf*. The album was a minor sensation, covering the entire history of the blues from the early rural acoustic blues to the modern electric sound he had helped make famous. Despite this brief triumph, an automobile accident in 1973 put a damper on his achievements. Heart attacks and kidney problems, a result of the car accident, marked a sharp decline in his health.

On January 10, 1976, in a veteran's hospital while being operated on for an aneurysm, Chester Arthur Burnett, known better to the world as Howlin' Wolf, died. He had performed until his last few days, despite his failing health. His death was a severe blow to the blues as well as the international music community. He was sixty-six years old.

Howlin' Wolf was a blues superstar. Long before his death he was regarded as one of the most successful blues singers in history. He was an excellent interpreter of the songs Willie Dixon wrote for him. He was an institution and occupies a sacred place in the development of the Chicago blues sound as well as rock and roll. No other bluesman created the same excitement with his outlandish stage antics. Howlin' Wolf was a major influence on postwar music, and his impact on the rock generation cannot be emphasized enough.

Though not a truly gifted musician, Wolf was an exceptional singer; this particular talent had a profound influence on the future course of popular music. There is scarcely a rocker in the last forty years who was not influenced in some way by Howlin' Wolf's passionate vocals. When one listens to a young Mick Jagger there is no doubt that he spent considerable time studying the vocal phrasings of Howlin' Wolf. The heavy metal shouters of hard rock, including Robert Plant, Ronnie James Dio, Ian Gillan, Sammy Hagar, Rob Helford, Ozzy Osbourne, and so many others owe an immeasurable debt to Howlin' Wolf's vocal style.

Howlin' Wolf was a stalking, brooding presence on stage. He had learned his trade from Charley Patton. The Wolf's stage antics became the foundation on which the styles of Mick Jagger, Jim Morrison, and the extremist Iggy Pop were built on. The Wolf could often be seen wriggling on the floor like a man in intense pain, a trick later perfected by arch-rebel Morrison.

Though many of the Wolf's best-known songs were supplied by Willie Dixon, the growlin' bluesman wrote many classics himself including "Killin' Floor," "Somestack Lightning," "Moanin' at Midnight" and "How Many More Years?" Like other bluesmen, many of his songs were covered by other bands. Cream did a version of "Sitting on Top of the World." The Grateful Dead and Electric Flag also dipped into the Wolf's extensive songbook. But the song "Killin' Floor" is most often associated with the name Howlin' Wolf. It became a staple among blues and rock musicians, and many different versions were recorded.

Of the many modern blues-rock artists on which Howlin' Wolf had a tremendous influence as a performer, songwriter, and vocalist, none was more important than Jimi Hendrix. All Hendrix did was take the passion and anger of the Wolf and channel it through his incredible guitar skills. As the ultimate tribute to one of his true blues heroes, Hendrix recorded a wild, up-tempo version of "Killin' Floor" that sounded like a freight train roaring down the tracks at breakneck speed.

Another blues-rock band that greatly benefited from the career of Howlin' Wolf was Led Zeppelin. Led Zeppelin turned the song "Killin' Floor" inside out by changing some of the lyrics and coupling it with a few poetic lines from Robert Johnson's "Traveling Riverside Blues" to create the "Lemon Song," a piece of total Zeppelin blast-off. Zeppelin also took "How Many More Years?," mixed it with Albert King's "The Hunter" and created "How Many More Times?" Zeppelin discovered the power of the Wolf's blues texture, which included intense rhythms and thundering riffs. By the time of the Wolf's death, heavy blues bands like Led Zeppelin had recycled many of his great songs and turned them into pure gold.

Though the Wolf never played rock music—he was a pure bluesman until the end—he was one of the few blues greats to benefit, however slightly, from the modern music he was instrumental in helping create. Arguably, some blues purists would insist that he was ripped off by rock bands who borrowed heavily from his original musical blueprint (including Led Zeppelin). While the financial rewards did not come his way, bands like Led Zeppelin, Cream, and the Jimi Hendrix Experience, by playing the Wolf's songs and re-creating the energy and passion he put into his music, paid homage to their idol. It also kept Howlin' Wolf's music fresh and expanded his legendary status.

Howlin' Wolf was a complex character who was suspicious of everyone around him. He possessed a brooding personality and an explosive temper that could be easily incited. He was a proud and private man whose feelings could be hurt very easily. He was also an American original, a bluesman of outstanding abilities who gave his audience a complete history lesson during a concert. However, until he was praised by the English blues scholars, his popularity in his home country (like so many other bluesmen) was regulated to a slim majority of the populace.

In 1980, Howlin' Wolf was elected to the Blues Foundation Hall of Fame and later, in 1991, to the Rock and Roll Hall of Fame. He played a major role in the development of Memphis blues, the electric urban

Chicago sound, and the development of rock and roll. His blues have endured the test of time and are an important part of the rich musical tradition of the twentieth century. Though he may be best remembered for a wealth of brilliant music that he gave to the world, the sheer power of his performances, and his sultry, gritty voice, the man will forever live in the pages of blues history as the growlin' bluesman, Howlin' Wolf.

Discography

The Back Door Wolf, Chess CHI 50045.
Chester Burnett AKA Howlin' Wolf, Chess 2CH60016.
Moaning in the Moonlight, Chess 1434.
Riding in the Moonlight, Kent 455.
A Howlin' Wolf, Chess 60016.
The Chess Box, Chess/MCA CHD 3-9332.
Howlin' Wolf: The Rockin' Chair Album, Chess/Vogue 600111.
Cadillac Daddy, Rounder 28.
Memphis Days: The Definitive Edition Vol. 1, Bear Family BCD 15460.
Memphis Days: Vol II, Bear Family BCD 15500.
Howlin' Wolf Rides Again, Capitol 86295.
Ain't Gonna Be Your Dog, Chess.
Original Folk Blues, Kent 526.
The Real Folk Blues, MCA-Chess 9273.
More Real Folk Blues, MCA-Chess 9279.
The London Howlin' Wolf Session, MCA-Chess 9297.
Change My Way, MCA-Chess 93001.
London Revisited (with Muddy Waters), Chess 60026.
Message to the Young, Phonogram (UK) 6310 108.
This Is Howlin' Wolf's New Album. He Doesn't Like It. He Didn't Like His Electric Guitar At First Either, Cadet 319.
Howlin' Wolf—Big City Blues, Crown 5140.
Evil, Chess 1540.
Live and Cooking at Alice's Revisited, Chess CH 50015.

ELMORE JAMES (1918–1963)

The Broomduster

An integral part of the Delta blues sound was the bottleneck slide guitar. The action of the metal (or glass) sliding across the guitar frets was similar to the motions of a sweeping broom. This is why the Delta slide guitarists were sometimes referred to as broomdusters. With the migration of blacks from the South to northern cities, there was an unspoken pact among all the transplanted Southern musicians to proudly carry on the Delta tradition. One of the most fervent disciples of the bottleneck style was also instrumental in passing its secrets to the next generation. He was the original broomduster, Elmore James.

Born Elmore Brooks on January 27, 1918, in Richmond, Mississippi, his early life wasn't much different than that of the other Delta bluesmen. He was a sharecropper's son who knew his way around a plow, but a career as a poor farmer did not interest him. Though he lacked the formal education to become a highly paid professional, he possessed the necessary fire and desire to become a bluesman.

Like so many other young poor black children, James lacked the money to buy a real guitar, so he fashioned a one-string instrument using an old broom wire. His simple, homemade invention was rather crude, but he did learn the rudiments of guitar playing. By the time he had saved enough money to buy his first real instrument he was already a semi-competent guitarist.

In every musician's life there is a turning point, a pinnacle moment where the entire universe of music is revealed, if only for a quick second. That moment occurred for James when he was traveling through the Belzoni area of Mississippi and met with the fabled Robert Johnson. The two became friends and roamed the Delta together, playing at juke joints and parties.

The musical friendship was an important one, but it was very brief. Approximately a year after their fateful meeting, Johnson died—but not before leaving an indelible mark on James's guitar progress. It was Johnson who taught Elmore the basics of slide guitar, the chilling energy that he would harness and mold into a successful blues career.

Around the time that he met Johnson, James also hooked up with harmonica player Sonny Boy Williamson II. The pair traveled the Delta and played parties together. James also played on Williamson's radio show and various recordings. Williamson, a bluesman with a mean streak, and James were a fearsome duo as they roamed the South delivering their coarse, down-home Delta blues.

When he was twenty-five James put his blues career on hold to serve Uncle Sam. After two years in the U.S. Navy fighting the Japanese in World War II, he was discharged and made his way back to the Delta. While he had been away (only for two years) from the music scene things had changed quite drastically. The electric guitar had been widely accepted, and James was a quick convert. He immediately formed an electric blues band.

By 1952, James had been playing around the Delta and other Southern regions for almost twenty years. He finally got his chance to record for Trumpet Records and put the classic "Dust My Broom" on vinyl, which guaranteed him instant recognition and eternal respectability as a blues artist.

While "Dust My Broom" became one of the biggest hits on the R&B charts in 1952, James was well aware that his opportunities in Mississippi were limited. Eager to have the chance to record more of his songs, he was persuaded to make the trek up north to Chicago. Once in the Windy City, he continued to record and performed in the clubs on the city's south side for the rest of the decade. He became an important member of the golden era of the Chicago blues and was instrumental in the evolution of the hard-edged rock sound that emerged in the late sixties.

James often played with his band, the Broomdusters, which included different musicians throughout the years. The most consistent lineup consisted of the rhythm section of Odie Payne Jr. and Homesick James, the sax talents of J. T. Brown, and the piano touch of Johnny Jones. A serious rival to the Muddy Waters Band, the Broomdusters were one of the marquee groups in Chicago in the 1950s. Although very focused, James was never able to duplicate the success that Muddy, Little Walter, and Howlin' Wolf enjoyed with their bands.

By the early 1960s, Elmore James was the distinguished master of the slide guitar and was on the verge of being discovered by the generation of white British blues scholars when he died of a fatal heart attack on May 24, 1963, in Chicago, Illinois. He was only forty-five years old.

Elmore James was a bona fide blues star. But there is no doubt that his biggest contribution was as torchbearer and innovator. James became the most important slide guitar player in the postwar era, ensuring that the art of Delta bottleneck guitar was passed on to the next generation. But he just didn't play standard slide guitar, he practically reinvented the technique. Over the years a devoted cult has championed his guitar heroics.

Elmore James gave the world several blues gems, including "Shake Your Moneymaker" and "Done Somebody Wrong," which the Allman Brothers included on their smash *Live at the Fillmore* album. James also penned the classic "The Sky Is Crying," a song covered by George Thorogood as well as the late, great Stevie Ray Vaughan. On the posthumous album *Jimi Hendrix Concerts*, Hendrix pays tribute to James, one of his idols, with the song "Blues in C Sharp."

But the song James will always be attached to is "Dust My Broom." He loved that blues lick so much he created a number of songs based on it, including "I Believe," "Dust My Blues," and "Wild about My Baby." That hypnotic riff was a piece of musical language that hundreds of future axmen incorporated into their guitar vocabulary.

The song "Dust My Broom" was originally by a Robert Johnson composition. James never paid a dime in royalties when he recorded the song because of Johnson's untimely death and the fact that the song had fallen out of copyright protection. Arguably, this can be perceived two different ways: Did James rob Johnson and his family of royalties, or was he paying homage to his mentor? He may be accused of stealing from Johnson, but there is no denying that Elmore was also a firm Robert Johnson disciple. Along with Robert Jr. Lockwood and Robert Shines, Elmore was responsible for keeping the Johnson guitar legacy alive.

Though James changed the original lyrics to "Dust My Broom," the theme remained pure Johnsonian. The central theme of the song is the treachery of an evil-hearted woman who forces the bluesman to move on in search of a more honest love. The singer claims that he is leaving because his woman has been unfaithful, but in reality it is he who didn't treat her right, which prompted her cheating. It is a basic blues love song until the last verse, which turns everything inside out. The singer believes that his time on earth is limited and foreshadows the morbid thought of his early death, which became a Johnson lyrical trademark.

Because of the repetitive blues lick of "Dust My Broom," many critics have dismissed James as a minor bluesman, a one-riff guitar player with a weak voice whose success was a genuine rip off of Johnson's guitar inventions. Although it is true that James borrowed from Johnson and owed a great debt to the Delta blues master, Elmore was an important musician in his own right.

In different ways, Elmore James has been one of the biggest influences on the guitar heroes of the past thirty years. As the torchbearer of the slide guitar technique, he has no equal. One of his brightest pupils was Duane Allman, arguably the best slide guitarist in rock history. But Allman was a gifted student who just didn't play by rote the treasured guitar licks of Elmore James; he took the slide guitar to places it had never gone before. Allman proudly wore his slide guitar powers like a badge of honor and performed the same task as James by passing on the secrets of bottleneck to other generations. James and Allman proved that slide guitarists occupy a special place in twentieth-century music.

Elmore James—along with Muddy Waters, Little Walter, Willie Dixon, and Howlin' Wolf—was one of the prime architects of the Chicago blues school, one of the most important influences on the British blues bands of the early 1960s including the Rolling Stones, the Animals, the Yardbirds, and the early incarnation of Fleetwood Mac. Elmore's ringing electric guitar sound swept away the diligent British blues pundits. A partial list of rockers deeply affected by Elmore's guitar style includes Eric Clapton, Peter Green, John Mayall, Rory Gallagher, Jimmy Page, Jeff Beck, and Mick Taylor.

Elmore James was in many ways a genuine rocker. His hard-driving blues guitar work is one of the prime roots of modern rock music. A large number of rock acts can trace their lineage directly from James, including ZZ Top, George Thorogood, Stevie Ray Vaughan, and Southern rock bands like the Allman Brothers and Lynyrd Skynyrd.

The thunderous blast of the Elmore James guitar sound is also one of the base roots of heavy metal. His slashing antics have been adopted by an entire legion of hard rock guitarists, who owe a great debt to James. Elmore's exceptional slide guitar work added an exciting new dimension to rock and tied it even closer to the blues.

Elmore James belongs to the same league of blues-rock pioneers as Albert King and Freddy King. Their influence on Jimi Hendrix, Richie Blackmore, Jimmy Page, Jeff Beck, Eric Clapton, Duane Allman, Dickie Betts, Stevie Ray Vaughan, and many more is immeasurable. If he had lived, Elmore would have basked in the same royal fraternity where Albert and Freddie King held court.

Elmore James also had a special influence on the new crop of guitarists that arrived on the scene at the tail end of the golden era of Chicago blues. Buddy Guy, Otis Rush, and Magic Sam all owe a certain debt to Elmore James. Though none were great slide guitarists, they all incorporated his harder rock sound into their own style.

Elmore James is a blues cult hero. This enthusiastic voice of support contrasts sharply with Elmore's detractors, and the difference of their opinions has created some interest in James's blues legacy. His true status as a bluesman is one that will never be agreed upon.

In 1980, Elmore James was elected to the Blues Foundation Hall of Fame. In 1992, James was elected to the Rock and Roll Hall of Fame, an honor he richly deserved. Despite questionable shortcomings as a guitarist, Elmore James is without doubt the most vital slide guitarist of the electric Chicago blues scene. While the name Elmore James conjures up different emotions in blues circles, there is no denying the broomduster's precious contributions to the music he loved so much.

Discography

Elmore James: King of the Slide Guitar (box set), Capricorn 42006-2.
Dust My Broom, Tomato R2-70389.
Let's Cut It: The Very Best of Elmore James, Flair (Virgin) 2-91800.
The Sky Is Crying: The History of Elmore James, Rhino 71190.
The Best of Elmore James, Kent 57 9001.
Blues after Hours, Crown 5168.
Original Folk Blues, Kent KLP 522.
Shake Your Moneymaker, Charly 31.
Come Go with Me, Charly 180.
The Original, Meteor & Flair Sides 112.
Rollin' and Tumblin'—The Best of Elmore James, Relic 7026.
Got to Move, Charly CRB 1017.
Whose Muddy Shoes (with John Brim), MCA-Chess CHD 9114.

SONNY BOY WILLIAMSON II
(1910–1965)

One Way Out Blues

It is those special individuals who burned with a fierce intensity that influenced the course of popular music. Many of these musicians were eccentric characters living on the edge of life, and too often their bodies gave out before their fiery spirits. One of the most independent bluesmen in history, whose vocabulary did not contain the word *compromise*, was nevertheless able to make a large contribution to the music playing his precious "One Way Out Blues." His nom de blues was Sonny Boy Williamson II.

Sonny Boy Williamson II, often known as Rice Miller, was born Aleck Miller in Glendora, Mississippi, in 1910. The details of Miller's early life are sketchy; however, it is known that he was born poor and became well acquainted with the meaning of hard work at early age. His experiences weren't much different than those of other future bluesmen from the poverty-stricken Mississippi Delta. Miller was not enchanted with the life of a sharecropper and realized that music was his only true escape.

A self-taught harmonica player, by his early teens Miller was roaming the South playing juke joints and house parties. In his travels, Miller met and jammed with Elmore James, Howlin' Wolf, Robert Jr. Lockwood, and Robert Johnson. Rumors persist that Miller may have been present the night that Johnson drank from the strychnine-laced whiskey bottle, which caused his death three days later.

Aware that his opportunities to record and gain fame in his native Mississippi were limited, Miller moved to Helena, Arkansas. He worked hard to establish himself in the musical scene in Helena and caught a break in the late 1930s, when he landed a job as a disc jockey on radio station KFFA in West Memphis, Arkansas. Sonny Boy II's show was known as the King Biscuit Radio Show (named after the show's sponsor) and became an instrumental part of blues history (see the end of this chapter for a list of performers).

The radio show allowed Sonny Boy to further expand his name as well as that of others. He had Robert Jr. Lockwood, Robert Johnson's stepson, as his main guitar player. Elmore James also made an appearance on the King Biscuit Radio Show, as did Willie Love, Joe Willie Wilkins, Hound Dog Taylor, Houston Stackhouse, and Peck Curtis. Sonny Boy II also gave a young, unknown Mississippi blues guitarist his first break. His name was B. B. King.

Sonny Boy II built up a considerable following through his radio shows, establishing himself as the best harmonica player in the West Memphis area. With the death of the original Sonny Boy in 1948 (he was murdered in Chicago) and a few years before the emergence of Little Walter, Sonny Boy II reigned supreme among harmonica players for a brief time.

Although the radio show provided some job security, Miller, who had by now adopted the name Sonny Boy, was eager to resume his traveling ways. In 1944, he quit his radio show to satiate his wandering appetite; however, he returned sporadically to the West Memphis area to reclaim his disc jockey spot.

Williamson was thirty-one before he was finally given the chance to record his songs. The first label he recorded for was Trumpet; although the songs were rough, it was apparent that he was an exciting performer able to transmit the same energy that he exhibited in his live shows on record.

In 1954, Williamson entered an unstable period in his life when he moved out of West Memphis and headed north. He lived in Detroit, Milwaukee, and Cleveland for brief periods before settling in Chicago. Though he made his home in different parts of the country, Williamson always returned to the Helena area. Although Sonny Boy II was eager to advance his blues career, he was not ready to sever his Southern blues roots.

In 1955, Williamson cut a few sides with Checker, a part of the Chess recording empire. In the studio, he was backed by Robert Jr. Lockwood, Willie Dixon, and Otis Spann. It was in the songs that he recorded for Checker that Sonny Boy II demonstrated his incredible harmonica skills and a style that had greatly matured from his Trumpet days. Although he was making his own records, Williamson was also doing session work for various other artists, including Elmore James. In 1952, Sonny Boy II played on James's classic "Dust My Broom."

Throughout the rest of the decade, Sonny Boy II was a fixture on Chicago's south side. He participated in hundreds of sessions and also toured the country with Robert Jr. Lockwood, Otis Spann, or Willie

Dixon. In the early 1960s, Sonny Boy II joined the long list of American bluesmen who traveled overseas to entertain blues-starved English and European audiences. Across the Atlantic, Sonny Boy II discovered an entirely new audience that was eager to listen to his riveting harmonica performances. Sonny Boy II's popularity was so widespread in England that he returned several times in order to record with eager English blues musicians.

His first recording session took place with the Yardbirds and featured the guitar talents of a very young Eric Clapton. Clapton, a devoted blues scholar, was thrilled at the chance of recording with Sonny Boy II, who was already a blues legend. Two years later, Sonny Boy II, returned to England and walked into the recording studio where session drummer Micky Waller, organist Brian Auger, and future Led Zeppelin guitarist Jimmy Page stood in awe of the famous bluesman. The sessions were very loose, and the product was a little disappointing. Later, Sonny Boy II claimed that he was unsatisfied with the recordings he did with the English blues players.

Sonny continued to record and perform, including a concert in Birmingham, England. It was one of the last engagements he played. On May 25, 1965, Rice Miller, known to the blues world as Sonny Boy Williamson II, passed away in Helena, Arkansas. He was fifty-five years old.

Rice Miller, aka Sonny Boy Williamson II, was a blues star of great importance. Along with Little Walter, Sonny Boy II helped establish the modern blues harmonica sound. With his inspired blues, Williamson raised the level of respect for the harmonica in blues circles and in other styles of music.

The essential key to Sonny Boy II's harmonica was tension. He was able to masterfully set sharp tones against shrill notes in a manner that created pure excitement. He used a variety of techniques, like vibrato, tone, emotion, and timing, to give his playing a unique styling. He was able to solo effectively, never prolonging the duration of his expertly flowing torrents of notes, but he also filled in open space nicely, giving his songs a burning edge.

Sonny Boy Williamson II was an authentic bluesman with direct links to Robert Johnson, B. B. King, Robert Jr. Lockwood, and Elmore James. His music served as a bridge that fused the styles of Sonny Boy Williamson, the first truly great blues harmonica player, and Little Walter, acknowledged as the greatest blues harmonica player of all time.

Even though he didn't score as many hits as Little Walter, Sonny Boy II was a prolific songwriter, providing the world with such blues classics as "Eyesight to the Blind," "One Way Out," "Help Me," "Goodnight Everybody," "Don't Start Me Talking," "Nine Below Zero," and "Your Funeral and My Trial."

Although "Eyesight to the Blind" is regarded as his most famous composition, his song "One Way Out" brought him to the attention of the rock crowd due to the dynamic version that the Allman Brothers recorded during their famous live appearance at the Fillmore East. The song was eventually included on the album *Eat a Peach*. Although the Allman Brothers changed the song into something new and exciting, they retained the fire of the original as well as the first opening lines.

Sonny Boy II's influence on the harmonica players in rock and roll is equal to that of Little Walter. Of the many rock bands to feature a harmonica as an integral part of their sound, none did it better than Magic Dick Selwitz of the J. Geils Band. It took several studio albums before the band really clicked with the rock crowd, but their live shows were always hot. At the forefront of their dynamic act was Magic Dick with his intense playing. The song "Whammer Jammer/Hard Drivin' Man" is a mind-blowing blues-rock number.

Sonny Boy Williamson II was keenly aware of the value of showmanship. He acquired his knowledge firsthand from Charley Patton. Sonny Boy II's antics were to the harmonica what Patton's tricks were to the guitar. Sonny Boy II played the harmonica with his nostrils and flipped the instrument around his mouth with his tongue. Although he played sitting down, he used his feet to create rhythm. He choose every note he blew with great care, like a sculptor creating a masterpiece. Sonny Boy II gave his all in every show because he knew it might be his last.

Sonny Boy Williamson II's legend is built on more than just his dynamic, electric harmonica sound. A complex character who even confused those around him, Sonny Boy II epitomized the life of a bluesman. He cut an intimidating figure, standing six foot two with a bluesman's penchant for hard liquor. He was a dangerous man with an explosive temper, usually armed, who would angrily challenge one (or all) the patrons in a crowded juke joint. He was a man of many personalities who could exhibit moments of pure tenderness, then without warning, lash out at those around him.

Despite his unique and unpredictable character, he gave the world a treasure trove of harmonica classics, including "Good Evening Everybody,"

"You Killing Me (On My Feet)," "Don't Lose Your Eye," "Have You Ever Been in Love," "Born Blind," "Little Village," "She Got Next to Me," "Let Your Conscience Be Your Guide," "The Goat," "Too Close Together," "Trying to Get Back on My Feet," "Find Another Woman," "Peach Tree," "Lonesome Cabin," "Temperature 110," and "This Is My Apartment." Sonny Boy II serious rival was Little Walter, who died a young man.

Sonny Boy Williamson II was inducted into the Blues Foundation Hall of Fame in 1980. Despite his odd behavior, he still managed to become one of the greatest harmonica players in the history of the blues. Only Little Walter can be said to have surpassed Sonny Boy II in imagination and fire. Although he may be best remembered as a colorful figure, his "One Way Out Blues" earned Rice Miller, aka Sonny Boy Williamson II, his credentials as a blues legend.

The Rise of Live Radio—King Biscuit Flour Hour—KFFA Helena, Arkansas (1941)*

Sonny Boy Williamson II (Rice Miller) 1941–1950		
Robert Jr. Lockwood, guitar 1941–1950	Elmore James, guitar 1941–1943	Houston Stackhouse, guitar 1944–?
Hound Dog Taylor, guitar 1945–1950	Dudlow Taylor, piano 1941–1942	Willie Love, piano 1942–1945
Pinetop Perkins, piano 1945–1950	Peck Curtis, drummer 1942–1944	Joe Willie Wilkins, guitar 1943–1945
Willie Nix, drummer 1944–1950		

*The musicians were members of the live radio show at various times originally hosted by Sonny Boy Williamson II.

In the beginning, only Williamson and Robert Jr. Lockwood were on the live radio show. With the rising popularity of the show the band was expanded to include a pianist, a drummer, and another guitar player.

Many of the above-mentioned bluesmen toured with Sonny Boy II and recorded with him on the Tempest sessions. They include Willie Love, Joe Willie Wilkins, Willie Nix, and Elmore James. They often called themselves the King Biscuit Boys.

Sonny Boy Williamson II left the show in 1944, but returned periodically to resume his role as disc jockey.

Discography

Sonny Boy Williamson The Chess Box, Chess CH 9257.
King Biscuit Time, Arhoolie 310.
One Way Out Blues, MCA-Chess 9116.
The Real Folk Blues, MCA-Chess 9272.
More Real Folk Blues, MCA-Chess 9277.
Bummer Road, MCA-Chess 324.
Sonny Boy Williamson and the Yardbirds: Live in London, Optimism LR CD 2020.
Keep It to Ourselves, Alligator 4787.
Going in Your Direction, Alligator 2801.
Essential Sonny Boy Williamson, MCA 9343.
Down and Out Blues, Chess 31272.
Clownin' with the World, Trumpet 700.
"The Original" Sonny Boy Williamson, Blues Classics BC 9.
The Best of Sonny Boy Williamson, Charly CD RED 23.

====

JIMMY REED (1925–1976)

The Sweet Blues

The words often used to describe the Chicago blues styles of Muddy Waters, Howlin' Wolf, and others are *gritty, urgent, nasty,* and *citified.* The Chicago blues school was the "college" that all of the British blues-rock pupils of the 1960s figuratively attended to learn their craft. But there was another blues course in the curriculum that many students studied rather closely. With a more laid-back approach that included casual instrumental touches and soothing vocals, the sweet blues were a gentler side to the ferocious attack of Muddy and the Wolf. The dean of the sweet blues was Jimmy Reed.

Mathias James Reed was born on September 6, 1925, in Dunleith, Mississippi. He was acquainted with hard work, performing all the duties of a sharecropper, like milking the cows, picking cotton, plowing the field behind a mule, and other farm chores. But a career as a farmer was not Reed's major ambition in life. He wanted to become a blues musician.

Reed struck up a friendship with Eddie Taylor,[1] and although the latter was a slightly better guitar player, they unlocked the mysteries of the blues together. They became inseparable because they both shared the same dream of becoming melody makers. Their friendship lasted for forty years. There was a musical chemistry between the two, a unity that was quite remarkable. It was as if they had been born to play guitar together.

At age eighteen, with his sights firmly set on a musical career, Reed moved to Chicago, the Northern blues capital. However, before he could begin the necessary steps into realizing his musical goals, he was deterred for three years while serving in the army. On his discharge at the end of the World War II, Reed returned to Chicago for a brief time before settling in Gary, Indiana. His blues career seemed at a standstill, and a frustrated Reed was relieved when he renewed his friendship with Eddie Taylor in 1949.

The friendship between Jimmy Reed and Eddie Taylor is reminiscent of the partnership between Mick Jagger and Keith Richards of the Rolling Stones. (Jagger and Richards met when they were young boys and became fast friends, only to be separated. Some ten years later they bumped into each other at a train station and realized their similar musical interests.) When Reed and Taylor reunited after a long separation, they each discovered that the other was pursuing a career in music. They decided to join forces like in the good old days back in Mississippi.

Reed and Taylor began playing small clubs, and the magic on stage between the two friends created a warm, musical universe that was virtually guaranteed to bring them fame. With Taylor on rhythm guitar, and Reed on guitar, harmonica, and vocals the duo were pure dynamite. The music flowed so easily between the two that they often sounded like a single performer.

---

[1]*Eddie Taylor was born January 29, 1923, in Benoit, Mississippi. He developed an early interest in music following the great delta playes around and catching their acts any time he had the chance. Once he obtained his first guitar, Taylor quickly learned the basics and blossomed. By his late teens he was already playing house parties and fish fries. Taylor eventually drifted down to Memphis, where he carved out a regional name for himself. He moved to Chicago in the late 1940s and began his working partnership with Reed shortly thereafter. Although he had a solo career, Taylor is best remembered as the architect behind the scenes of the Jimmy Reed sound. He was inducted into the Blues Foundation Hall of Fame in 1987.*

Once Reed resettled in Chicago, in 1953, the two began to audition for various labels. Although Chance and Chess both turned them down, Vee-Jay Records saw a winning combination and signed the pair to a recording contract.

In 1955, Jimmy Reed began his run (which lasted into the next decade) as one of the best-selling recorded blues artists. Some of his biggest hits include "You Don't Have to Go," "Ain't That Lovin' You Baby," "You Got Me Dizzy," "Honest, I Do," "Baby, What Do You Want Me to Do," "Big Boss Man" and "Bright Lights, Big City." The songs "Honest, I Do" and "Baby What Do You Want Me to Do" both hit the pop charts, rising to the top forty. But it was the songs "Big Boss Man" and "Bright Lights, Big City" that gained Reed the most attention. Despite selling a large number of records, Reed was often forced to take a regular job in order to make ends meet.

Reed's studio work fueled demand for concert appearances, and he toured many of the important venues in the country, such as the Apollo Theatre in Harlem and Carnegie Hall. Though he was not a dynamic live act, Reed pleased audiences, and he eventually lined up a European tour. He used the same gentle approach across the Atlantic and became a favorite, gaining valuable international respect.

Reed's career began to slow down in the mid–1960s. His contract with Vee-Jay Records expired, and he wasn't re-signed. He did some recording for a few other labels, but it was clear that his best days were behind him. The biggest reason was not that the public's taste had changed; on the contrary, Reed was still very popular thanks to the numerous cover versions of his songs by Rolling Stones. It was Reed's legendary battle with the bottle that eroded his once fine career.

The late 1960s and early 1970s were not good years for Jimmy Reed. He was a frustrated man who had once been at the top of the blues world and was now being forced to play smaller venues, which was degrading. The decline of a fine blues singer is a very sad story.

By the mid–1970s Reed was barely recognizable as the bluesman who had scored so many important hits. His drinking had cost him his marriage, his friendship with Eddie Taylor, his thriving career, and eventually his life. On August 29, 1976, Jimmy Reed died in Oakland, California, a penniless alcoholic. He was fifty years old, a week shy of his fifty-first birthday.

At the zenith of his career, Jimmy Reed was a blues star of great magnitude. In his heyday, he was a regular hit machine. His sweet blues were accessible, smooth, and comforting, very much in the rural blues and boo-gie piano styles. Reed was one of only a handful of true bluesmen to score with crossover hits like "Honest, I Do" and "Big Boss Man." His soft voice and the hypnotic background rhythm guitar of Eddie Taylor appealed to music fans of all ages.

Although Reed was no wizard on the guitar or a harmonica genius, he managed to utilize all of his best qualities to achieve success. Like a brilliant musician, he was able to fuse all of the elements that he had at his disposal to create a successful sound. He possessed a light touch that got to people. He had a particular twinkle in his voice, a Southern accent that charmed and soothed the listener. His perfectly seamless guitar work was constantly in harmony with his delicious vocal delivery. Because he did not possess the harmonica talent of Little Walter, Reed did not use the instrument as an important solo device, but rather as the third gen-tle element of his style. He cleverly combined his groovy guitar work, inspired harmonica riffs, and tender voice, which served as the very essence of the appeal of his music.

In any praise of Jimmy Reed credit must also be extended to Eddie Taylor, who played a large role in Reed's best years. Taylor, the man who taught Reed how to play guitar in the first place, provided catchy, solid rhythms that gave the music a smooth, well-rounded edge. Because of the unique musical chemistry between Reed and Taylor, they were able to cre-ate a beautiful harmony that made the two guitars sound as if they were one.

Credit for Reed's success must also go to his wife, Mary Lee Reed, who wrote the lyrics to some of her husband's biggest hits. The trio of Jimmy, Eddie, and Mary discovered a winning formula and made a giant impact on the blues community for a few years. Reed was able to assim-ilate the talents of his best friend and wife with his own into one cohe-sive sound.

Despite his popularity and crossover appeal in the pop charts, Reed's success also was a result of exposure via the Rolling Stones. He was another example of an African-American blues artist being recognized by a larger audience through the cover versions of his song by a white blues band. However, unlike Arthur "Big Boy" Crudup, whose song "That's All Right Mama" launched Elvis Presley's career, but who did not receive any financial rewards for his striking influence, the Rolling Stones, like all the other British blues enthusiasts, were adamant about giving proper credit to the black bluesmen. The Rolling Stones cleverly recognized that Reed was an original and were strong supporters of him. His influence can be heard in such songs as "Tumbling Dice," "Honky Tonk Women," "You Can't Always Get What You Want," "Lady Jane," "Time Is on My Side," and "Waiting on a Friend." The Stones championed Reed at the height of his career, which spread his fame even wider.

Reed also influenced other early British blues bands, such as the Yardbirds and the Animals. Reed had a profound effect on Eric Clapton's guitar sound, a laid-back style that earned him the nickname "Slowhand," a moniker that would have fit Reed perfectly.

Reed was in many ways one of the founders of the soft, California rock sound. Reed's music contained catchy rhythms, but there was a relaxed quality about it, too. This formula was best imitated by Joni Mitchell, James Taylor, the Eagles and Crosby, Stills, Nash, and Young.

Reed also influenced Bob Dylan. Dylan's first album, which contained old blues standards, demonstrated his casual and soft approach to the blues à la Jimmy Reed. Reed was also important in Dylan's artistic development in another way. In order to play the harmonica and guitar simultaneously, Reed rigged up a mouth device. Dylan was also a dual instrumentalist. He copied the harmonica mouth structure Reed had created, and also improved on it.

Jimmy Reed became a member of the Blues Foundation Hall of Fame in 1980 and, in 1991, a member of the Rock and Roll Hall of Fame. With his cool southern drawl, choice of easy listening ballads and shuffles, and walking bass passages in the boogie-woogie piano style, Jimmy Reed wrote his own unique chapter and occupies a special place in blues history. Nobody possessed the Jimmy Reed touch. Without a doubt, he faded from the scene much too quickly and left us yearning for more of his tasty, sweet blues.

Discography

Eddie Taylor and Jimmy Reed, Ride 'em on Down, Charly 171.
The Best of Jimmy Reed, Vee-Jay 1039.
Upside Your Head, Charly CD 61.
I'm the Man Down There, Charly CRB 1028.
Jimmy Reed, Paula PCD 8.
Jimmy Reed at Carnegie Hall, Mobile Fidelity Sound Lab MFSL 566.
Live at Carnegie Hall/Best of Jimmy Reed, Suite Beat 3001.
The Best of Jimmy Reed, Vee-Jay VJS 9034.

The Greatest Hits, Volume 1, Kent K57 553.
The Greatest Hits, Volume 2, Kent K57 562.
Roots of the Blues, Kent 2KST 537.
Blues Is My Business, Vee-Jay VJX 7303.
High and Lonesome, Charly 1013.
Big Boss Blues, Charly 389.
Speak the Lyrics to Me Mama Reed, Vee-Jay 705.
The Best of the Blues, Vee-Jay VJ 1072.
The Bossman of the Blues, Vee-Jay VJ 1080.
Jimmy Reed, Archives of Folk 234.
Still Not Ready for Eddie, Antoine's 005.

LITTLE WALTER (1930–1968)

The Mississippi Saxophone

There have been three major figures in the development of the harmonica's rise from its original minor role to essential presence in the blues. John Lee "Sonny Boy" Williamson (the first Sonny Boy) took the instrument from relative obscurity to common acceptance. Rice Miller, who adopted the name Sonny Boy Williamson, was the first blues harmonica player to step out as a featured performer earning the instrument more than mere acceptance. But it was the man nicknamed the "Mississippi Saxophone" who redefined the parameters of the blues harmonica, ensuring the instrument its greatest respect. His name was Little Walter.

Little Walter was born Marion Walter Jacobs in Marksville, Louisiana, on May 1, 1930. He developed an interest in music at an early age, and instead of the guitar or the piano he chose the harmonica as his prime instrument. Little Walter cut his musical teeth playing on the street corners in downtown New Orleans. Although New Orleans is in itself an important blues hub, Little Walter's restless spirit drove him from his native state. He moved to Helena, Arkansas, for a brief time, then pushed on to St. Louis. His final destination was Chicago.

In his travels, he picked up a reputation as a fine harmonica player and jammed with fellow players Walter "Shaky" Horton and Sonny Boy Williamson II (Rice Miller). Little Walter became part of Miller's band on his radio show before continuing his travels. The exchange of ideas between the two great harmonica players was akin to Muddy Waters and John Lee Hooker trading guitar licks.

Little Walter arrived in Chicago in 1946 and immediately hooked up with Big Bill Broonzy and Tampa Red. He found work with these two old-style bluesmen and even did some recording with them. Because of his obviously extraordinary talent, he was snapped up by a young Muddy Waters to play in his band. Waters, a fair harmonica player himself, knew the possibilities of the instrument. Little Walter added a dimension to Waters's band that fitted perfectly with the harsh, gritty sound that the packed, noisy crowds demanded in the clubs on Chicago's south side.

The softer country-blues sounds of Big Bill Broonzy, Tampa Red, and others of that generation were rapidly being overshadowed by the raucous, electric, urban blues best delivered by the Muddy Waters Band. By the early 1950s, the Muddy Waters Band—which included Little Walter, Willie Dixon, Otis Spann and Jimmy Rogers—as well as the Howlin' Wolf Band, were the dominant blues forces in the city.

Little Walter made the same kind of impression on the boss of Chess studios as he had on Muddy Waters. He became one of the label's biggest sellers right from the start, with a song with the curious title of "Your Cat Will Play." For commercial reasons the song was retitled "Juke" and became a smash hit. The song catapulted Little Walter into the spotlight and he immediately formed his own band, Little Walter and His Night Cats. The band consisted of Little Walter, Louis and David Myers on guitar, and Fred Below on drums. Louis Myers was later replaced by Robert Jr. Lockwood, the stepson of the late Robert Johnson. Lockwood had played with Sonny Boy Williamson II on the King Biscuit Hour radio show, so he held the unique distinction of playing with the two greatest harmonica players in blues history.

Little Walter changed the name of his band to Little Walter and His Jukes, and they became one of the hottest groups in the city. Little Walter's band was a serious rival to Muddy's group as well as Howlin' Wolf's and Elmore James's blues outfits. Although his band was very special, Little Walter never did completely overtake Muddy's group as the number one attraction on the Chicago blues scene.

Little Walter continued to make records and even played with Muddy Waters on certain occasions. Every major blues star of that particular era fronted his own band, but the blues singers on the Chess label were not above sitting in with each other for recording sessions or performances. As the record company boasted both Sonny Boy II and Little Walter on their roster, Muddy, Wolf, Dixon, Elmore James, and others had the difficult choice of having Sonny Boy II or Little Walter for the harmonica.

Many of the songs that Muddy Waters, Howlin' Wolf, and Little Walter turned into gold were written by Willie Dixon. In 1955, Little Walter recorded a Willie Dixon tune called "My Baby," which raced to number one on the rhythm and blues charts. The song was one of many hits for Little Walter, which also included the aforementioned "Juke" as well as "Blues with a Feeling" and "Sad Hours."

In 1962, Little Walter had the opportunity to play across the Atlantic, and he conquered much of continental Europe as well as Great Britain. His popularity was international. He was in so much demand in England that he returned a couple of years later to tour as the opening act for one of the country's most popular blues bands, the Rolling Stones.

His touring pace slackened in the mid–1960s, and he continued to record, but only sparingly. Little Walter had led a hectic life since the mid–1950s and his hard living and fast ways were catching up with him. Like another popular harmonica player of his time, Sonny Boy Williamson II, Little Walter indulged in whiskey, women, and good times. A musician who had once been very popular, the decline of the brilliant harmonica player from Louisiana is one of the saddest stories in blues history.

Little Walter, who had a mean streak like Sonny Boy Williamson II, never backed down from a fight. This belligerent attitude led to his death. On February 18, 1968, in Chicago the great Little Walter, only thirty-eight years old, passed away, a victim of his own self-indulgence.

Little Walter was for a brief time (1953–1964) a superstar of the blues. His huge popularity in the 1950s is surpassed only by that of Muddy Waters and Howlin' Wolf. He reached the top of the charts on many different occasions and was the most sought-after harmonica player of his day. He gave the world a treasure chest of songs and became a dominant blues figure as part of the Muddy Waters Band, as well as the bands he fronted with supreme leadership.

But Little Walter's true contribution to the blues was as an innovator. He was able to draw incredible sounds from the harmonica, and he influenced others who followed in his footsteps. He took the basic sound of the harmonica and expanded its boundaries far and wide, creating new tones that had never been heard before or since. In his hands, the harmonica was not the simple country instrument it had been at the turn of the century, but a powerful solo instrument that challenged the mighty lead guitar for supremacy. He had a genuinely golden touch on the harmonica that astounded not only his fellow blues singers but also many jazz musicians.

Although he was an excellent soloist, his solos were carefully constructed masterpieces of energy that were never self-indulgent. The one prime factor that separates Little Walter from all other harmonica players in blues history was his precise and expert control. Little Walter was able to regulate the length, power, and sharpness of every note he played with furious, yet calculated, speed. He was able to exercise the authority over the sounds he produced with superior breathing techniques in the same manner that all excellent guitarists were able to dominate their guitars with clever, dexterous fingers.

Little Walter was definitely one of the prime architects of the Chicago blues school. Although Muddy Waters and Elmore James established the definitive electric slide guitar sound, Willie Dixon occupied the bass throne, and Howlin' Wolf became the ultimate frontman, Little Walter was the sultan of the mouth saxophone. Although Sonny Boy Williamson II was a serious competitor for Little Walter's exotic title, the sultan eclipsed Sonny Boy II in talent and inspiration.

Unlike Muddy Waters, Howlin' Wolf, Elmore James, Willie Dixon, Robert Johnson, B. B. King, T-Bone Walker, Blind Lemon Jefferson, Freddie King, Albert King, and other blues greats, Little Walter's songs have rarely been covered by other artists. The reason for this is quite simple: No one possesses the necessary harmonica talents to reproduce the desired texture of the songs.

Of all the great bluesmen who were part of the Chicago blues school, the only one that has never been imitated is Little Walter. Duane Allman was a great slide guitarist and began where Muddy and Elmore left off. There have been half a dozen great bass players in the past forty years, including Jack Bruce, John Entwistle, and John Paul Jones. Many rock performers exhibited stage antics that were far more excessive than Howlin' Wolf's act. But no one has ever come close to accomplishing on the harmonica what Little Walter was able to do.

There have, of course, been those who tried. James Cotton, Junior

Wells, and Big Walter Horton are respected harmonica players, but none of them was ever on a par with Little Walter. In rock, Paul Butterfield and Magic Dick (of the J. Geils Band) are the best the genre has produced. Paul Butterfield, a protegé of Little Walter, was in his own right a fine harmonica player, though not in the same league as his mentor. Butterfield and his bandmate Mike Bloomfield were two white boys who entered the black-dominated blues world of Chicago's south side and won everyone over with their gritty, inspired talent. Magic Dick, one of the mainstays of the J. Geils Band during the group's long reign, is a supreme bluesmen who added a dangerous dimension to the fiery blues-rock that the band displayed with brilliance and intensity.

Little Walter's influence goes beyond harmonica players. Anyone with an appreciation of the blues can easily recognize the unique talent that was Little Walter. Eric Clapton, B. B. King, Jimi Hendrix, Jimmy Page, Robert Plant (who played harmonica on some of Led Zeppelin's earliest cuts), John Mayall, Buddy Guy, Magic Sam, Stevie Ray Vaughan, and countless others have acknowledged Little Walter's major contributions to the blues.

In 1980, Little Walter was elected to the Blues Foundation Hall of Fame, an honor befitting the man's pure talent and vital influence on so many other blues, rock, and jazz musicians. His contribution to the blues as musician, session man, recording artist, arranger, and band leader are solid. He was an original bluesman who, through a combination of talent, imagination, and passion, earned the rightful distinction of being called the Mississippi Saxophone.

Discography

The Best of Little Walter, Chess/MCA CHD 9192.
The Best of Little Walter, Vol. 2, Chess/MCA CHD 9292.
Hate to See You Go, Chess 9321.
Little Walter 1952–1960, Chess-Vogue.
The Blues World of Little Walter, Delmark 648.
The Essential Little Walter, MCA.
The Best of Little Walter, Chess 1428.
Little Walter, Chess 2A CMB 202.

OTIS SPANN (1930-1970)

A Blues Story

The history of the blues is built on a collection of life stories that are poignant tales of the human spirit. The blues are a saga of a special family whose ties are more often musical than biological. Unfortunately, too often, blues singers have been the victims of blatant stereotyping, their lives painted as examples of tragedy. After all, many critics reason, how can a singer of sad songs lead a happy life? The fact is that many blues singers experienced a great amount of joy in their lives. Although it is true that he left us much too early, Otis Spann led a prosperous life. His is one of the more enchanting personal blues stories.

Otis Spann was born on March 21, 1930, in Jackson, Mississippi, the son of a Baptist minister. As the church played such a central role in his young life, it was only natural for Spann to be heavily influenced by gospel music. He began his musical career playing piano in the church where his father preached. Although the ministry was a definite career option, Spann had other choices available. He was an athlete of some repute, playing semiprofessional football, and was also a promising amateur boxer. But the world of the blues promised fewer bruises and broken bones than his athletic interests, so Spann kept up his musical chops.

Unable to decide between the life of a musician or athlete, Spann divided time between playing juke joints and house parties and pursuing his sports interests. In 1946, he put all career aspirations aside when he joined the army to serve his country. He was discharged in 1951 at the tender age of twenty-one, a young man who no longer pondered the future course of his life. Spann had decided to become a bluesman like his half-brother, Muddy Waters, and moved to Chicago to fulfill his burning ambitions.

Once in Chicago, Spann performed at various blues clubs on the south side. It wasn't long before he found himself in the number one group in the city, the Muddy Waters Band. Spann's flexible piano skills added the final touch to the standard style that Waters fashioned into the electric, citified Chicago blues sound.

Spann also became the session pianist for Chess Records and was part of the legendary group of bluesmen who made Chicago the greatest blues attraction in the world. Although he didn't record his own material until much later, Spann participated in a number of sessions that included blues giants Waters, Howlin' Wolf, Little Walter, Willie Dixon, and others.

It wasn't until 1960, after hundreds of sessions, that Spann was given the opportunity to begin his solo career. The debut album *Otis Spann Is the Blues* demonstrated his superb talent, which had sparkled the recordings of his colleagues at Chess in the previous decade. Although his solo career was very successful, Spann remained an official member of the Muddy Waters Band.

The debut album contained many of his best-known songs, including "The Hard Way," "Otis in the Dark," "Country Boy," "Great Northern Stomp," and "Worried Life Blues." The record also featured the distinctive guitar touch of Robert Jr. Lockwood. The combined talents of Spann and Lockwood created a dynamite package of blues.

It was also in 1960 that the Muddy Waters Band roared into the Newport Jazz Festival and blew everyone's mind with their hard-driving, wicked, electric Chicago blues, of which Spann was an integral part. Spann's major contribution, besides his usual hard-rocking piano style, was his smashing vocals on "Goodbye Newport Blues," a song included on the album *Muddy Waters Live in Newport*.

The decade of the 1960s was very good to Otis Spann. He continued to record extensively due to the success of his first album. Other albums he recorded in the decade included *The Blues Never Die*, *Otis Walking the Blues*, and *Otis Spann's Chicago Blues*, all of which defined the modern blues piano style. He recorded for a variety of record companies, but no matter what the label his albums always retained a high quality because of his incredible piano skills.

Spann also took part in the numerous recordings with some of the great legends of the blues. In 1963, he toured Europe with Lonnie Johnson; while in Copenhagen they recorded some of Johnson's old standards, including "Swing with Lonnie," "Tomorrow Night," and the blues chestnut "See See Rider." Spann also participated in an interesting session (Super Black Blues) that featured the great Texas blues guitar legend T-Bone Walker.

Spann also toured Europe as a member of the Muddy Waters Band. No matter how successful he became as a solo artist, he was always cast in the shadow of Muddy Waters. But, no matter what the situation, Spann delighted crowds everywhere he went with his delivery of tasty, south-ern-fried blues. His ability to play boogie woogie, barrelhouse, ragtime, jazz-tinged, and thick, electric Chicago rhythms made him a favorite at many of the blues festivals in the United States.

Throughout the decade, Spann made his presence felt and became a dominant force in blues circles. He was as visible as Muddy Waters, Howlin' Wolf, Willie Dixon, Buddy Guy, Otis Rush, and Magic Sam, and he deserved as much of the spotlight as any of them. Without a doubt, as the 1960s came to an end, Otis Spann could look back with a feeling of pure satisfaction.

As the next decade beckoned and promised to be even better, Spann could only look on in anticipation. However, it was not to be. He was diagnosed with cancer and quickly succumbed to the disease. On April 25, 1970, in Chicago, Otis Spann died. He was only forty years old.

Otis Spann was a blues star during the 1950s and the 1960s. He was one of the prime architects of the golden age of the Chicago blues, and though he didn't enjoy quite the same recording success as Muddy Waters, Little Walter, and Howlin' Wolf, his albums always sold well. Spann may well be remembered more for his live appearances like the Newport Jazz Festival and various tours in Europe than his studio material.

Otis Spann was not so much an innovator as a synthesis of all the piano players that came before him. He could pound out boogie-woogie rhythm with the best of them and was heavily influenced by the work of Pete Johnson, Albert Ammons, and Meade "Lux" Lewis, the boogie-woo-gie kings of the 1930s and 1940s. Spann was also comfortable with the slow blues style developed by Roosevelt Sykes, the great pianist originally from Arkansas who was a huge influence on many piano players of the postwar era.

Spann's musical brilliance existed in his ability to absorb what the great early piano geniuses—men like Roosevelt Sykes, Pete Johnson, Leroy Carr, and Sunnyland Slim—had to offer, incorporate their ideas into his own playing, and pass on the lessons to the next generation. Because of his exceptional versatility he left his mark on future piano players in two different ways.

Spann was a terrific band leader and directed his group from his piano stool like a five-star general. His ability to carry a band with his dazzling talents heavily influenced the great modern keyboard virtuosos, such as Keith Emerson (of Emerson, Lake, and Palmer), Jon Lord of

Deep Purple, Rick Wakeman of Yes, Ray Manzerek of the Doors, and Seth Justman of the J. Geils Band. All of them were the focal points of their groups and pushed the boundaries of piano/organ first established by Spann.

Also, because the Chicago blues school had such a large influence on rock, Spann—along with Johnny Johnson, the longtime piano player in Chuck Berry's combo—was an important pioneer and served as the bridge between the earliest of blues piano players and the modern pianist/keyboard players of the rock generation, including the aforementioned names and the Southern boogie piano players, including Billy Powell of Lynyrd Skynyrd and Chuck Leavell and Mike Lawler of the Allman Brothers Band. There is scarcely a piano player today who has not been touched by the Spann magic in some shape or form. All rock and roll piano players owe a large debt to him.

Spann was also the single most important piano player of his era. From 1951 to 1970, there was not a more important piano player on the blues scene; he was the undisputed champion. Because of his versatility and influence on later generations, he is without doubt the most important postwar blues piano player. In Chicago's blues hierarchy, Spann inherited Big Maceo Merriweather's piano stool.

In many ways, Spann was the perfect, complete pianist. He was comfortable as the center of attention as well as in a lesser role, giving a chance to the other musicians in his band to show off their own talents. He could pump out regular rhythm patterns and work in time with the drummer and bass player. He could hold the bottom part of a song with his left hand while playing intricate chords and flashy solos with his right hand. He could stun listeners with excellent solo work, playing complicated jazz chords or romping blues riffs. As a member of the Muddy Waters Band, Spann played the dual role of rhythmic accompanist as well as featured solo performer. On his own records he demonstrated his ability to blend all the elements into one complete sound.

In 1980, Spann was inducted into the Blues Foundation Hall of Fame. His death was a tragic blow to the blues community, and he has never been properly replaced. His death, along with that of Little Walter a few years before, put a final end to the dominance of the Chicago blues school that had been so powerful in the 1950s. It is unfortunate that Spann did not live longer. With his deep understanding of blues textures and complete command of the piano, he would have become a genuine superstar. Because of the countless people that he touched with his warmth and sincerity, Otis Spann remains one of the most enchanting stories of the blues.

Discography

Otis Spann's Chicago Blues, Testament 2211.
Otis Spann Is the Blues, Story of Blues 79001.
The Blues Never Die, Prestige 7719.
Otis Walking the Blues, Story of the Blues 79025.
Otis Spann, Mosaic MD3-139.
Heart Loaded with Trouble, Bluesway BLS 6063.
The Blues Is Where It's At, Bluesway BL 6003.
The Bottom of the Blues, Bluesway BL 6013.
Walking the Blues, Barnaby 31290.
Cryin' Time, Vanguard 6514.
Sweet Giant of the Blues, Bluestime 29006.
The Complete Candid Otis Spann/Lightnin' Hopkins Sessions, Mosaic MD-3/139
Willie Dixon The Chess Box, MCA-Chess CHD2-16500.

OTIS RUSH (1934–   )

Double Trouble Blues

Fame is a fickle mistress. Sometimes, those who deserve to be successful are overlooked in place of other, less talented individuals. It is unfortunate that Otis Rush, despite his important contribution to the west side Chicago blues, has never been blessed by fame's special touch, but only by the double trouble blues.

Otis Rush was born on April 29, 1934, in Philadelphia, Mississippi. Like so many other blues singers born and raised in Mississippi, Rush grew up surrounded by the state's rich musical tradition, which had a profound effect on his career selection. He learned the basics of the harmonica before settling on the guitar as his instrument of choice. In the tradition of Albert King, Rush was a natural lefty who played the instrument upside down. He jammed with other musicians around his home town, absorbing different musical ideas that he later used to create his own sound.

In 1948, at the tender age of fourteen, Rush, like other aspiring blues-men, moved from the Delta up North to Chicago. His timing could not have been better because he arrived in the Windy City on the eve of the golden age of the electric blues. As a blossoming guitarist whose style was not yet completely formed, Rush greatly benefited from listening to the dynamic live performances of Muddy Waters, Howlin' Wolf, Willie Dixon, Elmore James, Little Walter, B. B. King, and Albert King. Waters, Wolf, Albert and B. B. King were all important influences in the devel-opment of Rush's burgeoning guitar style.

It took six years before he was ready to make his mark on the Chicago blues scene. He had carefully studied the big stars of the day and assumed his special spot in the city's blues hierarchy. Though he was able to win over a large fan base with his unique guitar style, it wasn't until the mid–1950s that he signed a recording contract with Cobra. The new label was seeking young talent and benefited from the guidance of blues giant Willie Dixon.

Rush's first taste of success was a cover version of Dixon's "I Can't Quit You Baby," recorded on Cobra Records through arrangements by Dixon himself. The record marked the arrival of Otis Rush as a respected blues artist—the song reached number nine on the charts. Rush cut more sides for Cobra Records, including some of his best-known songs "All Your Love," "Three Times a Fool," "Jump Sister Bessie," "If You Were Mine," "Keep on Loving My Baby," "She's a Good 'Un Parts 1 & 2," "Dou-ble Trouble," and "Groaning the Blues." The songs helped solidify his position as one of the prime forces of the West Side Chicago blues school. However, Cobra Records went bankrupt, leaving him and other artists out in the cold.

Despite this stroke of misfortune, Rush was keenly aware that it was an exciting time to be a bluesman. The Delta-based blues, which was an integral part of 1950s Chicago blues, was grudgingly giving way to the postmodern blues era. Although heavily influenced by their forebears, the young crop of modern bluesmen set out to develop their own sound.

From Texas came the behemoth Freddie King, who could cut a mountain in half with his ferocious guitar playing. From Louisiana came Buddy Guy, who possessed the unique talent of mimicking any blues char-acter in history while delivering torrid, inspired solos that were his per-sonal creations. From Mississippi came Magic Sam, who put more pure emotion into his playing and singing than many quartets. From Houston came Albert Collins, who froze audiences with his chilling guitar work and would later be dubbed the "Ice Picker." Otis Rush was the fifth member of this rat pack of Chicago-based guitar players, and he held as much promise as any of them.

The Muddy Waters Band and other blues greats of the 1950s had made the South Side of Chicago the most famous blues scene in the world, but the new, young blues singers decided to adopt the West Side of Chicago as their turf. Magic Sam, Buddy Guy, Freddie King, and Otis Rush were headliners in clubs all over the West Side and created their own special blues world. However, their live performances were not regulated strictly to the West Side. They still played clubs on the South Side as well.

Shortly after Cobra Records went bankrupt, Rush was signed to the Chess label with the help of his good friend and former producer, Willie Dixon. However, Chess decided to release only one track, "So Many Roads, So Many Trains," during a two-year time span, which prompted Rush to find another recording company. In 1962, he signed with Duke Records, and the future looked brighter. However, like Chess, Duke only released one song that Rush recorded, entitled "Homework."

It seemed that Rush's luck had changed when some of his best songs were included on the album *Chicago/The Blues/Today!* Because of the commercial and critical success of this album, Rush was suddenly a hot ticket again. The album gained so much attention that it landed Rush a manager, the famous Albert Grossman, who had directed the careers of Bob Dylan and the Paul Butterfield Blues Band and would later manage blues-rock queen Janis Joplin.

Through Grossman's connections, Rush was signed to Cotillion in 1969. For the first time in a long while, Rush's future looked truly promising. He recorded the *Mourning for the Morning* album, which fell sharply from anticipated sales. Grossman, still acting as Rush's manager, was able to sign his client to Capitol Records. For his new label, Rush cut the *Right Place, Wrong Time* album. For unknown reasons, executives decided to keep the record on the shelf, and it wasn't until five years later that the album was finally available to the public on a small independent label. However, by then the blues were enduring one of the driest spells in popularity, and Rush's dynamic efforts went virtually unnoticed.

Throughout the 1970s and the 1980s, Rush sustained his waning blues career with live performances. A gifted performer, Rush has always been able to give the audience more than their money's worth. He performed in hundreds of blues clubs throughout the country, including Antoine's in Austin, Texas (Jimmy Reed, Buddy Guy, and B. B. King also played there). Although Rush's career on the concert circuit remained strong, his recording career never got back on track.

In the 1980s, Rush quit the music business out of frustration. However, his self-imposed retirement did not last long; by the middle of the decade he had returned doing what he does best. Since then, he has performed in Chicago and other parts of the country.

Otis Rush is a genuine star in the eyes of dedicated and knowledgeable blues fans. In the Chicago blues clubs he is a revered performer and a legend. Though he has never fulfilled the promise that he showed back in 1960 when his record did so well, Rush has continued to dazzle crowds with his blazing guitar style. Arguably, Rush has been severely underrecorded, to the point that it is absolutely ridiculous. Despite the neglect he has suffered at the hands of record companies, he has remained one of the prime movers of the second generation of Chicago blues bands. Rush's contribution to the blues has not gone unnoticed by his fellow musicians.

Although he has never been recognized as a great blues guitarist, Rush's special phrasing and expressive vocal style makes it difficult to understand why he has not become a bigger blues star. Why do some blues singers strike gold while others remain underappreciated? There are no easy answers to that question, but it would go a long way in explaining why Rush has been ignored by the music industry. Somewhere, lurking on some dark shelf, unfairly collecting dust, are the songs of a true guitar master. If released, they would not only give Rush's career a much-needed boost but also add another dimension to the modern blues sound.

Despite little recorded material available, Rush has still made a large impact on fellow blues singers, as well as rock guitarists. With his blistering riffs and sound knowledge of the guitar fretboard, Rush creates a very unique blues magic with his guitar skills. His guitar style, which is based on the single-string runs of B. B. King, also features Rush's own vivid imagination. Like a magician, he has the ability to pull unexpected licks out of his guitar that are fresh and exciting. Able to express any emotion of the human condition on the guitar, Rush will forever be known for his intricate, brooding lines of pure self-expression. An explosive singer whose voice is tailor-made to sing the hard, electric Chicago blues, Rush remains one of the best-kept secrets in the blues.

Not only did Rush have an immediate and profound effect on Buddy Guy and Magic Sam but he was also a major influence on the greatest guitar hero of the modern era, Jimi Hendrix. They were both left-handed players whose musical roots were deeply embedded in the Delta blues. Rush based his style not only on the expressive guitar work of B. B. King but also on the raw, Delta-drenched sound of Muddy Waters. Rush understood the subtle text of the deepest strains of country-blues. Hendrix took the best all three artists had to offer to create his own guitar style.

Rush, along with so many other architects of the dynamic, electric Chicago blues style, had a profound impact on future rockers Jimmy Page, Eric Clapton, Jeff Beck, Keith Richards, Robert Cray, and Jimmy and Stevie Ray Vaughan. John Mayall and his band, the Bluesbreakers, often played songs from the limited Otis Rush catalog.

Rush created a sophisticated, modern blues sound that has been imitated, but never duplicated. His lack of commercial appeal in no way deflects from the contributions of this very talented individual. His strong urban sensibility reflects the life of the African American person living in America.

Because of his limited recorded contributions he has never received his proper due. Despite being overlooked by the powers that be, Rush has managed to carve out a name for himself among blues aficionados, and he remains one of the major blues cult heroes. Those who remember him for his contributions to the blues back in the late 1950s and early 1960s keep a special secret. Throughout his career it seems as if Rush was destined to miss out on the big time. It is unfortunate that he has not been luckier throughout his career, or he might be singing a different song than the double trouble blues.

Discography

Right Place, Wrong Time, Hightone 8007.
Otis Rush, 1956–1958—His Cobra Recordings, Paula PCD 01.
Lost in the Blues, Alligator ALCD 4797.
A Cold Day in Hell, Delmark DD 638.
Mourning for the Morning, Atlantic 82367.
Door to Door (with Albert King), Chess 9322.
Screamin' and Cryin', Evidence 26014.
This Way, Mercury.
The Classic Recordings—Otis Rush, Charly CD 217.
Otis Rush Blues Live, Trio 3086.

BUDDY GUY (1936–   )

The First Time I Met the Blues

A first encounter with the blues is often an earth-shattering experience that changes a person forever. The blues have been known to have strange effects on people. The first time he met the blues, one little boy immediately fell under the power of the music and remains spellbound by its invincible grip to this day. His name is Buddy Guy.

George "Buddy" Guy was born on July 30, 1936, in Lettsworth, Louisiana. The Bayou State, home to Alonso "Lonnie" Johnson, Marion "Little" Walter, and Professor Longhair, has always been a hotbed for the blues, and it provided a solid training ground for young Buddy. He was exposed early to Louisiana's rich musical heritage and made the most of this special advantage.

Buddy was also enchanted by the pounding, driving rhythms of the spring and summer rains, the thumping bass notes of the giant bullfrogs, the singing wind rushing through the lonely cypress trees, and the frenetic energy of the watchful, hungry alligators, whose angry thrashing could be heard during feeding time. The rhythms, harmonies, melodies, and power of the natural sounds of the bayou are the combined elements that eventually supplied the essential spark in Buddy's blues.

Buddy learned to incorporate all of the natural sounds into his guitar playing; by his late teens he was good enough to perform at various clubs throughout the state. Louisiana presented many opportunities for an aspiring bluesman, but Buddy felt otherwise. He set his sights for Chicago and arrived there in 1957, smack in the middle of the city's golden era.

The most important friend a young bluesman could make in Chicago in 1957 was Muddy Waters. Buddy's search for the dean of electric Chicago blues was successful and impressed the veteran bluesman with his polished guitar skills, which ensured that Buddy would not starve. Guy became a regular performer at the 700 Club, one of the city's most noted blues spots. He also appeared at different venues around Chicago.

A year later, Guy entered a "Battle of the Blues" contest and triumphed over formidable opponents Otis Rush and Magic Sam. It was this victory that led to Guy's first recording contract with Artistic Records. Buddy cut two sides for the financially troubled label, "Sit and Cry" and "This Is the End." Neither single made him an overnight sensation.

In 1960, Guy signed with Chess Records, where he established a solid reputation as a session man by backing such blues greats as Muddy Waters, Willie Dixon, Little Walter, Koko Taylor, and Sonny Boy Williamson II, among others. His fine guitar skills can be heard on numerous recordings made by these and other blues artists who belonged to the label's roster of stars. Guy became a fixture in the studio and began to establish his reputation as one of the prime forces of modern blues.

After playing on the records of other Chess artists, Guy finally had a chance to record his own music, and he scored with one of his own compositions, "Stone Crazy," in 1962, which topped at number twelve on the R&B charts. Other songs he recorded during this period include "Broken Hearted Blues," "First Time I Met the Blues," "Hully Gully," "Every Girl I See," "She Suits Me to a Tee," and "Mother-In-Law Blues" to name a few.

Guy's departure from Chess Records in 1967 was a positive step in his career. For his new record label, Vanguard, Guy recorded three respected albums: *A Man and His Blues*, *This Is Buddy Guy* and *Hold That Plane!* Though all three were solid efforts, they did not match his Chess material.

Guy was a tireless performer and even supported the Rolling Stones in France on the first leg of their European tour. He also played the rock venues because a core part of his fan base were the rabid white blues audience who adopted him as one of their favorite artists. Guy also appeared at numerous blues festivals in the United States and Europe.

His partnership with Junior Wells in the late 1960s was an interesting career move. Their sound, based on Buddy's stirring guitar work and Junior's inspired harmonica tones, ensured them a steady concert schedule as they became regulars in blues clubs around the country. Not since Sonny Terry and Brownie McGhee had two blues companions made such an impact. Guy and Wells also recorded an album of acoustic numbers in France called *Going Back*. The record was remarkable for its high technical standards and authentic blues sound. The special magic that existed between the two dynamic performers delighted crowds wherever they went, but the artistic partnership did not prove to be commercially successful.

Like many other blues artists, Guy suffered a loss of popularity in the 1970s as the white audiences that had wholeheartedly supported the blues in the previous decade became enamored with different kinds of music. But Guy continued to record and make live appearances, plugging away like a good blues soldier. Although his live shows kept his name prominent in blues circles, his records were somewhat disappointing, suffering from lack of direction. His appearance at blues festivals in America and Europe enhanced his already solid reputation.

At the beginning of the 1980s, Buddy Guy had become one of the most respected live blues artist; however, his albums were poorly received by a lukewarm public. The blues boom of the 1980s did not do much to resurrect his sagging recording career. It seems as if he was entrenched in a rut from which he could not escape that had him singing the blues.

He had first come to Chicago with his guitar and a burning ambition, but Guy was fully aware of the difficulties that new blues acts faced when trying to establish a name for themselves. So, in 1989, Buddy Guy added "entrepreneur" to his already impressive list of accomplishments with the opening of his blues club Legends in Chicago. It became a hangout for passing blues and rock musicians, much like Chess Studios had been for blues singers in the 1950s and 1960s. On any given night a genuine who's who of blues musicians can be found on stage, kicking out the old blues classics to the utter delight of the lucky patrons inside.

The club also provided new acts with a venue where they could be guaranteed to gain some recognition by opening up for some established blues act or being sandwiched in between Robert Cray and Eric Clapton, B. B. King and John Lee Hooker, Koko Taylor and Etta James, Taj Mahal and Joe Louis Walker, or even appearing on stage with Buddy himself. Guy, who uses a 200+-foot guitar cord, often roams through the audience and even into the street, chatting with passersby.

By the beginning of the 1990s, Buddy Guy had been playing the blues professionally for nearly forty years. He had delivered his blues to appreciative crowds on every major continent, including East and Central Africa, a rarity among blues performers.

In 1991, Guy reached another milestone when he was included in Eric Clapton's performance at Albert Hall. This resurgence led to Guy's acclaimed comeback album *Damn Right I've Got the Blues*, which featured the contributions of Eric Clapton, Jeff Beck, and Mark Knopfler (of Dire Straits). That these three incredible guitarists would guest on Guy's albums is a strong indication of the respect that Buddy commands among the rock-blues crowd.

In 1993, Guy released *Feels Like Rain*, which helped solidify his position as one of the top bluesmen in the world. He remains an active blues participant with his concert tours and recent album releases.

Buddy Guy is a blues superstar. He has been carrying the blues torch as long as anyone else except for John Lee Hooker and B. B. King, and he continues to do so with distinction and enthusiasm. His long and prosperous career has earned him a well-deserved reputation. His importance to the blues exists on many different levels.

Like many other blues artists, Buddy Guy is a channel. As a young musician he absorbed the styles of the older bluesmen like B. B. King, Muddy Waters, John Lee Hooker, and Elmore James, and incorporated all of their ideas into his own playing. In turn, since the late 1950s and 1960s, Guy has become the inspiration for the young bluesmen who have studied the elements of his style and incorporated them into their own guitar vocabulary.

Eric Clapton is a huge Buddy Guy fan and considers the Louisiana bluesman a great influence. Buddy Guy also had a major influence on another great rock guitarist, Jimi Hendrix. Hendrix, one of the great students of music, knew Buddy Guy was special and paid close attention. Buddy's tasteful version of "Red House," recorded for the Hendrix tribute album *Stone Free* is one of the highlights of this heartfelt effort of respect. Although Hendrix and Guy built their careers around the blues, each headed in a different direction. Yet there remains an uncanny relationship between their playing, and the two have often been compared to each other. Despite their different styles, both Hendrix and Guy were able to produce frenetic solos that have often been imitated, but never perfectly copied.

Buddy Guy is a survivor. In 1958, a new crop of young and upcoming bluesmen burst on the scene. The group included Albert Collins, Magic Sam, Otis Rush, Freddie King, and Guy. While they were heavily influenced by past blues singers, they did more than just reinvent the lessons they had learned from their forebears. Each developed his own distinct style. Of the five, Collins, Magic Sam, and King are all dead. Otis Rush never managed to sustain any continued recording success. Guy remains as one of the primary voices of modern blues guitar. Buddy has also outlived Jimi Hendrix, Stevie Ray Vaughan, and Mike Bloomfield, three of the more brilliant young blues-rock guitarists of the past thirty years.

What has enabled Guy to survive as one of the favorite blues performers the last forty years is the special energy of his live concerts. Though his recording output has been somewhat erratic throughout his career, he has maintained a consistent level in his performances. A normal-looking man off stage, when he steps under the spotlight he undergoes a transformation. He is no longer a poor, talented kid from Louisiana trying to make it in the music business. He is the incarnation of every blues singer ever to pick up the guitar. This is the secret of Buddy Guy's live performances.

An exceptional live performer, Guy has always displayed the chameleon-like ability to play in any style and imitate an entire legion of bluesmen. His schizophrenic act is a truly mesmerizing. One minute he could be playing regional down-home blues in the same style as Blind Boy Fuller or Blind Willie McTell. In another instant he can churn out the heavy, electric blues sound that made Muddy Waters, Howlin' Wolf, Willie Dixon, Elmore James, and Little Walter legends. He can imitate Otis Rush, T-Bone Walker, and Robert Cray or pay a special tribute to one of his deceased friends like Magic Sam, Stevie Ray Vaughan, or Freddie King. He can play any style of blues, including New Orleans, Chicago, Memphis, Piedmont, Texas, jump, modern electric, modern acoustic, and Louisiana.

Guy has proven over and over again that the blues is a musical force that can capture one's soul and never relinquish it. When he was a young boy growing up in Louisiana the blues spoke to him through the natural surroundings, and he has used those sounds to forge his distinct style. For Guy, hearing the blues for the first time was a turning point in his life, and he has passed the fire on to two generations of blues fans through the sheer power of his music.

Discography

The Complete Chess Studio Recordings, MCA-Chess CHD2-9337.
Damn Right, I've Got the Blues, Silvertone 1462-2-J.
Alone and Acoustic, Alligator AL 4802.
I Was Walking Through the Woods, MCA-Chess 9315.
A Man and His Blues, Vanguard VMD 79272.
Stone Crazy, Alligator 4723.
Hold That Plane!, Vanguard VMD 79323.
This Is Buddy Guy, Vanguard VMD 79290.

My Time After Awhile, Vanguard VMD 141/42.
The Very Best of Buddy Guy, Rhino R2-70280.
Feels Like Rain, Silvertone 01241-41-2.
Pleading the Blues, Evidence
Drinkin' TNT 'n' Smokin' Dynamite, Blind Pig 71182.
I Left My Blues in San Francisco, Chess 31265.
Buddy Guy and Junior Wells Play the Blues, Rhino 70299.
In the Beginning, Red Lightnin' RL 001.

======

MAGIC SAM (1937–1969)

West Side Guitar Blues

At the end of the 1950s the Chicago blues scene began to change. The fire and energy created by the first generation of postwar electric bluesman that had made the city's south side the blues capital of the world was fading. The new blues sound emerged from Chicago's West Side and featured a cavalcade of young, exciting musicians who were passionately dedicated to carrying on the Windy City's legendary reputation as the Northern capital of the blues. This new crop of enthusiastic and gifted blues artists helped usher in the era of the postmodern blues. One of the leaders of the new west side guitar blues sound was Magic Sam.

Magic Sam was born Sam Maghett on February 14, 1937, in Grenada, Mississippi. Another entry in the long list of Mississippi-born bluesmen, Maghett was deeply affected by the state's rich musical heritage, which he absorbed like a sponge. From a very young age he burned to be a famous blues singer like his heroes Charley Patton, Son House, and Robert Johnson. He was a keen student of music and began to create blues songs even before he owned a manufactured guitar. Like so many before him, Sam's earliest apprenticeship consisted of watching and learning from the country-blues guitar players at church picnics, fish fries, and other social events.

Once he possessed a factory-built guitar, he began to forge his own musical identity. Although his chances at a formal education were better than those of the earlier generation of Delta bluesmen, he was so consumed with the idea of becoming a famous blues guitarist in Chicago that he left home in his early teens to fulfill his dream.

Maghett arrived in the middle of the golden age of Chicago blues, the heyday of Muddy Waters, Howlin' Wolf, Willie Dixon, Little Walter, Elmore James, and all the other Chess recording stars. Though he was just in his teens, Sam was determined to succeed in Chicago. As he had done back in the Delta, he frequented the blues clubs around town, observing the masters at play. He was confident of his musical abilities, so it was only a matter of time before he found work in his chosen field. He impressed many important people in the tight Chicago blues circle enough to gain a spot in Homesick James's[1] band.

Once Magic Sam had served a brief apprenticeship in Homesick's band he formed his own group to play in the blues clubs around town. That Magic Sam was something special is obvious by the fact that he was quickly signed to a recording contract with Cobra Records. Yet, despite the careful guidance of Willie Dixon in the recording studio, Sam's records did not attract public attention. His presence, however, did not go unnoticed by the U.S. Army who drafted him in 1959. Sam showed how much he liked army routine by running away. He was caught and served a couple of years in jail for desertion before he was dishonorably discharged.

Sam returned to Chicago in 1961 to resume his blues career. Although he enjoyed some success, the interruption caused by his military stint is something from which never really totally recovered. After a two-year absence, Sam's only logical move to reinstate himself into the competitive blues scene was live performances, which had always been his suit.

He did make a considerable comeback on the club circuit, but his recording career remained dormant. Although Sam cut sides for Chief, Delmark, and other small labels, he never achieved any substantial studio success. His inability to record a critically acclaimed album hurt his overall stature. He remained, however, one of the most exciting live blues acts in the country.

The blues boom of the 1960s provided a gigantic window of opportunity for old and new blues artists. Suddenly, they were no longer playing tiny venues for spare change. They were booked on the prestigious

[1]*Homesick James, whose real name was James Williamson, was born around the turn of the century and hailed from Tennessee. He is best remembered for his imaginative approach to the slide guitar. Homesick permanently joined his cousin Elmore James's band, the Broom-dusters, in the late 1950s as the bass player. Elmore suffered his fatal heart attack in Homesick's apartment. Homesick continued to perform in Chicago after his cousin's death, but eventually moved back home to Nashville.*

rock and roll money tours and were finally receiving the recognition they deserved for creating the foundation of rock. Magic Sam was one of the many blues masters adored by white rock audiences, who had a special sweet tooth for his brand of energetic West Side Chicago blues. He played in the Bay Area at the famed Fillmore West and the Avalon Ballroom. With his frenzied live shows, Magic Sam developed a special relationship with the rock-blues generation.

Some of the most lucrative venues that were opened to blues singers as a result of the 1960s blues boom were the major rock festivals. It was at an Ann Arbor, Michigan, Blues Festival that Magic Sam achieved legendary status in the pages of blues history. The festival was established to celebrate the state's fine blues heritage (in Detroit a young, traveling, Mississippi Delta rhythm ace named John Lee Hooker recorded "Boogie Chillen," the song that launched his fantastic career).

Magic Sam had gained some much needed exposure by jamming in the San Francisco Bay area, and he roared into Ann Arbor and dazzled the crowd with his expert feel and love for the blues. As the undisputed champion of the Ann Arbor Blues Festival, he gained considerable recognition, which had been long overdue. Although stardom is never achieved overnight, it seemed that in the space of twenty-four hours Magic Sam had gone from a reputable blues act to a major star.

It is unfortunate that all blues stories do not have happy endings. Before Magic Sam could capitalize on the many tours of the United States and Europe that came his way as a result of his spellbinding performance at Ann Arbor, he died of a massive heart attack on December 1, 1969, in Chicago. He was only thirty-two years old.

Magic Sam was a blues star and an important modern blues guitarist on the verge of superstardom just before his death. Undoubtedly, if he had lived, his star would have shone that much more brightly in the blues universe. There is no way of predicting how great his stature in blues history would have been if he had lived. However, although he wasn't with us for a long time, Magic Sam left his own personal stamp on the blues. His influence on future blues guitarists is unquestionable.

Like Robert Johnson's, Magic Sam's recording output is noticeably limited. His only studio album, *West Side Soul,* is a definite collector's item and showcases the incredible talent of one of the premiere west side Chicago bluesmen. Another one of his classic albums is *Magic Sam Live,* a double disc containing his famous concert appearance at the Ann Arbor Blues Festival.

The appeal of Magic Sam's music centered around his incredible guitar skills. His two biggest influences were Muddy Waters and B. B. King. Sam was able to incorporate into his own style the slashing, raw, electric power of the Muddy Waters guitar sound and the single-note, fast-break runs and expert control of vibrato that were the staples of B. B. King's guitar technique. By combining the best elements of his two primary influences and borrowing some of the musical innovations of fellow bluesman Otis Rush, Sam possessed a truly unique guitar style. He used a Stratocaster for its clear, ringing tone. His ability to play a screaming run of hard notes and chord phrasings with as much emotion as a roomful of guitar players ensures him a special place in the blues guitarists' hall of fame.

As an instrumentalist, Magic Sam was in many ways cut from the same cloth as hard-rocking guitarists Freddie King, Albert King, and Elmore James. The frenetic attack for which the aforementioned blues players were famous influenced many of the British rockers of the late 1960s and 1970s, who were dedicated blues scholars. Perhaps the largest influence that Magic Sam exerted on anyone was on Buddy Guy, who learned much from his good friend.

Although Sam didn't possess the greatest range or a true dominant blues bark, he vocally exerted the same energy he demonstrated on the guitar, which is essentially the story of Magic Sam. He was one of the most intense bluesmen who not only sang the blues but lived them and was able to transmit his spectrum of feelings to a live audience. In his hands, the blues were simplified into a universal message that touched everyone who came in contact with his music because of its humane and personal quality.

Though it is easy to reflect on Magic Sam's musical legacy during his brief career, one can only surmise what he would have accomplished if he had not suffered that fatal heart attack. There is no doubt that Magic Sam was on the edge of breaking through to superstardom before his tragic death. He had just dazzled the crowd and the critics at the Ann Arbor Blues Festival. Suddenly, the entire world was at his feet. If he had been able to fulfill the scheduled tours of Europe and the United States, he would have become a blues megastar.

Magic Sam belonged to the last original group of bluesmen, which included Albert Collins, Buddy Guy, Freddie King, and Otis Rush. As a group that held so much promise, they never fulfilled their destiny. Albert Collins and Buddy Guy became big stars, but Freddie King and Magic

Sam died young. Otis Rush has never been able to get his blues career on track despite an abundance of talent.

Magic Sam lived hard and played hard. He also gave the world many blues treasures, which are our only permanent link to the man. The songs "All My Whole Life," "Everything Gonna Be Alright," "Easy Baby," "Look Watcha Done," "All Your Love," "Every Night About This Time," "Roll Your Moneymaker," "Call Me if You Need Me," "Magic Maker," and "21 Days in Jail" are just a few.

Magic Sam was inducted into the Blues Foundation Hall of Fame in 1982. His story is both a triumph and a tragedy. Despite the fact that Magic Sam left us much too early, there is no denying his status as one of the most exciting blues performers of the West Side Chicago blues school.

Discography

West Side Story, Delmark 615.
Black Magic, Delmark 620.
Magic Sam Live, Delmark DE 645.
West Side Guitar, Paula PCD 02.
Give Me Time, Delmark DD 654.
Magic Touch, Black Top BT 1085.
Otis Rush and Magic Sam, Flyright 562.
Live at Ann Arbor & in Chicago, Delmark 645.
Live at Ann Arbor & in Chicago, Delmark 646.
1957–66 Recordings from Cobra and Crash Recordings, Paula 2.
Back Country Blues, Savoy 14019.
Magic Sam Genius: The Final Session, Intermediate 5041.
Magic Blues Genius, Intermediate 5025.

PART THREE

The Texas Blues Tradition

Texas has produced as many important blues singers as any other region in the world except the Mississippi Delta. The practitioners of the Texas blues style are some of the most gifted and fiercely independent characters in the history of the genre. From the beginning of the century, the Texas bluesmen have played an integral part in the development of American blues.

There is a definite brotherhood between the Texas Bluesmen. Blind Lemon Jefferson had a profound and direct influence on Huddie "Leadbelly" Ledbetter, T-Bone Walker, and Sam "Lightnin'" Hopkins. Hopkins and Texas Alexander were cousins, as were Hopkins and Albert Collins. Collins, Johnny Copeland, and Johnny "Guitar" Watson often shared the same Houston stage and were the first generation of Texas bluesmen to benefit from seeing T-Bone Walker perform live. Walker's heir apparent was Clarence "Gatemouth" Brown. Freddie King took what he learned from Jefferson and Hopkins and brought it up to Chicago, spreading the Texas blues tradition even further.

Another branch of the Lone Star State blues that was transplanted to a different part of the country is the West Coast blues style, which was built around the colony of Texas expatriates, including Charles Brown, Pee Wee Crayton, Lowell Fulson, and Percy Mayfield. The subgenre was an important catalyst in the development of rock and roll.

Other important Texas blues singers include Johnny "Guitar" Watson, Mance Lipscomb, Texas Alexander, Smokey Hogg, Victoria Spivey, Sippie Wallace, Janis Joplin, and the modern electric blues-rockers, ZZ Top, Johnny Winter, the Fabulous Thunderbirds, and Stevie Ray Vaughan, who can all draw a straight line from Jefferson, Walker, and Hopkins.

The Texas blues are a rich, long, and proud tradition that deserves as much attention as any other style. This tradition has produced some of the greatest musicians of the twentieth century, who have been instrumental in shaping the course of domestic and international music.

Long live the Texas blues!

======

BLIND LEMON JEFFERSON (1897–1929)

The Blues Comet

In blues history careers are not always measured by length, but often by their impact on other blues artists. Take, for instance, the Texas blues tradition. T-Bone Walker and Sam "Lightnin'" Hopkins both enjoyed long, prosperous careers. Albert Collins and Johnny Copeland emerged from the Houston blues scene in the late 1950s, but it wasn't until the 1980s blues boom that they gained any serious attention. Clarence Gatemouth Brown has been performing for fifty years and continues strong even today. Sadly, due to imprisonment and a heart failure, the respective careers of Huddie "Leadbelly" Ledbetter and Freddie King were cut short; but they still made monstrous contributions to the blues. Ironically, the man who had the deepest influence on his fellow Texas bluesmen, earning him the prestigious title "Father of Texas Blues," was a flashing comet in the sky. His name was Blind Lemon Jefferson.

Blind Lemon Jefferson was born in July 1897, in Couchman, Texas, a small community outside of Wortham in Freestone County. Jefferson, blind at birth, was one of eight children, the son of hard-working sharecroppers. His early childhood prepared him well for the life of a bluesman; when he was ten years old, Blind Lemon's brother was tragically killed in a train accident.

He discovered the guitar in his early teens and began his musical career by playing at barn dances and parties. He also performed on street corners and in front of the local barbershop every Saturday, gratefully accepting any spare change thrown his way. Primarily a self-taught guitarist, Blind Lemon did not let his obvious handicap deter his ambition to be a country-blues musician.

In true bluesman fashion, by his late teens he was traveling through-out Texas to deliver his highly individual brand of blues to appreciative audiences. During his train travels to the Deep Ellum area of Dallas, Blind Lemon first hooked up with folk-blues legend Huddie "Leadbelly" Ledbetter.

The two were an unlikely pair. Blind Lemon, a genuine country bluesman, was a portly fellow who wore glasses for some unknown rea-son, giving him an owlish appearance. Leadbelly, more of a songster than a true bluesman, was a tall, muscular man from Louisiana who looked dan-gerous. He played the twelve-string guitar and the mandolin.

Yet despite the obvious physical and musical differences between the two, they became quick friends and traveling partners, riding the rails and playing their music at every whistle stop. Although their time together was brief, Blind Lemon had a strong influence on Leadbelly's develop-ment as a musician. Leadbelly, who arrived in Texas as a young man, was still shaping his overall blues sound when he met up with Jefferson. A quick study, he picked up on many of Jefferson's guitar techniques, which can be heard in his later recordings. When Leadbelly was convicted of killing a man in a brawl, the musical partnership prematurely ended. Arguably, if the duo had stayed together for a longer period of time they might well have become the most famous blues duo in history. Despite their short time together the so-called father of the Texas blues managed to successfully tutor his first pupil.

In 1917, at the tender age of twenty, but already a well-seasoned per-former, Jefferson made the Deep Ellum section of Dallas his permanent home. At the corner of Central and Elm Streets he began to establish a reputation as an entertaining and clever bluesman. His fame was such that he was able to support the wife he married in 1922, as well as a child, from the money he earned as a street musician.

In Dallas he encountered his second pupil, a young boy who worked as a guide for the blind. Although Jefferson's sense of direction was uncanny, he sometimes required assistance. The youth's name was Aaron Thibeau Walker, and his father was a friend of Jefferson's. Blind Lemon was more than happy to teach the young T-Bone the basics of blues gui-tar. Walker remembered his private lessons well because not only did he go on to become one of the greatest bluesmen in history but he also became one of the greatest musicians of any genre of the twentieth century.

Blind Lemon, a spiritual man, belonged to the Shiloh Baptist Church. He played at many church picnics, and on one particular

Sunday in Buffalo, Texas, a young, impressionable Sam "Lightnin'" Hopkins was touched by Blind Lemon's magic. Hopkins, who would later become one of the greatest exponents of the Texas blues tradition, cited that special day as one that changed his life.

Aside from his brief partnership with Leadbelly, Blind Lemon was chiefly a solo artist, a lonely man whose personal life began to unravel in the mid–1920s. He began to drink and court other women, putting considerable strain on his marriage. His wife eventually left him. Another factor that contributed to his failed marriage was his nomadic ways. Despite being blind, Jefferson traveled to Oklahoma, the Mississippi Delta, Atlanta, the Carolinas, and even up North to Chicago.

Only after his lengthy apprenticeship as a roamer and street musician was Jefferson finally given a chance to make records. In 1925, Jefferson cut his first two sides for Paramount, "Old Rounder's Blues" and "Begging Back." Neither song was immediately released. A year later, he recorded two spiritual songs, "I Want to Be Like Jesus in My Heart" and "All I Want Is that Pure Religion," using the curious pseudonym Deacon L. J. Bates. Neither song provided him with the breakthrough he prayed for. On his third attempt, using his given name, he recorded "Got the Blues" and "Long, Lonesome Blues," which became the first of his many hits.

The 1920s, the first golden age of the blues, was dominated by female blues singers like Bessie Smith, Ma Rainey, Ida Cox, and Victoria Spivey. Blind Lemon's breakthrough opened the door for other male blues artists—like Blind Blake—who were then able to secure a recording contract with Paramount. The two first-generation blues guitarists were instrumental in arousing interest in country-blues, which led to the discovery and recording in the 1930s of Delta bluesmen Charley Patton, Eddie "Son" House, Skip James, and Robert Johnson, among others.

Though Blind Lemon was forced to share the spotlight with the classic female blues singers, he was also one step ahead of them. Many of the female singers depended on other people for their songs; but from the start, Blind Lemon was determined to write and record his own material. He set the standard, and soon many of the most popular female singers such as Cox, Spivey, and Wallace began to write their own songs.

He became a huge favorite in the "race" market, selling large quantities of records. His next release, "Matchbox Blues," was also a hit. A genuine portrait of a bluesman's hard life, "Matchbox Blues" is one of the most poetically imaginative, yet sadly thematic songs to be found in the blues canon.

From 1926 to 1929, Blind Lemon Jefferson was in his prime. He was the best-selling blues artist, male or female, in the United States. Although he didn't receive his fair share of royalties from his songs, he was able to build up a sizable bank account before his death. He also owned a car and was wealthy enough to hire his own chauffeur. Undoubtedly, he was one of the brightest stars of that first golden age of the blues.

The secret of Jefferson's success was in his unique ability to turn his self-penned songs into stories. His songwriting reflected the hope, misery, anger, and frustration of his audience. Although he sang about other people's misfortunes, many of the songs were autobiographical, which gave them a powerful emotional depth. He was acknowledging the pain of his generation while exposing his own through the brilliance of his lyrics. Many of his songs provided an escape from the hardships of daily life.

One of the prettiest songs in the Jefferson catalog was a blues spiritual entitled "See That My Grave Is Kept Clean." The song became a country-blues classic and has found its way into the repertoire of countless folk singers. The song was also very prophetic.

His climb to fame was not an overnight event, and Jefferson's time in the public spotlight was brief. By 1929, his best writing and recording days were behind him. Fittingly, the decline of the first great country-blues artist coincided with the end of the first great blues era.

In December 1929, during a terrible blizzard in Chicago, Blind Lemon Jefferson froze to death. The exact circumstances of his demise were never revealed and have been the subject of much speculation among blues historians. No official record of his death was ever found, which only compounds the mystery. Blind Lemon Jefferson was thirty-two years old when he died.

By the standards of his day, Blind Lemon Jefferson was not only an important country-blues star but also a superstar. He sold hundreds of thousands of records and was a popular entertainer everywhere he went. Blind Lemon Jefferson—along with Blind Blake—was the first important country-blues artist whose initial achievements paved the way for later blues artists like Charley Patton, Son House, and Skip James.

Arguably, Blind Lemon Jefferson must be considered as the first true blues pop star. His record releases featured an A and B side, which created a trend in the music business. Although his sound was deeply rooted in the blues, there was a commercial quality to his songs that was lacking in the efforts of other blues singers of that era. Also, like many other pop acts of the past fifty years, Jefferson's popularity was powerful, but very brief.

But Blind Lemon's importance in blues history is based on more than just the number of records he sold. He was a pioneer and reigns as one of the greatest influences the genre has ever known. Jefferson is the father of Texas blues and directly touched the lives of Ledbetter, Walker, and Hopkins. He also influenced three generations of Texas musicians including Albert Collins, Mance Lipscomb, Texas Alexander, Freddie King, Stevie Ray Vaughan, Johnny Winter, ZZ Top, Clarence "Gatemouth" Brown, and many other blues hopefuls from the Lone Star State.

But Blind Lemon's influence stretched past the boundaries of his native Texas and spilled into every corner of the globe. B. B. King, Charley Patton, Son House, Robert Johnson, Muddy Waters, Blind Willie McTell, and Reverend Blind Gary Davis are just a few of the blues artists who cited Jefferson as a prime influence. They in turn had a strong impact on other blues artists who toured the world spreading the message first initiated by Jefferson.

His reputation is based on many different aspects of his blues career, including his many guitar innovations. He played structured harmonies, single-string runs, and clear bass lines that gave his style dimensions never heard before in the blues. He was also the first to incorporate jazz chords into his style, which had a profound effect on one of his main disciples, T-Bone Walker.

He possessed an original fluency on the guitar that when matched with his thin, high-pitched, distinctive voice created a total blues package that hundreds of future blues singers have tried to imitate. His song "Matchbox Blues" was recorded by both Elvis Presley and the Beatles. Leadbelly covered some of his songs as did numerous other country-blues artists, especially Hopkins. Jefferson's songs covered a wide range of topics. The aforementioned "Matchbox Blues" and "Sunshine Special" explore the attraction of the loneliness of the road versus the security of home. The choice between travel and putting down roots was a balancing act that Jefferson struggled with his entire life, but was never able to resolve in a comfortable compromise.

One of the major themes of Blind Lemon's song catalog was his ambiguous feeling toward women. His lyrics portray a confused man who was enchanted, but at the same time repulsed by the female persuasion. In such songs as "Elder Green," "Got the Blues," "Piney Woods Money Mama," and "Deceitful Brownskin Blues" Jefferson perceives women as being both good and evil.

His uneasy feelings toward women are also evident in some more sexually explicit compositions. In his songs "Baker Shop Blues," "Oil Well Blues," "That Black Snake Moan," "That Black Snake Moan, No. 2," and "Peach Orchard Mama" his frustrations about women are clearly stated. The lyrics, however, are not bitter, but humorous and clever. The analogies Jefferson used are not blatantly chauvinistic observations; they are written in a way that does not offend, but entertains. One can only marvel at the poetic prowess of Blind Lemon's lyrical genius.

Jefferson's "Jack O' Diamonds," a song later recorded by his good friend Ledbetter, warned against the evils of gambling. Like so many of his other songs, "Jack O' Diamonds" was autobiographical—Blind Lemon was known to gamble away large sums of money.

"Tin Cup Blues," "Broke and Hungry," and "One Dime Blues" emphasize the desperate situation of the blues singer as well as a large portion of the black population in the country at that time. The songs, recorded just a few years before the Great Depression, served as fitting messages of the hardships endured in the 1930s not only by blacks but also by people throughout the United States and the world.

Blind Lemon also endeared himself to his fellow Texans with "Boll Weevil Blues," a song depicting the destructive insect that ravaged the cotton fields of his home state. He also wrote "Rising High Water Blues," which dealt with the constant threat of flooding, a common occurrence in Texas during Jefferson's time and one that continues to this day. The latter song is an another example of the universal appeal of Jefferson's music.

Another major theme in his music was the decidedly unjust court system, which convicted a black person before the beginning of the trial. "Hangman's Blues," "Prison Cell Blues," "'Lectric Chair Blues," "Lockstep Blues," and "Blind Lemon's Penitentiary Blues" all express Jefferson's clear point of view on the sensitive subject. Perhaps, when he wrote these songs, he was thinking of his good friend and previous traveling companion Leadbelly, who was cooling off in a Huntsville prison for murder.

Jefferson also recorded "Low Down Mojo Blues," "Pneumonia Blues" "Lemon's Worried Blues," "Bootin' Me 'Bout," and "Black Horse Blues," which indicate the wide range of his songwriting abilities. Jefferson proved that blues lyrics could be more sophisticated than the usual sad stories of some guy's woman leaving him and promising not to come back.

When his original songs weren't copied outright, other blues artists wrote tunes that resembled Blind Lemon compositions. His lyrics influenced numerous blues composers because they contained phrases that were so delicately crafted that it was impossible *not* to copy them. He set a high standard for songwriting that influenced many blues singers and rock acts.

The Robert Johnson gem "Terraplane Blues," which compares car parts to a woman's anatomy, was written in the same vein as Blind Lemon's "Oil Well Blues." T-Bone Walker's first record, "Trinity River Blues," and Bessie Smith's "Back Water Blues" bear a striking resemblance in theme to Jefferson's original flood song, "Rising High Water Blues." There is an uncanny relationship between the disciplined lyrical structure of Blind Lemon's songwriting and the classics penned by Chuck Berry. The street-wise, punchy lyrics that made Willie Dixon one of the greatest composers in blues history bear a close resemblance to the verbal efficiency of Jefferson's best efforts.

Blind Lemon Jefferson was inducted into the Blues Foundation Hall of Fame in 1980. Although other blues singers enjoyed longer careers, sold more records, and played larger venues for greater sums of money, none had a more vital impact on the overall development of the blues as Blind Lemon Jefferson. He may have been the greatest of them all. Although he was with us for only a short time, the blues comet made the world take notice of him. All this from a guitar player who couldn't even see the notes he played.

Discography

The Classic Folk Blues of Blind Lemon Jefferson, Riverside 12-125.
The Classic Folk Blues of Blind Lemon Jefferson, Riverside 12-126.
The Immortal Blind Lemon Jefferson, Milestone 2004.
Blind Lemon Jefferson, Milestone 47022.
King of the Country Blues, Yazoo 1069.
Blind Lemon Jefferson/Son House, Biograph BLP 12040.
Complete Recorded Works, Volume 1, Document 5020.
Complete Recorded Works, Volume 2, Document 5021.
Complete Recorded Works, Volume 3, Document 5022.
Complete Recorded Works, Volume 4, Document 5023.
One Dime Blues, Aldabra 1006.
All I Want Is That Pure Religion/I Want to Be Like Jesus in My Heart (as Deacon L. J. Bates), Paramount 12386.

HUDDIE "LEADBELLY" LEDBETTER (1889–1949)

'Lectric Chair Blues

When one considers the fact that most blues singers lived life on the edge, it is a true miracle that none ever ended up in the electric chair. A turbulent life of violence, fleeting love affairs, loneliness, depression, and alcohol abuse often sparked skirmishes with the law. Many blues artists wrote songs about the horror of the gallows, but none as hauntingly vivid as Blind Lemon Jefferson. Ironically, Jefferson's earliest blues partner almost did end up singing the 'Lectric Chair Blues on more than one occasion. His name was Huddie "Leadbelly" Ledbetter.

Huddie Ledbetter was born on January 20, 1889, in Morringsport, Louisiana. Very few concrete details are known about his early years, but there are two facts about him that are quite evident: Leadbelly was a gifted musician who learned to play the mandolin, piano, accordion, and six- and twelve-string guitar; and he possessed a bluesman's penchant for travel. This wanderlust eventually brought him to Texas.

Sometime around 1912 or 1915 Leadbelly encountered Blind Lemon Jefferson in the eastern part of Texas. The pair hit it off and became quick friends. They traveled together, with the fierce Huddie looking out for his blind friend. The duo was more interested in keeping body and soul together than creating history, yet they unknowingly became the pioneers of the Texas blues tradition.

Although they were often broke, it was a time of good music and good friendship. There is no telling how great an impact they would have made if fate hadn't intervened. When it seemed that the two were just beginning to make some progress, Leadbelly killed a man in Texas and was sentenced to thirty-five years in prison for the crime. After a failed escape attempt, six more years were added to his sentence.

But Leadbelly was no ordinary prisoner. He used his musical talents like a magical key to gain his freedom. He was set free in 1925 by Texas governor Pat Neff. (Sent to prison in 1917, Leadbelly would normally not have been eligible for parole until 1958.)

In an attempt to put his troubled past behind him, Leadbelly returned to his native Louisiana and resumed his musical career, playing parties and country events. But his temper flared once up again in 1939; Leadbelly was sentenced to serve time in prison for assault with intent to kill. While at the Angola Prison Farm he was discovered by Alan Lomax, who was scouting the South for blues musicians to record for the Library of Congress. With Lomax's help, Leadbelly was released from prison in 1934. He went to work for Lomax as a chauffeur while performing the occasional concert.

In 1935, Leadbelly, accompanied by his new bride, traveled to New York City. Although the blues were prominent in the South, the biggest city on the East Coast was home to the pioneer folk singers Pete Seeger and Woodie Guthrie. He appeared on stage with Seeger, Guthrie, and the folk-blues duo Sonny Terry and Brownie McGhee. He gained a white audience, but Leadbelly paid a heavy price.

Becuase he had cut himself off from his black musical roots those who attended his concerts were mostly white folk music enthusiasts. Leadbelly was essentially a bluesman forgotten by the very black audiences he often sang about. The genius of Leadbelly Ledbetter was one of the best-kept secrets in the blues for decades.

Life in New York presented a drastic change from his early years of roaming through the South, including Shreveport's red-light district, the vast state of Texas, down the dusty roads of Arkansas and Mississippi and Lake Caddo of Louisiana. The big city was initially a difficult adjustment for a freewheeling Southern man to make, but he eventually made a life for himself. The frantic metropolitan lifestyle as well as his partnership with folk-protesters Seeger and Guthrie influenced Leadbelly's musical philosophy.

In the following years, Leadbelly, who had been a carefree bluesman, developed a political vision. He wrote "Bourgeois Blues" and "Scottsboro Boys"; both songs containing strong messages of change. Despite his new-found musical outlook, Leadbelly just eked out an existence in the big city. He recorded for RCA, Columbia, and Folkways as well as the Library of Congress.

His live appearances were interesting shows because they contained a variety of musical styles. He played blues tunes, spirituals, pop, prison songs, politically flavored tunes, and old-fashioned American folk favorites. He was an entertainer who pleased his audiences with his versatility and natural musical ability.

Leadbelly became a staple on the folk singing circuit in the late 1930s and 1940s. While he was singing his protest songs on the east coast, Robert Johnson was establishing his reputation in the Mississippi Delta, and Big Bill Broonzy was in Chicago laying down the foundation for the future invasion of Delta bluesmen. At the same time in Kansas City, Missouri, Big Joe Turner was shouting the blues with unmatched authority, often teaming up with boogie-woogie piano virtuoso Pete Johnson.

In 1949, Leadbelly became one of the first bluesmen to travel to Europe. There is no doubt that his presence in France must have caused quite a stir. After all, what would the French say about a huge, muscular black man with a threatening glare and a hair-trigger temper among them? Unfortunately, Leadbelly's European jaunt was unsuccessful—the French were unprepared to accept the strange sound of an American songster.

In 1949, on the occasion of his sixty-first birthday (a ripe old age for someone with a fierce temper who lived on the edge and had gone over more than once), Leadbelly Ledbetter was diagnosed with Lou Gehrig's disease. He died later that year on December 6, in New York City.

Huddie "Leadbelly" Ledbetter was one of the most important songsters in American musical history. Ironically, the man whose songs glorified the life of blacks from the Old South played in front of almost entirely white audiences, virtually ignored by his own people. Although he possessed a wealth of talent, made enormous contributions to American folk music, and has since been recognized as a national treasure by intelligent blues scholars, he died virtually penniless.

Leadbelly was an innovator of the highest order. He developed a folk-blues structure that was later copied by many folk singers. Leadbelly, along with Woody Guthrie and Pete Seeger, planted the musical seeds that would blossom into the folk-blues craze of the early 1960s and enabled performers such as Joan Baez, Arlo Guthrie, and, of course, Bob Dylan to attain the fame that Leadbelly himself never enjoyed.

Leadbelly's initial efforts also enabled forgotten bluesmen to return in the musical spotlight, if only for a brief time. Skip James, Eddie "Son" House, Mance Lipscomb, Sippie Wallace, Big Joe Williams, Johnny Shines, Robert Jr. Lockwood, Sam "Lightnin'" Hopkins, Mississippi Fred McDowell, and a host of others were "discovered" by white college students. Many of the old bluesmen benefited financially and artistically from their return to the music world.

Leadbelly also laid down the foundation for the introspective, soft rock sound that drifted from Laurel Canyon, California, beginning in the late 1960s and best played by James Taylor; Joni Mitchell; Crosby, Stills, Nash, and Young; and, later, the Eagles.

In many ways, Leadbelly was way ahead of his time. For decades, black music was relegated to a "race" market, which severely handicapped black singers. But Leadbelly was performing in front of white audiences long before the color barrier was broken. He was one of the pioneers who paved the way for the introduction of black music into a white market.

Arguably, Leadbelly captured and contained the very essence of the blues. In the beginning, the heart of the blues was the musical chants used to alleviate the hard labor of the slaves who had been brought over from Africa to work on the Southern plantations. With his stirring twelve-string guitar work and gentle folk ballads, Leadbelly immortalized the daily life of the South he had left behind. He retained this particular blues strain in his folkish work songs and hollers, of which he had firsthand knowledge because of the decade or so he spent in prison working on the chain gangs.

Because of time spent incarcerated, Leadbelly's recording career is erratic. He managed to provide the world with the classics "Ella Speed," "Rock Island Line," "John Henry," "Good Morning Blues," "Midnight Special," and "Goodnight Irene." The songs "Midnight Special" and "On a Monday" describe in sharp detail prison life in the South during the 1920s and early 1930s.

Although he was a riveting performer, Leadbelly never made much money in his career. Ironically, the year after his death, his song "Goodnight Irene" was recorded by a group called the Weavers, led by Pete Seeger, and it sold two million copies. The fact that he missed out on that pot of gold summarizes Leadbelly's music career. He seemed destined to miss out on the big time.

He spent approximately fifteen years in Texas (and eight of those years in prison), and Leadbelly is an important part of the Lone Star State blues tradition. His partnership with Blind Lemon Jefferson, the so-called father of Texas blues, and the influence that each had on the other is incalculable. He learned how to play guitar in Louisiana, but he polished his musical skills in Texas and became part of the sophisticated and highly technical Texas blues school of guitarists. Leadbelly perfected a rhythmic guitar style and incorporated the bass figures of the barrelhouse piano players into his overall sound. Though he was proficient on the six-string guitar, he rejected the instrument in favor of a twelve-string. With double the strings, he reasoned, a person could play twice as much music.

Leadbelly made an impact on the entire Texas blues tradition. His folkish bent can be heard in the styles of Sam "Lightnin'" Hopkins. Leadbelly could also play swing, and this musical element was copied by T-Bone Walker and Gatemouth Brown. Leadbelly was able to incorporate many different musical ideas into one coherent style, which is a trademark of every Texas bluesman.

Leadbelly's contributions have not gone entirely unnoticed. He was elected to the Blues Foundation Hall of Fame in 1986 and the Rock and Roll Hall of Fame in 1988. Many of his songs have been recorded by other artists, and his influence is as fresh today as it was sixty years ago. Janis Joplin cited Leadbelly as one of her main inspirations.

Huddie "Leadbelly" Ledbetter was in many ways like the hungry alligators that patrolled the bayous of his native Louisiana. He roamed his native Southern habitat freely with a surly disposition, never backing down from a fight. Like the gator, Leadbelly was an original who became part of American folklore, despite almost suffering from the electric chair blues.

Discography

Midnight Special, Rounder 1044.
Gwine Dig a Hole to Put the Devil In, Rounder 1045.
Let it Shine on Me, Rounder 1046.
King of the 12-string Guitar, Columbia CK 46776.
Alabama Bound, RCA 9600-2.
Leadbelly Sings Folk Songs, Smithsonian/Folkways SF 40010.
Pick up on This, Rounder Records.
Convict Blues, Aldabra 1004.
Congress Blues, Aldabra 1007.
The Titanic, Rounder Records.
The Legend of Leadbelly, Tradition TRD 2093.
Leadbelly Soundtrack, ABC ABDP 939.
Huddie "Leadbelly" Ledbetter Memorial, Stinson 17/19/48/51.
Last Sessions Volume 1, Folkways FA 2941.
Last Sessions Volume 2, Folkways FA 2942.
Shout On, Folkways F75 31030.
Skip to My Lou, ASCH SC-79 Disc 5071.
Huddie Ledbetter, Fantasy F24715.
Good Night Irene, Allegro LEG 9025.

Huddie Ledbetter's Best, Capitol 92078-2.
Good Mornin' Blues (1936–40), Biograph 12013.
Nobody Knows The Trouble I've Seen, Rounder Records.
Leadbelly The Library of Congress Recordings, Elektra.
Leadbelly's Legacy, Folkways.
Blues Songs by the Lonesome Blues Singer, Royale.
Leadbelly, His Guitar, His Voice, His Piano, Capitol.
Leadbelly—Keep Your Hands off Her, Verve.
Take This Hammer, Verve.
Rock Island Line, Folkways.

AARON T-BONE WALKER
(1910–1975)

Stormy Monday Blues

The invention of the electric guitar brought many innovations to the blues sound. The amplification of the instrument hinted at previously unknown possibilities that were impossible to duplicate on the old acoustic guitars cherished by the dedicated pioneers. The modern blues style required someone who could combine all of the essential elements of the country-blues with the slick urban sound. The champion came from Texas, and he established the electric guitar style stunning the world with his Stormy Monday Blues. His name was T-Bone Walker.

Aaron Thibeaux "T-Bone" Walker was born in 1910 in Linden, Texas, a land of sawmills, cotton, and cattle. When he was barely a year old his mother, bored with the stifling country ways of a small town, moved to the exciting urban center of Dallas, taking Aaron with her. The escape from Linden rescued Aaron from a childhood of hard field labor and pointed his future toward a musical direction.

T-Bone's mother played guitar, and his uncles were street musicians. When he was barely ten years old, Walker joined his uncles and danced up a storm. By his early teens he had already acquired his first guitar.

Though it is true his family fed his musical appetite, perhaps the greatest early influence on Walker was the first important country-blues star from Texas, Blind Lemon Jefferson. Walker acted as a lead boy and often accompanied Jefferson around town. Blind Lemon not only taught his young pupil the rudiments of Texas style guitar but he also passed down the sacred secrets of show business.

It was only natural that T-Bone decided to pursue a musical career. He was an acrobatic dancer and inventive guitarist and songwriter, and he possessed a warm, friendly voice. Music had been the single greatest force throughout his young life, and he was drawn by its powerful magnetism.

In 1929, after spending time in Lawson Brooke's band, Walker entered an amateur show at the Majestic Theatre with first prize being a one-week guest spot in Cab Calloway's band. Walker won the contest, and the experience was a brief, but rewarding one.

At this time Walker made his first recordings for Columbia Records. The two songs, "Wichita Falls" and "Trinity River Blues," did not make him an overnight star. It was almost a decade before he recorded again. In the interim, there were drastic changes in his personal and professional life that would forever alter the course of popular music.

Walker continued to scuffle around, spending time in different groups including a spot in Count Biloxi's band. T-Bone had already developed a bluesman's taste for traveling, and he toured the Southwest and other parts of the country. Walker eventually returned to the Fort Worth area of Texas. To continue his musical career, he formed a quartet. At this time he met his future wife, Vida Lee. It was also at this time, in the middle of the decade, that the first electric guitars became available.

But the biggest change in T-Bone's life was his desire to head west. In 1934, Walker moved to California, which began a pattern of Texas bluesmen migrating to the Golden State. In Los Angeles Walker first started to experiment with the possibilities of the electric guitar. He led his own band, whose lineup included Big Jim Wynn on baritone saxophone and Zutty Singleton on drums. The band played the black ghetto of Watts and established a strong following. His later engagements in Chicago enhanced his reputation.

In Los Angeles in 1946, Walker cut some fifty sides for the Black & White label, including his masterpiece, "Stormy Monday." Other songs he added to his catalog were "T-Bone Shuffle," "Hypin' Woman Blues," "I Want a Little Girl," and "Lonesome Blues," which featured jazz musicians like Al Killian, Bumps Myers, Teddy Buckner, and Jack McVea.

Although Walker had been playing many of these songs for some time, the new amplified sound captivated listeners. No one had ever heard electric blues like "T-Bone Shuffle," "Stormy Monday Blues," "Lonesome Blues," and "I Want a Little Girl" simply because no one had created them yet. The amplification of the rural blues ushered in the modern postwar blues era, and because he was credited with being the first to constantly utilize the instrument in recordings, T-Bone was recognized as the father of the electric guitar style.

Walker, backed by a veteran Los Angeles jazz band, went on to record "Evil Hearted Woman," "Railroad Station Blues," "Strollin' with Bones," "Blue Mood," and "Love Is a Gamble." These songs established his reputation as the first electric guitar stylist, an opinion that still exists today. After much success with Black & White Records, Walker signed with Imperial in 1950.

In the part of the decade he recorded "You Don't Love Me," "Alimony Blues," "I'm About to Lose My Mind," "Blues Is a Woman," "Blue Mood," "Love Is a Gamble," "Railroad Station Blues," "Got no Use for You," and "Bye-Bye Baby," to name just a few gems. Later, Walker recorded for Atlantic Records. With the release of the album *T-Bone Blues* he not only solidified his already powerful standing but also gained eternal fame.

His smooth, friendly voice, jazz-influenced guitar lines, and incredible showmanship had made him one of the most exciting and popular blues singers of the 1940s and early 1950s. However, by the late '50s, his recording output began to decline, though he continued to perform despite increasing health problems. T-Bone was always pushing himself to the limits, and his drinking problem certainly didn't help matters.

By 1960, Walker had been in show business for four decades and could look back on a glorious career. Arguably, his best days were over, but the electric Texan wasn't totally used up just yet. He appeared with Count Basie as part of a package tour that also featured the great Ruth Brown. In 1962, he was part of another concert package called Rhythm and Blues U.S.A., along with John Lee Hooker, Willie Dixon, Memphis Slim, and the duo of Sonny Terry and Brownie McGhee. They played many European countries including France, Italy, Germany, Denmark, Sweden, Switzerland, and England. The band recorded an album with T-Bone in the unusual guise of piano player. He also appeared in an all-star session with Joe Turner and Otis Spann on the album *Super Black Blues*. T-Bone took part in many collaboration albums with other blues singers. He also made some recordings in Europe during this period.

In 1967, Walker appeared in the 1967 concert for Norman Granz, "The Greatest Jazz Concert in the World," where he sang and played in the company of Oscar Peterson, Johnny Hodges, Clark Terry, and Paul Gonsalves. Throughout his career, Walker never lost his love for jazz stylings and recorded the album *Funky Town* with a Basie-like big band. On his album *Very Rare*, he was backed by top jazz instrumentalists like Gerry Muligan, Dizzy Gillespie, Zoot Sims, Al Cohn, and Wilton Felder. Other Walker albums which featured the horn-driven, jazz sound were *T-Bone Jumps Again, Plain Ole Blues, The Natural Blues* and *Sings the Blues*.

By the mid–1960s and early 1970s Walker had slowed down considerably. His recording and performance dates were unevenly spaced out due to his increasingly poor health. Walker had indulged in the good life, and his carefree ways had taken their toll on his fragile body.

However, despite his ill health he pushed on. In 1972, Walker won a Grammy for his album *Good Feelin'*, and this brief taste of success gave him new energy. Around this time the definite cover version of his classic song "Stormy Monday" was released by the Allman Brothers Band on their album *Live at the Fillmore*. At the time Walker was working with younger musicians and trying to revive the old spirit. But, like a doomed cat, he had used up nearly all of his nine lives. A car accident in which he suffered serious injuries only added to his troubles.

He played his last concert in Pittsburgh in 1974. For those in attendance, it was a very sad sight to see one of America's greatest musical legends slip away. The career of the father of the electric guitar style was finished. Stormy Monday had arrived with a vengeance, and it was time for T-Bone to pay the bill.

Near the end of 1974, he suffered a stroke and entered a nursing home in Los Angeles. Three months later, he died on March 15, 1975. He was sixty-five years old.

T-Bone Walker was a blues superstar whose genius cannot be overstated. His innovations on the electric guitar are numerous, and he is responsible for the modern sound in rock, blues, and jazz. Not only was he the first bluesman to make use of amplification but he defined the modern electric guitar style. All modern blues guitarists can quickly point to T-Bone Walker as one of their main inspirations.

He brought to blues guitar jazz lines that were smooth and concise. His ability to swing between straight-note feel and swing is another innovation. Nobody was doing this before T-Bone. His friendship with Charlie Christian was an important one for both men and an even more important one for modern music. The two learned from each other and borrowed ideas that fused blues and jazz sounds together, the very foundations of rock.

T-Bone brought a delicate sensitivity to the electric guitar, a special touch that no one has ever been able to imitate, though many have tried. He understood the subtle textures of dynamics and tone and was able to fuse them together in harmony with heartfelt lyrics in a casual style.

His ability to create tension and excitement with the use of sixteenth notes created the deft shift between light and heavy sounds, a skill he acquired while experimenting with the new electric guitar. This unique use of amplification would later become a trademark of nearly every successful blues-rock band, including the Beatles, the Rolling Stones, Led Zeppelin, the Doors, the Who, the Yardbirds, and countless others.

T-Bone also had a unique way of holding his guitar—not parallel to his body, but perpendicular to it. This was one of the essential elements of his overall sound. He was able to roll out the smooth jazz lines that he became famous for with this unusual posturing. A slightly built man, he was a sharp dresser who elevated the image of the lowly blues singer from unsavory character to professional musician. But he was much more than that.

T-Bone Walker was a complete package. He possessed incredible guitar skills; a warm, reassuring voice; a superb songwriting ability; and a keen sense of showmanship. It was T-Bone Walker who imitated the splits and other athletic maneuvers of Charley Patton, which he later passed on to Chuck Berry and Jimi Hendrix.

But Walker was part of another important blues chain. He was one of the seminal figures of the rich Texas blues tradition. His major contribution to the genre was the creation of his "Texas shuffle," which added a new dimension to the Texas sound. His special feeling for funky blues had a profound effect on a galaxy of Texas guitarists, including Freddie King, Albert Collins, Johnny Copeland, Johnny "Guitar" Watson, Johnny Winter, Billy Gibbons, and the late Stevie Ray Vaughan.

But T-Bone's deep influence spilled over the Texas border. He was a special source of inspiration to B. B. King, the most important bluesman of the postwar era. King began where T-Bone left off. Much of King's style—the jazzy single-line solos, the fusion of country and city sounds, the expert use of timing and emotions—are all a direct result from listening to Walker's music for countless hours.

T-Bone's unique sound also played a large role in the development of the styles of Muddy Waters, John Lee Hooker, Jimmy Reed, and others of the Chicago blues school. He was also the pioneer in the development of the West Coast blues, which was primarily a piano-based, jazz-influenced sound. Many of the Texas expatriates who relocated to California (including Charles Brown, Pee Wee Crayton, Lowell Fulson, Jesse Fuller, Floyd Dixon, Johnny Otis, Jimmy Witherspoon, and Percy Mayfield) owe a great debt to T-Bone Walker.

T-Bone worked with Ida Cox, Ma Rainey, Bessie Smith, and Clara Smith, as well as Lonnie Johnson. He was also connected with some of the immortals of jazz, including Dizzy Gillespie and Charlie Parker, the inventors of be-bop. He toured with rock and rollers like Jerry Lee Lewis and Little Richard. It is quite possible that Walker had more influence on more musical styles than any other artist of the twentieth century.

In 1980, T-Bone Walker was inducted into the Blues Foundation Hall of Fame, and in 1987 to the Rock and Roll Hall of Fame. Both were fitting tributes to man often tagged as the greatest blues guitar player. Although this honor is like arguing who is the greatest baseball player that ever lived, without a doubt, the man who gave the world his "Stormy Monday Blues" occupies a very special place in the hierarchy of twentieth-century musicians.

Discography

The Complete Recordings of T-Bone Walker, Mosaic Records MR6-130.
Low Down Blues, Charly CD 7.
I Want a Little Girl, Delmark DD 633.
The Inventor of the Electric Guitar Blues, Blues Boy BB-304.
His Original 1945–50 Performances, Capitol T-1958.
Classic in Jazz, Capitol H 370.
Classic in Jazz, Capitol LC 6681.
His Original 1945–1950 Performances, Capitol 8185.
Too Much Trouble Blues, Capitol 062-80732.
Plain Ole Blues, Charly CRB 1037.
The Natural Blues, Charly CRB 1057.
The Complete Imperial Recordings, 1950–1954, EMI CDP 7-96737-2.
The Blues of T-Bone Walker, MFP 1043.
Home of the Blues, Volume 3, Polydor 46867.
Classics of Modern Blues, Blue Note BN-LA-522-H2.

T-Bone Jumps Again, Charly CRB 1019.
Well Done, Home Cookin' HC S-103.
The Truth, Brunswick 754126.
Stormy Monday Blues, BluesWay BLS 6008.
Funky Town, BluesWay BLS 6014.
Dirty Mistreater, BluesWay BLS 6058.
Feeling the Blues, Black & Blue 33019.
T-Bone Blues, Atlantic 8020-2.
Good Feelin', Polydor 658158.
Stormy Monday Blues, Wet Soul 1002.
Every Day I Have the Blues, Blues Time 29004.
Fly Walker Airlines, Polydor PD-5521.
Very Rare, Reprise 6483.

SAM "LIGHTNIN'" HOPKINS
(1912–1985)

Lightnin' Strikes

The blues fever can attack anyone, anywhere, anytime. Take for instance, one sunny Sunday afternoon in 1920 at a church picnic in Buffalo, Texas, when an impressionable eight-year-old boy sat mesmerized by the performance of country-blues star Blind Lemon Jefferson. History has indicated that blues fever struck that boy hard that day because he grew up to be a blues legend. His name was Sam "Lightnin'" Hopkins.

Sam Hopkins was born on March 18, 1912, in Centreville, part of Leona County in the very heart of east Texas. Hopkins suffered a Dickensian life of hardship: a murdered father, hard labor, extreme poverty, and no education. Music was his sole salvation. His brother owned a real guitar, but Hopkins was denied access to it, so he made one out of a cigar box. Later, when he finally acquired his first manufactured guitar, he started making up blues songs.

Hopkins received lessons from a variety of sources, including his brother, Joel, who was also a bluesman. An old blues singer who courted his mother also taught young Sam a few chords. But that fateful meeting at age eight dictated the path of Sam's future. At the church that day Blind Lemon allowed Sam to play along and whispered golden words of encouragement. This was all Hopkins needed.

Despite possessing the burning blues fire in his stomach, there was no overnight success for Hopkins. For the next twenty-five years, he paid his dues. As a teen he played with a fiddler friend on street corners for spare change. He later hooked up with his cousin Texas Alexander, who had once played on a session with the immortal Lonnie Johnson. Hopkins and Alexander played parties throughout the Houston area. Hopkins also hoboed through other parts of Texas, playing at juke joints and parties.

While he was developing his distinctive sound, Hopkins was also turning the soil behind the mule, which was hard, punishing work. He was also traveling down the road his father had gone down—drinking, fighting, and gambling excessively, which earned him a personal invitation on the chain gain. Hopkins was headed on a direct path of self-destruction with his hard-living ways. Music would temporarily alleviate his plight, but Hopkins would relapse into periods of heavy drinking and fighting, which only landed him back on the chain gang. Thirty years after his last stint of doing hard labor the scars of the chains were still apparent on his wrists—the lasting personal tattoo of a man's wasted youth.

In 1938, he made a giant step toward getting his life back together when he moved to Houston to be with his cousin Texas Alexander. To keep a roof over his head Hopkins played on street corners and parties around the Houston area, with his cousin or by himself. He also traveled throughout the South to play his blues, riding the rails and moving from one small town to the next. Although the temptations on the road were many, Hopkins managed to stay out of trouble. It seemed, after much punishment, that he had finally learned the hardest lessons in life and was eager to pursue his musical ambitions.

It wasn't until 1946, when he was thirty-four years old, that he made his first recordings and quickly found a ready audience that was enthusiastic for his rough, gritty voice and dizzying guitar speed. He cut his first two singles, "Katie Mae Blues" and "That Mean Old Twister," for Aladdin Records, which was based in Los Angeles. Hopkins made the trip to the Golden State with pianist Wilson Smith, and the pair recorded together. Because of his thumping bass notes and hard-driving sound, Smith was nicknamed "Thunder" and Hopkins was dubbed "Lightnin'."

Encouraged by the first sides he cut, which became minor hits, Hopkins returned to the studio to record "Short Haired Woman," which also attracted some attention. Back in Houston, the recognition translated into increased performances and more opportunities to record. Because of his ready ability to invent whole songs at a moment's notice, Hopkins was able to walk into any recording studio, at any time, and record a clever tune. The quick cash was more than enough incentive for him to visit the recording booth often. By the end of his career, he was recognized as one of the most prolific recording artists in blues history.

A partial list of the labels Hopkins recorded for includes Aladdin/ Imperial, Imperial, Gold Star, Modern, RPM, Jax/Sittin' With, United, Kent, Crown, Verve, Dart, Time, Mercury, Folkways, Mainstream, Blues Classics, Decca, Herald, and Arhoolie. Although he demonstrated an incredible versatility by recording for so many companies, he also created major headaches for all biographers, collectors, and blues historians.

Hopkins continued to record in the 1950s, although his country-blues were often overlooked in favor of the harsher, electric Chicago blues sound. He only produced three singles in 1955 and 1956, and he did not record in 1957 and 1958 at all. Yet he still retained a strong base of popularity among blues purists, who clung to their country-blues roots. Hopkins continued to perform within the small circuit where his Texas country-blues were well received, but his career faded to the point that he was almost out of the music business entirely.

But around 1959, the musical tastes of the country began to shift in his favor. The traditional folk blues, the music that ran through the veins of Lightnin' Hopkins, became the new rage of educated white audiences who were eager to experience the music from direct sources. Seemingly overnight, the careers of such forgotten blues artists like Hopkins were resurrected from desperation. Hopkins was reportedly "discovered" by Sam Charters in the early 1960s, living in a Houston ghetto, a bitter and dejected man. Determined to cash in on the sudden popularity of folk music, he returned to the recording studio and made his first album for Folkways.

The record included a tribute song to his prime influence, "Reminiscences of Blind Lemon," as well as a couple of Jefferson originals: the haunting "Penitentiary Blues" and the spiritual "See That My Grave Is Kept Clean." Hopkins, a proud individual, was paying his respects to the man who introduced him to the blues and guided him spiritually throughout his entire career.

In 1960, Hopkins along with fellow folk blues artists Sonny Terry, Brownie McGhee, and Big Joe Williams (who was also enjoying a career revival) convened in Los Angeles to record together for World Pacific. Hopkins, who had done little to advance his career during the last half of the previous decade, was now a man on fire. He appeared with Joan Baez and Pete Seeger at Carnegie Hall and later in the year recorded what became his signature song, "Mojo Hand," for Fire Records.

Hopkins continued to record and perform at a furious rate throughout the 1960s and increased his sphere of fame with each passing concert and album. He became a favorite on the college campus circuit, providing eager audiences with authentic folk-blues. Because of his remarkable talent for making up witty blues songs up on the spot (often about everyday subjects that touched each member of the audience in a very real personal way), Hopkins remained in demand even after the folk-blues craze had subsided.

In the 1970s, Hopkins slowed down some, but continued to record, providing the world with such songs as "California Mudslide," "Keeps on Rainin'," "Hootin' the Blues," and "Gotta Move Your Baby" with Sonny Terry. He also provided the soundtrack to the movie *Sounder* in 1972, as well as taking part in several blues documentaries.

By the beginning of the 1980s it was evident that Hopkins was one of a dying breed. His folkish blues style was considered passé. Hopkins, approaching his seventieth birthday, was one of the last links to the country-blues, the very foundation of the music that artists like Blind Lemon Jefferson, Charley Patton, Son House, Robert Johnson, Skip James, Blind Willie McTell, Blind Boy Fuller, and Lonnie Johnson had popularized.

In 1982, on January 30, after a long bout with cancer, Sam "Lightnin'," Hopkins, the incorrigible blues rascal, died at age seventy. The death of Hopkins and of Muddy Waters a year later robbed the blues community of two of its greatest treasures.

Lightnin' Hopkins was an innovative blues singer deeply rooted in the Texas tradition, whose career spanned six decades, making him one of the most durable bluesmen. Because of his constant recording he also became one of the most prolific blues singers in history. With his creative abilities Hopkins made the blues fun. He was an American original, a national treasure as well as a Texas institution.

Hopkins possessed a natural rhythm, a superb dexterity, and an impeccable sense of timing. As a guitar player, he never received his proper due. The true cornerstone of the Hopkins sound was his powerful, fast-flowing guitar work, which was another possible source for his nick-name. His use of irregular meter and unconventional chord arrangements gave his music a unique appeal. There always existed an energy, a lively pulse to his sound that created a subtle tension that was the genuine dri-ving force of his music.

Hopkins possessed a voice that was dry and prickly like a cactus, yet also contained a warm familiarity. He played more than just country-blues with traditional themes. His songs were a mixture of humorous stories, tragic narratives, spirited ballads, and up-tempo swing numbers laced with sudden breaks and fast but controlled solos, which made him a blues leg-end. The high energy level of his blazing fingers was copied by countless guitar players, especially in the styles of blues-rockers Jimi Hendrix and Alvin Lee of the band Ten Years After.

Sam "Lightnin'" Hopkins was a genuine bluesman with a fervid indi-vidual spirit, which came through in his songs. A pure yarn spinner, he was a man who could make the common events in life seem interesting and humorous. His unmatched ability to instantly create a polished, catchy tune about everyday occurrences like his car breaking down, combing his hair, or mailing a letter, assured that Hopkins was constantly able to touch a communal nerve in his audience in a way few others have ever managed to do. On stage, he created a private world and held the audience spell-bound with his storytelling gift and guitar magic.

He gave the world such blues classics as "Unkind Blues," "Some-body's Got to Go," "Mad with You," "Airplane Blues," "Loretta Blues," "Whiskey Blues," "Ida Mae," "Organ Boogie," and "Bluebird Blues" to name only a few.

Hopkins was a man who knew his share of good times as well as bad times. His songs often contained humorous lyrics mixed with tinges of hardship. Yet, despite possessing a genuine blues sensibility, Hopkins never became a superstar. The main reason for his lack of strong com-mercial success was his refusal to sell out. Lightnin' Hopkins was his own man, a fiercely independent individual who was not interested in winning any popularity contests. His only wish was to play his concerts and to be left alone. Hopkins had his own perception of how the blues should sound, and he remained stubbornly faithful to the country-blues tradi-tion.

Despite his independent Texan stance, Hopkins made a large impact on a number of different singers. His popularization of the boogie-woo-gie accompaniment can be found in the music of such early rockers as

Chuck Berry and Elvis Presley, as well as fellow Texans Johnny Winter, ZZ Top, and the late Stevie Ray Vaughan.

But Hopkins was more than just a country-blues artist. He played international music with a Texas flavor. Aside from Blind Lemon Jefferson and T-Bone Walker, Hopkins is the most important exponent of the Texas blues tradition. Though his place as one of the great pioneers of Texas blues is assured, Hopkins holds still another honor.

In the long, illustrious American folk music tradition, Hopkins occupies a regal position. He is in the same company as Huddie "Leadbelly" Ledbetter, Pete Seeger, Woodie and Arlo Guthrie, Joan Baez, Bob Dylan, Brownie McGhee, Sonny Terry, Harry Chapin, Don McLean, and others who wrote political and social songs that mattered to their country. Hopkins reflected the life of the poor, common black person in his songs, and he fostered awareness of their plight. When a Who's Who of folk singers is compiled, the name Sam "Lightnin'" Hopkins is a most natural selection.

In 1980, Lightnin' Hopkins was inducted into the Blues Foundation Hall of Fame, a well-deserved honor. Hopkins remains one of the most charming stories of the blues. He was a musical gem and an intriguing personality. He was a man who lived on his own principles and never worried what was said about him. He possessed a unique gift and was quick to share it with anyone who was willing to listen. He was an authentic country bluesman. To forget men such as Lightnin' Hopkins is to turn our backs on the entire blues tradition. Any aspiring bluesman today who listens to his recordings will undoubtedly prove that lightning can strike again.

Discography

How Many More Years I Got, Fantasy 24725.
In New York 1970, Candid 79010.
The Herald Material 1954–1988, Collectables 5121.
The Herald Material Volume 2, 5181.
The Gold Star Sessions, Vol. 1, Arhoolie CD 330.
The Gold Star Sessions, Vol. 2, Arhoolie CD 337.
Sittin' in With, Mainstream 905.
Mojo Hand: The Anthology Man, Rhino.
Lightnin' Hopkins and the Blues, Imperial 12211.
Lightnin' and the Blues, Herald 1012.

The Blues Giant, Olympic 7110.
Early Recordings Volume 1, Arhoolie 2007.
Early Recordings Volume 2, Arhoolie 2008.
Early Recordings Volume 3, Arhoolie 2009.
Early Recordings Volume 4, Arhoolie 2010.
Fast Life Woman, Verve V 8543.
Double Blues, Fantasy 24702.
The Roots of Lightnin' Hopkins, Verve/Folkways VLP 5003.
The Complete Prestige/Bluesville Recordings, Prestige/Bluesville 7PCD
    4406-2.
The Complete Aladdin Recordings, EMI CDP 7-96843-2.
Lightnin' Hopkins, Smithsonian/Folkways CD SF 40019.
Texas Blues, Arhoolie CD 302.
The Herald Recordings—1954, Collectables Col. -CD 5121.
The Lost Texas Tapes, Vol. 1-5, Collectables Col. 5201, 5202, 5203, 5204,
    5205.
Drinkin' in the Blues, Collectables Col.-CD 5143.
Prison Blues, Collectables Col.-CD 5144.
Mama and Papa Hopkins, Collectables Col.-CD 5145.
Nothin' but the Blues, Collectables Col.-CD 5146.
Mojo Hand, Collectables Col.-CD 5111.
Houston's King of the Blues, Blues Classics 30.
Lightnin' New York, Story of Blues 79010.
The Complete Candid Otis Spann/Lightnin' Hopkins Sessions, Mosaic
    Records MD #-139.

CLARENCE "GATEMOUTH" BROWN
(1924–   )

Gatemouth's Blues

The Texas blues experience is a melting pot of numerous influences.
Jazz, swing, Cajun, bluegrass, country, folk, spiritual, work songs, rocka-
billy, and Mexican are just some of the elements that have been blended

together to create that lowdown Texas blues sound. In the annals of Texas blues a number of different musicians have tried to assimilate all of these styles into one cohesive sound while still retaining their individuality. No other Texas musician has worked harder to incorporate many different musical ideas into his own style than the man responsible for creating Gatemouth's blues. His name is Clarence "Gatemouth" Brown.

Clarence Brown was born on April 18, 1924, in Vinton, Louisiana. Brown became a resident of the Lone Star State very early in his life. The biggest musical influence on him was his father, a capable musician who passed on his love of music to his son. Because of his father Gatemouth learned how to play a variety of instruments—enough to become a one-man band. His multi-instrumental talents make him an anomaly in the blues world.

Gatemouth often jammed with his father and friends around his home in Orange, Texas. But he grew bored; by his mid-teens, he was ready to strike out on his own to earn fame and fortune. After years of watching his father, Gatemouth was well prepared. He left home armed with his old Washburn guitar, his father's precious words of wisdom, and raw determination. Brown landed his first gig with W. M. Barbo and the Brownskin Models, an old-time traveling show. It was a good, but brief experience for young Clarence, who stayed behind in Norfolk, Virginia, when the rest of the troupe moved to the next town. In Norfolk, he found work at the El Dorado Club as a drummer with the house band. This job didn't last much longer than his previous gig because his budding musical career was interrupted by a call to arms.

Gatemouth served for six months in the army before his discharge. He headed to San Antonio, where he performed with Hart Hodge's twenty-three-piece orchestra. Though some blues singers would be lost in such a large ensemble, Gatemouth thrived on the opportunity and was nicknamed "The Singing Drummer." Early in his career, Brown was already demonstrating a strong liking for big band jazz ensembles.

Undoubtedly, the turning point in Gatemouth's career occurred one night at the Bronze Peacock, owned by Don Robey, the kingpin of the Texas blues scene for many years. At the time, T-Bone Walker's star was as big as the state of Texas itself. Walker suffered from vicious ulcers throughout his career, and appeared too sick to play. Gatemouth, seeing his golden opportunity, seized Walker's seat and invented on the spot a riveting Texas boogie tune that captivated the audience as well as Robey. In fact, Robey was so enthralled by Gatemouth's performance that he immediately took him under his wing.

Not long after, Gatemouth found himself in a recording studio with the chance to record his songs. Backed by the Maxwell Davis Band, Gatemouth cut four songs for Aladdin Records in 1947. Despite the fact that they were swinging numbers the album sold poorly because of limited promotion.

When Robey formed his own label, Peacock Records, Brown was one of the first artists to be signed. His 1953 release, *Boogie Uproar*, as well as his 1954 effort *Midnight Hour* quickly established Gatemouth as one of the bright blues stars. While Muddy and his mates were burning down Chicago with their citified sound, Gatemouth was doing his own Texas swing thing.

The productive partnership between Gatemouth and Peacock lasted from 1947 until 1960 and produced such songs as "Mary Is Fine," "Dirty Work at the Crossroads," "Just Got Lucky," "Pale Dry Boogie," and the blues cult classic "Okie Dokie Stomp." Despite the distinct appeal of his boogie/stomp blues, Gatemouth's music was never truly commercial. His only stab at success was "Mary Is Fine," which made the top ten on the rhythm and blues charts in 1949.

By 1961, Gatemouth was experiencing some hard times. His recording career was at a standstill, and he carved out a meager existence by grinding it out on the small-club circuit. This harsh life soon took its toll and Gatemouth decided to leave Texas in search of a fresh start.

He moved to Nashville, Tennessee, one of the world's greatest musical centers, and found work on the television show *The Beat*. He also had the opportunity to record with country superstar Roy Clark. Despite a certain degree of success in Nashville, Brown never made a serious impact.

In the early 1970s, Gatemouth toured Europe and was able to breathe new life into his dormant career. Charged by the spark of being able to earn a living recording his songs again, he cut a few sides with the label Black and Blue, a French record company. His constant touring of Europe was partly responsible for the renewed interest in his electric blues at home. A musician with a traveling bug, Gatemouth performed in Africa and the Soviet Union as a representative of the U.S. State Department. Like a Texas minister spreading the gospel, Brown delivered his funky music to the deprived masses who had not been fortunate enough to experience his blues.

By the late 1970s, after a long drought, Gatemouth's recording career was back on track when he secured a contract with Rounder Records. For his new label, Brown recorded *Alright Again, One More Nite*, and *Real*

Life. Despite his success on Rounder, Brown moved to Alligator Records. His first venture on Alligator produced *Pressure Cooker.* In 1989, he added *Standing My Ground* to his list of credits.

The *Standing My Ground* effort showed Brown's true versatility as a musician. The record includes hard blues, swing, and Texas funk. Many cuts on the album featured his multitalented abilities. Despite strong commercial success with Alligator, Gatemouth switched labels again and recorded *Gate Swings* for Verve Records.

The CD *Gate Swings* is destined to be a classic. Backed by his road band and a thirteen-piece horn section, Gatemouth revisits the big band days. Standard songs such as "Midnight Hour" and "Too Late Baby" are mixed in with other original Brown creations, such as "Gate's Blues Waltz," "Take the A Train," "Caldonia," "One o'clock Jump," and "Flyin' Home." The entire effort burns with a fierce intensity and proves that the old master has lost nothing over the years.

Clarence "Gatemouth" Brown is in many ways one of the best-kept secrets of the blues. He has been entertaining audiences throughout the world for over fifty years; yet, in all fairness, he has never received proper credit. This is in part because of the fact that he has never been a great commercial success. However, his contributions to Texas blues as well as international music are undeniable.

Brown is fiercely independent; he is his own man. He vehemently denies he is a "bluesman," but insists he is a capable musician who plays international music with a Lone Star flavor. This defiant attitude is not only an example of Brown's independent Texas attitude but is also perhaps derived from the fact that his father, also a musician, was more of a songster than a bluesman. In Texas, as well as the other Southern states bluesmen were looked down on as lowdown, shiftless characters.

There is also the fact that Brown plays more than just straight blues. His sound is a fusion of musical ideas that includes jazz, swing, Cajun and Creole, Mexican, European, and rural white. Also, his remarkable versatility as a musician separates him from most bluesmen, who play at most just a couple of instruments. Brown, a proud man, has no desire to be chained to a narrow category only convenient for blues pundits.

But Gatemouth is more than just an incredibly versatile musician. He is an eccentric character, a man with great charisma and an incredible understanding of a variety of musical styles. He is a serious student of music and possesses a unique musical vision. His approach to life is unique.

The essential ingredient to Gatemouth's sound is his philosophy of a hornlike approach to playing the electric guitar. He plays without a pick so he can maintain better control. By using his bare fingers, Gatemouth can make his guitar sound like an authentic horn. By using his intelligent, dexterous fingers, Gatemouth has always been able to get that horn sound he desires. He can play long, sustained notes or short, choppy ones with ease.

Gatemouth's contribution to Texas blues is enormous. By expanding its parameters, he has given the Texas sound a rougher edge. In his music, strains of jazz, country, and Cajun are clearly audible. His interesting use of the fiddle, an instrument seldom used in blues music, earns him important innovation credentials. His striking, self-reliant approach to creating music places his name alongside other Texas notables, including Blind Lemon Jefferson, Lightnin' Hopkins, T-Bone Walker, and Stevie Ray Vaughan. No matter where he has performed in the world, Gatemouth has always worn his Texas heritage proudly.

The biggest Texas influence on Brown was without a doubt T-Bone Walker. When he was "discovered" in 1947 by Don Robey, Brown was hailed as Walker's heir apparent. Like T-Bone, Gatemouth thrived in a big band atmosphere, and his unique skills allowed him to excel in such a situation. Although he may have not attained the commercial success that Walker did, Brown has nevertheless carved out his own special niche.

But Brown didn't just expand the Texas sound, he also added a special dimension to international blues. While the blues are American-dominated with the British claiming second place, the music has reached global heights. In every corner of the world the blues are being played, and traveling mavericks like Gatemouth Brown are responsible for spreading the message.

Clarence "Gatemouth" Brown has touched many listeners with his abundant skills and continues today, although he is well into his seventies. He has an abundance of charisma that shines through in his music. By stubbornly following his own musical course, he has provided a global audience with the unique sound of Gatemouth's blues, and the world is a much better place for it.

Discography

Alright Again, Rounder 2028.
The Original Peacock Recordings, Rounder 2039.

One More Nite, Rounder 2034.
Real Life, Rounder 2054.
Texas Swing, Rounder 11527.
Pressure Cooker, Alligator AL 4745.
Standing My Ground, Alligator AL 4779.
Makin' Music with Roy Clark, MCA 3009.
San Antonio Ballbuster, Red Lightnin' 0010.
No Looking Back, Alligator AL 4804

ALBERT COLLINS (1932–1993)

The Iceman Cometh

In the 1980s, the blues enjoyed a sparkling revival. The blues had fallen out of public favor for much of the 1970s, due in part to the untimely deaths of T-Bone Walker, Howlin' Wolf, Freddie King, and Jimmy Reed within an eighteen-month period in the middle of the decade. But the blues regained its old audience members and was discovered by new ones. The blues renaissance was spearheaded by three Texans—Stevie Ray Vaughan, Johnny Copeland, and the Iceman, who arrived on the scene with icy guitar tones. His name was Albert Collins.

Collins was born on October 1, 1932, in Leona, Texas. If bloodlines count for anything in blues history, then Collins had a head start on many of his contemporaries because he was a cousin of legendary Texas blues storyteller Lightnin' Hopkins. There are no clear indications of how much direct influence Hopkins had on his cousin; in young Albert's eyes, Cousin Sam must have seemed like a mythical figure. After all, Hopkins was a living, breathing, genuine bluesman, which was Albert's burning desire.

Collins studied piano and guitar at an early age and was deeply influenced by the lords of the Texas tradition, including his aforementioned cousin plus Blind Lemon Jefferson, T-Bone Walker, and Gatemouth Brown. Collins spent part of his youth in Houston, where he was exposed to the city's rich musical heritage. Both Sippie Wallace and Victoria Spivey were born in Houston, and from the turn of the century this city has boasted a thriving blues scene that continues even today. Collins gained valuable experience playing in a number of pick-up and garage bands in his early teens, developing and mastering the guitar skills that would someday earn him the nicknames the Iceman and the Ice Picker.

Eventually, Collins graduated to the Houston club circuit and formed his first professional band, the Rhythm Rockers. In his days with the Rhythm Rockers, Collins—along with Johnny Copeland and Johnny "Guitar" Watson—tried to break out of the grinding Texas bar circuit.

After the demise of the Rhythm Rockers, Collins joined the Piney Brown Orchestra, adding his distinctive guitar touch to the band's sound. They toured extensively throughout Texas and other Southern states. By this time Collins had blossomed into a truly magnificent virtuoso with one of the most unique guitar sounds on the Texas blues scene. Despite achieving a local following and sporting an impressive résumé it wasn't until 1958 that Albert was able to record some of his own material.

Collins, a crafty bluesman, was fully aware that every musician possessed some clear characteristic that separated him or her from other blues artists. With this in mind, he decided to build his career on pure blues by capitalizing on his unusually sparse guitar sound. It seemed only natural to write songs with icy titles that reflected his cool playing style.

For Kangaroo Records, Collins recorded the instrumental "The Freeze," which was a regional hit, and continued the "cold" trend with such songs as "Frosty," "Frost-Bite," "Thaw Out," "Icy Blues," and "Sno-cone." Unfortunately, his intelligent marketing strategy did not catapult him into stardom, although he managed to earn the respect of his fellow bluesmen. Whereas many modern blues guitarists were offshoots of the B. B. King or Muddy Waters school of guitar, Collins was his own private institution and practically impossible to copy.

In 1966, in an effort to boost a stagnant career, Collins moved to Kansas City. Although he lived far away in another state, Collins was reluctant to completely sever his Texas ties, and he returned to Houston periodically to play an occasional gig. At one of these Houston concerts he caught the attention of Bob "Bear" Hite of Canned Heat fame. Through this important connection Collins secured a contract with Imperial Records.

In 1969, Collins moved to Los Angeles, the home base of Imperial. The musical marriage between Collins and this label produced three albums: *Love Can Be Found Anywhere (Even in a Guitar)*, *Trash Talkin*, and *The Complete Albert Collins*. None of the three records were the break-through album that he hoped for, and the relationship between the Iceman and Imperial ended in 1972.

Always a spirited individual, Collins tried his hand at recording again, this time for Tumbleweed Records. The aptly titled *There's Gotta Be a Change* was not a critical or commercial success and left him without a recording contract. At this point, Collins disappeared from the recording scene for a while, relying on live performances to pay the bills.

After a five-year absence from the studio, he was ready to record once again. He secured a contract with Alligator Records and delivered the strongest effort since his days on the Kangaroo label. The album, *Ice Pickin'*, saw Collins return to his Iceman identity, and it earned him a Grammy nomination. More important, the album enabled Collins to regain some of the popularity he had lost during his absence from the recording scene.

But the album had even greater significance. In 1977, the punk explosion was dominating the music industry, and eager record executives were quick to offer large sums of money to bands that barely knew how to play their instruments. The punk movement stands out as one of the rare musical directions in the twentieth century whose backbone was <u>not</u> based on the blues. But there was something stirring underneath the fractured musical scene. The pure blues artists, who had suffered a commercial drought during much of the decade, were strategically planting the necessary musical seeds that would ripen into a full bloom in the next decade. The album *Ice Pickin'* was one of those essential seeds.

Encouraged by the success of his previous release, Collins followed with *Frostbite!* in 1980 and *Frozen Alive* in 1981. *Frozen Alive* was also nominated for a Grammy. The two albums helped set the stage for the dominant role in the blues revival that Collins would play later on in the decade.

The identity of the Iceman that Collins had forged during his recording days with Kangaroo had never been rightfully accepted by the record-buying public. But twenty years later it was the right time for the Iceman, and his "cool" formula won him a W. C. Handy award in 1983 for his album *Don't Lose Your Cool*. His follow-up album, *Live in Japan*, captured the magic of Collins in front of a screaming audience.

By the mid–1980s, fellow Texas blues great Stevie Ray Vaughan had joined Collins in the battle to raise the blues flag high above the music that was playing on the radio at the time. The high point of Albert Collins's career came in 1985 when he appeared with George Thorogood at Live Aid in front of a television audience of almost two billion people. It wasn't some punk/new wave band that excited the crowd that night, it was the blues as played by the Delaware Destroyer and the Iceman.

Collins recorded two more albums with Alligator Records, *Showdown* and *Cold Snap*. *Showdown* was a special effort because it featured the combined guitar sounds of Collins, Robert Cray, and Johnny Copeland. The album won a Grammy and helped define the contemporary blues sound. It also gave Collins the blues status that he had been seeking ever since his early days.

The success of his albums opened new performance opportunities, and Collins appeared at numerous blues venues throughout the United States and Europe. Always a dynamic live artist on stage, he created a special world of chills and thrills. One of the major advantages of playing pure music like Collins did was that he could reproduce on stage any sound that he recorded in the studio. He proved that his icy guitar sound was something genuine, not created by a mixing machine.

In 1991, Collins recorded the album *Albert Collins* on the Point Blank-Charisma label. It was a solid effort and an important one in the wake of the death of Stevie Ray Vaughan in late summer 1990. Three years after the tragic loss of his Texas blues friend, Albert Collins himself died of heart failure. He was sixty-three years old.

The blues career of Albert Collins is a study in perseverance. He struggled for years to establish himself as a premier blues force only to enjoy a brief time in the sun. From the late 1970s and throughout the 1980s, Collins was a blues star. He was instrumental in the blues boom of the 1980s and became one of the leading exponents of the contemporary blues scene.

As a stylist, Collins was not only one of the most remarkable guitarists to ever play the blues but also an important innovator. He used minor instead of major tunings. He had an individual picking style that was based on the Delta and Texas sound. He placed a capo at different strategic points on the neck of his guitar, which made his style almost impossible to copy. His solos were built not on note-infested, orgasmic outbursts but on the sparse, sinister qualities of the brooding, boundless beauty of winter landscapes, which earned him the nicknames the Iceman and the Ice Picker. Collins possessed impeccable timing as well as a comforting singing voice.

Collins was important on the international blues scene, and he also played a vital role in Texas blues. He is, along with Freddie King, the bridge that spans between the early Texas bluesmen—Blind Lemon Jefferson, Leadbelly Ledbetter, T-Bone Walker, and Lightnin' Hopkins— and the later Texas blues-rockers, Johnny Winter, ZZ Top, and Stevie

Ray Vaughan. Collins is perhaps the only Lone Star State bluesmen who had the opportunity to play with the entire gamut of Texas bluesmen, including Ledbetter, Walker, Hopkins, Freddie King, Gatemouth Brown, Johnny "Guitar" Watson, Texas Alexander, Vaughan, Winter, and ZZ Top.

He gave many classic blues grooves to the world, including "When the Welfare Turns Its Back on You," "Ice Pick," "Cold, Cold Feeling," "Avalanche," and "Collins's Shuffle" to name only a few. The song "Collins's Shuffle" was a tribute to T-Bone Walker and his "T-Bone Shuffle." Collins's shuffle song added a new dimension to the funky Texas sound first developed by Walker.

But Collins was more than a gifted guitarist who played Texas blues. He was an international musician who helped shape the course of popular music in the 1980s and the 1990s. His love for the blues was expressed in his calculated playing and raw patience. After all, how many musicians would hang around until they were forty-five years old before finally tasting stardom? While each decade during the past century has featured some blues phenomenon, the 1980s will be remembered as the era of the Iceman.

Discography

Truckin' with Albert Collins, MCA 10423.
The Complete Imperial Recordings, EMI CDP 7-96740-2.
Ice Pickin', Alligator AL 4713.
Frostbite, Alligator AL 4719.
Frozen Alive, Alligator AL 4725.
Don't Lose Your Cool, Alligator Al 4730.
Live in Japan, Alligator AL 4733.
Cold Snap, Alligator AL 4752.
Albert Collins, Point Blank-Charisma 2-91583.
Albert Collins Deluxe Edition, Alligator AL 5601

FREDDIE KING (1934–1976)

A Link in the Chain

An abundance of talent does not always translate into guaranteed fame. The history of the blues is filled with individuals who possessed a special musical gift and made enormous contributions to the blues, but never received the proper recognition they deserved. However, fame may include a few who might otherwise be overlooked. Sometimes an individual who is thought to be a mere link in the chain of something much bigger and more important manages to become a legend. It happened to Freddie King.

Freddie King was born Freddie Christian on September 3, 1934, in Gilmer, Texas. Along with Albert Collins, King made up the second generation of great Texas blues singers and was lucky enough to enjoy T-Bone Walker, Lightnin' Hopkins, and Gatemouth Brown in their prime. The music of Blind Lemon Jefferson and Lonnie Johnson was also pivotal in influencing King's career choice.

He finished school when he was sixteen years old and decided to forego further academic pursuits to fully concentrate on his musical ambitions. He performed around the Texas area and spent some time in Little Sonny Copper's Band. Although Texas was a hotbed of blues, King felt that better opportunities existed in Chicago; in 1954, with his guitar on his back, he headed north. This was King's third trip to Chicago, and this time he was determined to find his idol, Muddy Waters.

It didn't take long for King to immerse himself in the Chicago blues scene, and he was eventually accepted by Waters, Howlin' Wolf, Willie Dixon, Elmore James, Little Walter, Eddie Taylor, Robert Jr. Lockwood, and Jimmy Rogers. In 1956 he got a chance to record on the El-Bee label and cut his first side, "Country Boy," backed with "That's What You Think." Although neither song became a big hit, Robert Jr. Lockwood provided energetic rhythm guitar on the session, which made the whole thing worthwhile for King.

Although he can claim an authentic Texas birth certificate, King owes more of his development as a blues musician to the electric Chicago blues school. However, no matter what the performance or recording, there was always a little Texas in King's music. He was indirectly linked to the Texas blues tradition, but he was often associated with the new breed of Chicago bluesmen that emerged in the early 1960s and hailed as the next generation of blues singers. The group included Magic Sam, Otis Rush, Albert Collins, Buddy Guy, and King.

By 1960, King was an established live performer, but was still seeking respectability as a recording artist. That day occurred on August 29, 1960, when King, with his talented band consisting of Bill Willis on bass, Phillip Paul on drums, Sonny Thompson on piano, and Freddie Jordan on guitar, recorded his first album for King Records in Cincinnati. The album *Freddie King Sings* contained the songs "Hide Away," "See See Baby," "I Love the Woman," "Have You Ever Loved a Woman?," "I'm Tore Down," and "Lonesome Whistle Blues."

The instrumental "Hide Away" climbed to number twenty-nine on Billboard's pop charts, earning King important crossover appeal. It was rare for blues artists to be exposed to more than the usual audience, but King was one of the first blues singers to change all that. Although the essential sound of his music was the blues, his songs were commercial enough to attract wider attention. Aware that the instrumental was his meal ticket, King made sure to include a healthy selection on his next album.

King's second recorded effort was in fact an entire album of instrumentals, including his classic "The Stumble," which sent aspiring guitar players running for their instruments to learn every note of his trademark blues licks. The album also included "San-Ho-Zay" and "Sen-Sa-Shun," and eight instrumental classics became a guitar Bible for thousands of hopeful blues/rock musicians. King, with his guitar gems, was leading the way during the first great era of rock instrumentals.

After the average album *Bossa Nova and Blues*, King struck back with *Freddie King Gives You a Bonanza of Instrumentals* which put him back on track. The *Bonanza* album also showed another side of King with the slow, mournful pieces "Sad Nite Owl" and "Freddie's Midnite Dream." The versatility that King displayed on his third album was solid proof of his incredible talent.

In the music industry good albums usually translate into better concert venues. For a time King was part of the rock and roll packages. Since King's music possessed a hard-edged sound, he had no trouble opening up for the rockers on any given night. Unfortunately, his ride on the rock and roll tour bus seemed over before it really started. By the last part of the decade he had slipped down to a circuit that contained an immense amount of talented acts, but consisted of clubs below the standard that he had played at in the past.

Another change in King's career was his new label, Atlantic's Cotillion branch. Freddie cut *Freddie King Is a Blues Master* and *My Feeling for the Blues*, but neither album was a big hit. The albums were produced by R&B sensation King Curtis and used the soulful Kingpins as the studio band. That special groove that had been the essential ingredient of King's earlier success was absent from the sessions for Cotillion Records.

In 1970, King signed with Shelter and released the album *Getting Ready*. The label, which featured producers Leon Russell and Denny Cordell, was the right step for King. He regained some of the momentum he had lost in the latter part of the 1960s. The album produced a stone classic in "Going Down." More important, *Getting Ready* also helped revive the performing side of King's career. He graduated from the so-called chittlin' circuit and appeared in the famous rock ballrooms like the Kinetic Circus in Chicago, the Boston Tea Party in Boston, the Grande Ballroom in Detroit, and the Fillmores, East and West. Because he had not lost his rocking edge, he was well received by the rock audiences.

King recorded two more albums for Shelter, *Texas Cannonball* and *Woman Across the River*. Texas Cannonball became a moniker for King. Although the latter two albums failed to match the overall success of *Getting Ready*, they still provided some great music, like "Ain't No Sunshine," "Lodi," and "Help Me Through the Day."

In the last few years of his career, King finally received the kudos that he richly deserved. However, the adulation came not from the blues community but from the rockers who knew a good thing when they heard one. Arguably, the best reason for this delayed recognition was that King was ahead of his time. The guitar hero who had became popular in the late 1960s and truly blossomed in the 1970s was a role that King had settled into comfortably on the release of his first album.

On Christmas Day, 1976, at a concert in Dallas, King fell ill. On December 27, 1976, Freddie King died of pancreatitis brought on by acute ulcers. His death was a shock to blues fans who had already lost T-Bone Walker, Howlin' Wolf, and Jimmy Reed in a short span of time. Walker and Wolf were going on in years, but Reed and King were relatively young men. Freddie King was only forty-two years old, and like so many other blues greats, he left us far too early.

During his lifetime, Freddie King was shown some respect, but never given the true credit he deserved as a major blues star and innovator. King was one of the first modern guitar heroes—long before the arrival of Jimi Hendrix, Eric Clapton, Jimmy Page, Jeff Beck, Duane Allman, Keith Richards, Stevie Ray Vaughan, Johnny Winter, Billy Gibbons, Mike Bloomfield, Robert Cray, and Kenny Wayne Shepherd. King possessed a good voice, kicked out funky instrumentals, and played slick guitar licks that inspired an entire generation.

Freddie King was one of the distinct stylists of the modern blues guitar era along with Otis Rush, Albert Collins, Magic Sam, and Buddy Guy. King was a vital member of the all-important link between the Chicago blues school and the rock-blues guitarists of the 1960s blues boom.

Particularly notable was King's influence on the best of all British blues guitarists, Eric Clapton. Clapton played on the album *Freddie King (1934–1976)* which includes the duo's dynamic version of "Further on up the Road," which is absolutely breathtaking. Clapton's respect for the Texas bluesman is evident in his playing and is reflected in personal interviews.

On Clapton's album *Layla and Assorted Love Songs* the song "Have You Ever Loved a Woman?" appears as a tribute to King. During the late 1960s and 1970s, King continued to record and was often backed by rock-blues musicians, including members of Derek and the Dominoes, Clapton's band on *Layla*. By championing the genius of Freddie King, Clapton was paying homage to one of the true blues masters.

Freddie King was a very large man who stood about six feet, seven inches tall and weighed close to 300 pounds. He was a metal worker by day and played venues like the 700 Club at night. He had an easygoing personality. He played a Les Paul Goldtop early in his career, then switched to a Gibson 345. He was confident of his abilities. In many ways, Freddie King was an average person. But when he strapped on his guitar, he became the center of attention with high-speed instrumental solos and hard-edged sound. Like a precise welder who was devoted to a high standard of craftmanship, King fused the Texas blues with a harsher rock sound into one cohesive unit. He didn't play just the blues, but international music with a Texas flavor.

With his stirring solos and driving sound, Freddie King was a definite rock and roller. King's guitar work sounds as fresh today as it does when he recorded thirty years ago because of the intensity he injected into every note. He recorded with a diverse group of musicians, including Leon Russell, King Curtis, Eric Clapton, Muddy Waters, Buddy Guy, Magic Sam, Otis Rush, and a plethora of rock musicians.

Freddie King was an American original who gave the world some of the greatest instrumental classics of all time. King remained in obscurity until blues-rockers began to champion his work and brought him the attention he had deserved for so long. To sum up his career, he was an astounding guitar player who became more than another mere link in the chain of minor, but talented musicians. Freddie King was the eminent link in the chain.

Discography

Freddy King Sings, Modern Blues 722.
Just Pickin', Modern Blues 721.
Getting Ready, Shelter 8003.
Larger than Life, Polydor 831 816-1.
Let's Hide Away and Dance Away with Freddie King, King Records 773.
17 Original Greatest Hits, Federal 1036.
Best of Freddie King, MCA 610.
17 Original Great Hits, King 5012.
Texas Sensation, Charly 242.
Takin' Care of Business, Charly 30.
Hide Away, Stein & Day 5033.
Texas Cannonball, Document 8018.
Woman Across the River, Document.
Hide Away: The Best of Freddie King, Rhino.

JOHNNY COPELAND (1937–1997)

The Fire Maker

The blues boom of the 1980s featured the searing guitar work of three Texas tornadoes. Stevie Ray Vaughan possessed a genuine blues soul and was the single most important musical figure of the decade. Albert Collins, the Ice Picker, rocked the house with his unique approach to playing the electric guitar. The third Texas guitar player was best known as the Fire Maker. His name was Johnny Copeland.

Johnny Clyde Copeland was born on March 27, 1937, in Haynesville, Louisiana. Though a native of the Bayou state, he was raised in neighboring Arkansas. He learned to play guitar at an early age, developing a special appetite for the blues. Arkansas provided ample opportunities, but he eyed the Lone Star State as the perfect training ground in his quest to become a successful blues musician.

He settled in Houston and immediately immersed himself in the local blues scene, frequenting the city's hottest clubs. One of his first regular gigs was with Joe Hughes and the Dukes of Rhythm, with whom he gained invaluable performing experience while touring with the band. Copeland was fortunate enough to back up such blues greats as Big Mama Willie Mae Thornton, Sonny Boy Williamson II, and fellow Texan Freddie King while he was a member of the Dukes of Rhythm.

Although he had proved himself on stage, earning a reputation as one of the brightest young guns on the Texas blues scene, Copeland's recording success developed at a much slower pace. It wasn't until 1958 that he was given a chance to record his own material. None of the songs from this period—with the exception of "Rock 'n' Roll Lily," which became a regional hit—gave him the exposure he desired at this early point in his career. Although he continued to record throughout the 1960s his songs were released on small, independent labels and raised little interest.

By the beginning of the 1970s, he had forged an identity as one of the most frenetic live performers to play Texas-style blues. Although he had been born in Louisiana and raised in Arkansas, it was the Texas tradition that he carried on with intense pride. Like other Texas bluesmen before him, he was a fire maker who had forged a burning guitar style that had the Lone Star State stamped all over it. Another Texan characteristic that he possessed was an adventurous spirit and a penchant for rambling in search of fresh blues scenes.

He had prospered in Texas, but Copeland realized that a change of venues was necessary if he was to expand his musical horizons. However, he did not follow Freddie King's trail north to the Windy City, nor did he partake in the exodus west to Los Angeles. T-Bone Walker, Lowell Fulson, Percy Mayfield, Charles Brown, Pee Wee Crayton, Floyd Dixon, and Jesse Fuller were all Texan bluesmen whose careers had prospered in the Golden State. Instead, Copeland headed east to New York City.

The Big Apple boasted some impressive blues credentials. It had been the home of Leadbelly Ledbetter in the latter part of his career, as well as serving as the prime stomping grounds of Sonny Terry and Brownie McGhee. Victoria Spivey, another Texas expatriate, had made New York city her home base throughout most of her career. The boogie-woogie piano trio of Pete Johnson, Albert Ammons, and Meade "Lux" Lewis had starred at the New York City Cafe in the late 1930s and early 1940s during the boogie-woogie craze. Despite the intense competition from jazz, folk, pop, and other forms of music, blues singers had carved their own niche in New York.

In his new home Copeland's career blossomed. In just a couple of years the transplanted Southerner was a major draw in the city's finest blues clubs, brandishing his sizzling guitar like a slick, sharp weapon and leaving his mark everywhere he went. In his inimitable way he was delivering the guitar-dominated Texas blues style that the East Coast had been missing out on for a long time.

There is an old street adage that states if you can make it in New York, you can make it anywhere in the world. He had proved beyond a shadow of a doubt that he could make it in one of the toughest blues markets in the country, and he had done it in grand style. His dogged perseverance did not go unnoticed—it eventually paid off handsomely when, in 1980, Rounder Records stepped in with an attractive contract offer for him.

Finally, twenty-two years after his first attempt at being a successful recording artist, he was given another chance at achieving his ambitions. His first effort for Rounder, entitled *Copeland Special*, was exactly what the title suggested. Johnny Copeland was a bluesman with a special touch and everyone was quick to notice. His second album, *Make My Home Where I Hang My Hat*, was also enthusiastically received.

His timing could not have been better. The blues were quietly building momentum, which would peak later on in the decade, and Copeland was an integral part of it all. His recording triumphs led to increased touring in both America and Europe. Copeland, always an adventurous soul, decided to record his third album in Africa using local musicians. The result was the album *Bringing It All Back Home*. The music connected Copeland with his ancestral musical roots.

At this point in his career he was undoubtedly one of the better-known blues singers. He was on the very edge of stardom and needed the right project to push him over the line. The blues gods were smiling on Copeland, and his next studio album was a smash breakthrough.

It was entitled *Showdown!* and featured Copeland as well as one of his oldest and best friends, Albert Collins. They were joined by the great contemporary blues talent Robert Cray. The album was exactly what blues fans craved—a hard-driving, inspired set that featured three of the biggest names in blues. The record leaves no doubt that all three were at their very best, and it became one of the greatest classic blues albums ever recorded.

Copeland followed the award winning *Showdown!* with *Ain't Nothin' but a Party* and later *Boom Boom*. Although neither became the explosive success that *Showdown!* had been, both recordings provided plenty of fiery Texas-style blues guitar, which had become Copeland's trademark. He continued to record and perform into the 1990s; although the decade was not as kind to him as the previous one, he remained one of the top blues acts on the scene.

On July 3, 1997, Johnny Copeland, the rapid-fire guitar player with the red-hot Texas licks, died. He was sixty years old.

Copeland did not achieve true stardom until he was almost fifty years old. After this point, it seemed that he could do no wrong, and he retained his high caliber status until his death. He will always be identified as a Texas bluesman even though he did not boast a genuine Lone Star State birth certificate. However, he carried on the Texas blues tradition with as much pride and soul as any native son.

Copeland's undeniable legacy was his blazing guitar work, which he could deliver with equal excellence on vinyl or in front of an audience. In his guitar sound the usual array of Texas influences can be heard, including Mexican, Cajun and Creole, jazz, soul, country-blues, boogie-woogie, and rock and roll. He was creative enough to assimilate all of the thick sounds he heard and shape them into his own unique battle cry.

In the Texas blues tradition, Copeland holds a special place. He was of the first generation of Texas guitar players who were able to see T-Bone Walker perform live. Copeland was also part of the Houston blues invasion that included Albert Collins and Johnny "Guitar" Watson. All three were part of the Third Ward neighborhood and went on to make their marks as Texas bluesmen and international musicians.

Without a doubt, Copeland's biggest influence was T-Bone Walker. Walker ranks as one of the greatest postwar modern guitarists, and he had a special touch that every aspiring bluesman craved to imitate. Like thousands

of other hopeful blues singers, Copeland was mesmerized by the electric dazzle of Walker's guitar sound. The song "Call It Stormy Monday" was released
in 1947 and had a huge impact on ten-year-old Copeland.

It was from Walker that Copeland inherited the Texas swing thing,
one of the most essential weapons in every Lone Star State bluesman's
arsenal. Walker, the ultimate showman, also influenced Copeland's stage
dynamics. Although he didn't dance on stage with the same acrobatic skill
as Walker, Copeland was a genuine pouncing tiger.

Other Texas bluesmen were also important in Copeland's development as a musician, including the father of Texas blues, Blind Lemon
Jefferson. From Jefferson Copeland acquired the secrets of Texas blues
guitar, the hammering of the strings, the boogie-woogie–influenced rep-
etition of bass figures, and the steaming run of open and fretted notes.
From Lightnin' Hopkins Copeland learned to write general, yet effective
lyrics.

Copeland was also touched by the special charisma of Gatemouth
Brown. Brown expanded the parameters of Texas blues by incorporating
a number of different musical styles into his own, and he was a hero to
the Houston blues-crazy crowd, which included Copeland. Another
dimension of Brown's popularity among Copeland's generation was his
live performances. The thrilling experience of seeing Brown in concert
was easy for Copeland, Collins, and Watson because Gatemouth often
played in and around the Houston area at the Bronze Peacock, Club Mati-
nee and Shady's Playhouse.

In turn, Copeland became a hero to a younger generation of blues
musicians, including Robert Cray. A generation of ambitious blues students can sit down and listen to albums such as *Showdown!*, *Copeland's Special*, and *Ain't Nothin' but a House Party* and learn from a true master.
Although perhaps not as great an influence as fellow Texan Stevie Ray
Vaughan, Copeland nevertheless was the real thing. His driving, rollicking blues sound is sure to inspire an entire group of future guitar warriors.

Johnny Copeland will someday be elected to the Blues Foundation
Hall of Fame, and it will be a very well-deserved honor. His career, which
included tours in numerous countries, made him an international star. He
was the first American bluesman to record an album in Africa. He was
also one of only a handful of blues singers to ever perform behind the iron
curtain during the Cold War. However, Copeland will best be remembered for his integral part during the blues boom of the 1980s, when his
burning guitar licks earned him the nickname the Fire Maker.

Discography

Copeland Special, Rounder 2025.
Make My Home Where I Hang My Hat, Rounder 2030.
Bringing It All Back Home, Rounder 2050.
Ain't Nothin but a Party, Rounder 205.
Boom Boom, Rounder 2060.

PART FOUR

Women of the Blues

The vast contributions made by female blues singers in the past century constitute one of the most important chapters in blues history. The first blues phonograph record released to the public was by a woman, Mamie Smith, who in 1920 sang about her "Crazy Blues." The recording sold a million copies in six months, a remarkable achievement considering the economic condition of those who bought her record, the lack of promotion, and that Smith was relegated to the narrow race market.

Without a doubt, the golden era of the female blues singer was the 1920s. Until the arrival of Blind Lemon Jefferson and Blind Blake in the middle of the decade, the women singers dominated the blues scene, outselling the men by a wide margin. Because of their utter dominance during this period, the years from 1923 to 1929 have been labeled as the era of the classic female blues singers.

Although many of the phonograph records released by the legion of female blues singers became classics, the term *classic* when used to describe the group of female singers of this period is misleading because of the variety of styles practiced by each performer.

The first entry in this category, Gertrude "Ma" Rainey, possessed a forceful voice and a strong personality. She was a vaudeville singer who got her start in the tent shows and rarely played the Northern concert halls. Rainey's heir to her blues throne, Bessie Smith, considered the greatest female blues singer of them all, delivered the blues to a more citified audience. Ida Cox turned blues singing into a true art and was one of the first women to write her own material. Both Victoria Spivey and Sippie Wallace were from Texas, but each possessed a totally different style. Spivey, one of the finest cosmopolitan singers, moaned the blues whereas Wallace spiced her special delivery of blues with good, old-fashioned Texas appeal.

The last three women discussed in this section are more modern blues singers. Willie Mae Thornton belted out the blues with the ferocity of a lioness. Koko Taylor is from the Thornton school of blues belting, but is more refined than her idol. Etta James expanded the parameters of women's blues by incorporating soul and pop into her style.

The eight female blues singers discussed here represent a solid and tasteful sampling of a much larger circle. The contributions of Trixie Smith, Mamie Smith, Edith Wilson, Lucille Hegamin, Alberta Hunter, Ruth Brown, Clara Smith, Sarah Vaughan, Lucille Bogan, Sara Martin, and, more recently, Bonnie Raitt, Sue Foley, Rory Block, and Joanna Connor should never be forgotten.

The grand tradition of the female blues singers continues strong today. May they never be silenced.

MA RAINEY (1886–1939)

Mother of the Blues

The history of the blues is rich with pioneers—men and women who were instrumental in developing and shaping the course of popular music. The recording careers of these pace-setting blues artists began during the 1920s and exercised a profound influence on the second and third generations of blues singers. The establishment of the recording industry helped spread the blues to every corner of the world. However, at the turn of the century, long before the release of her phonograph records, one blues singer had already incorporated blues songs into her vaudeville stage act. For her efforts, this pioneer earned the title "Mother of the Blues." Her name was Ma Rainey.

Ma Rainey was born Gertrude Malissa Nix Pridgett on April 26, 1886, in Columbus, Georgia. Gertrude's parents were both in show business in the nineteenth century, and it is quite possible that she caught the show biz bug from them. Her first public appearance occurred when she was fourteen years old in "The Bunch of Blackberries" talent show. Her inclusion in the show marked the beginning of the career of the first great female blues singer.

In 1904, she married William "Pa" Rainey, also a minstrel song and dance man. Their dynamic live show earned them the title "Rainey and Rainey, Assassinators of the Blues." In certain blues circles they were simply known as Pa and Ma Rainey. They traveled all over the South with the Rabbit Foot Minstrel Revue, then with Tolliver's Circus and Musical Extravaganza.

Because of segregation, the Raineys were limited to the South's Negro vaudeville circuit, performing in theaters and barns while living in a house trailer. Despite the hardships, the Raineys provided a vital entertainment outlet for their audience, which was made up of poor black people. Pa and Ma Rainey were popular and important members of a black culture that struggled hard to survive.

In 1923, after almost a quarter of a century of performing throughout the South (including occasional spots on the Theater Owner's Booking Association circuit, a well-known venue for entertainers of the era), Ma Rainey signed a recording contract with Paramount. For the next six years she became one of the best-selling female singers in the country. Her six-year recording career produced some 100 sides, including the classic "See, See, Rider," which was later covered by numerous blues and blues-rock acts, including Leadbelly Ledbetter and Mitch Ryder and the Detroit Wheels some forty years after the song's initial release.

Some of the other gems that Rainey recorded during the period of 1923 to 1929 include "Jelly Bean Blues," "Daddy, Goodbye Blues," the sensual "Slow Driving Moan," "Shave 'Em Dry Blues," "Good Bye Daddy Blues," "Levee Camp Moan," "Booze and Blues," "Toad Frog Blues," and "Moonshine Blues," a song warning against the evils of drinking. She also gave the world the comic, autobiographical "Ma Rainey's Black Bottom" and "Bo Weevil Blues." The range of her material was outstanding and provided many glimpses into the life of the Southern black folk of that time period.

In 1928, she recorded "Hear Me Talking to You," "Deep Moanin' Blues," "Sweet Rough Man," "Tough Luck Blues," and "Leavin' this Morning" with Georgia Tom Dorsey and Tampa Red. Ma Rainey also garnered respect from noted jazz musicians. Louis Armstrong's cornet made a strong presence on "Jelly Bean Blues," "See, See, Rider," and "Countin' the Blues." John Smith's cornet was clearly evident on "Titanic Man Blues," "Stack o' Lee," "Wringin' and Twistin' Blues," "Chain Gang Blues," and "Bessemer Bound Blues." Tommy Ladnier was equally complementary to the Rainey declamatory style on other recordings like "Ma

Rainey's Mystery Record" and "Cell Bound Blues." Individual standouts on certain songs included Claude Hopkins on "Dead Drunk Blues," Jimmy Blythe on "Mountain Jack Blues," and Lil' Henderson on "Trust No Man."

Other sessions included noted pianists Fletcher Henderson and Lovie Austin, saxophonist Coleman Hawkins, clarinetist Buster Bailey, and Texas guitar legend T-Bone Walker. More often, Rainey was backed by the members of her Georgia band, which included Al Wynn, Dave Nelson, Ed Pollock, and Thomas A. Dorsey.

In 1930, she fronted her own show company called "Arkansas Swift Foot." It was a common practice among black female singers of the late 1920s and early 1930s to form their own song and dance traveling troupes so they could retain better control of their bookings and money. It was an adventurous enterprise becoming a business manager in that era, considering the tough economic pressures and the dual disadvantages of being black and female. Ma Rainey is a grand example of the brave nature that these blues ladies possessed.

Unfortunately, because of the Great Depression and the economic gloom that robbed the music industry of its vitality, Rainey's company fell apart. In 1930 she joined the Bleuse De Legge's Bandana Babies for three years.

But even as early as 1931, it was evident that Ma Rainey's singing career was over. In 1933, after the death of her mother and sister, she retired from the music industry. She had wisely saved enough from her singing career to retire comfortably in her hometown of Columbus, Georgia. Never one to stay idle, Rainey operated two theaters in Columbus until her death. On December 29, 1939, at the age of fifty-three, Gertrude "Ma" Rainey passed away, the victim of a massive heart attack.

Ma Rainey was in her own right a very important star, perhaps not of the same magnitude as Bessie Smith, but the pioneer of the blues was always extremely popular with black audiences. During her salad days she was one of the best female blues singers on the circuit. What she lacked in talent she made up for with enthusiasm, hard work, showmanship, and sincerity.

But Ma Rainey's true claim to fame was through her role of pioneer. Other female singers may have surpassed her achievements, but Rainey opened important doors for all others to follow, including Bessie Smith. Because she was, at the turn of the century, the first female singer to incorporate blues into her act, she is the equivalent of other blues pioneers, including Blind Lemon Jefferson, Charley Patton, Blind Willie McTell, Lonnie Johnson, and Eddie "Son" House.

Rainey believed the blues to be the sacred music of the poor blacks who toiled the soil from early morning until the sun melted into the Southern ground. No matter who backed her—whether a jug band featuring instruments like the kazoo and washboard or a gifted group of horn players—Ma Rainey always put her entire heart into every song. This essential quality persuaded people to keep coming back to see her perform.

Perhaps Rainey's greatest talent as a singer was her ability to draw songs and ideas from a variety of sources and tie them all together to create something that was truly unique. She was inspired by a variety of musical styles such as minstrel, vaudeville, burlesque, circus and carnival songs, folk ballads, and country-blues. She was able to blend all of these different ideas into an identifiable style that made her famous.

Ma Rainey was always a singer of the people because she shared with her audience the same painful plight. Songs about moonshine, levee camps, sex, love, relationships, poverty, disease, and illiteracy all reflected common experiences of blacks living in dreadful squalor throughout the Southern states.

Much of her success also had to do with her unique delivery. Rainey was steeped in the country-blues. Her singing was crude and unpolished, resembling more the field holler that existed before the turn of the century than the smooth urban sound of her cosmopolitan contemporaries. Rainey's blues was down-home authentic music sparked by a passionate and genuine emotional plea.

Ma Rainey was the single biggest influence on the greatest female blues singer of them all, Bessie Smith. It remains unclear, however, how large an impact Rainey had on Smith. It was Rainey who introduced Smith to the blues world. Perhaps it is just a piece of blues folklore, but varying reports insist that Rainey once kidnapped Smith when the latter was just eleven years old to appear on stage. It is quite possible that Rainey taught Smith a few dance steps, and Bessie probably picked up valuable lessons watching her idol performing on stage. Because of Bessie's natural voice, it is doubtful that Rainey actually taught her to sing.

It is almost certain that Rainey also inspired Smith's stage wardrobe. In a comparison of stage pictures, Smith obviously based many of her fashion choices on Rainey's look.

However, fashion was only a part of Rainey's performance package. Although not a truly beautiful woman, Ma Rainey had a chubby face and a friendly manner that charmed audiences. She wore sparkling accessories around her straight, black hair and earrings of gold and a chain of gold pieces around her neck. She also dressed in fashionable, long-flowing gowns and sometimes sported a huge fan of ostrich feathers. Although she was somewhat short and stocky, Rainey could dance up a storm. She was more than capable of putting on a show that was a staple of all black performers. She worked hard to impress her audience and did just that with her witty lyrics, performing savvy, powerful voice, and complete stage dress.

Ma Rainey was also fiercely determined, and her perseverance allowed her to sing the blues the way *she* wanted to. It was difficult for a black women to make it in the music business in the 1920s, no matter how superior her talent may have been. The individual spirit that Rainey possessed is a characteristic that all of the female blues singers evinced, including Bessie Smith, Ida Cox, Victoria Spivey, Dinah Washington, Koko Taylor, and Etta James. Such a stubborn streak was needed to compete and survive in a man's world.

Ma Rainey was inducted into the Blues Foundation Hall of Fame in 1983 and in 1990 to the Rock and Roll Hall of Fame. She also appeared in a book by Derrick Stewart-Baxter titled *Ma Rainey and the Classic Blues Singers*. She was one of the supreme blues queens of the classic female era and blazed the trail for all others to follow. But despite the great number of female blues singers who have appeared after her reign, Ma Rainey will always remain the mother of the blues.

Discography

Ma Rainey's Black Bottom, Yazoo 1071.
The Immortal Ma Rainey, Milestone 2001.
Ma Rainey, Milestone M-47021.
Ma Rainey, Riverside RLP 8807.
Ma Rainey Volume 3, London (E) AL 3558.

BESSIE SMITH (1894–1939)

Empress of the Blues

The 1920s belonged to the gallery of blues queens who dominated the early blues scene with their creative catalog of songs; earthy, plaintive, gold-speckled vocals; and sassy and sultry stage personas. The title of blues queen was coined to describe every major female star of that golden era. However, there was one blues singer who belonged beyond the realm of queen. Because of her obvious superiority, she was given the special title "Empress of the Blues." Her name was Bessie Smith.

Bessie Smith was born on April 15, 1894, in the Blue Goose Hollow section at the foot of Cameron Hill in Chattanooga, Tennessee. Her early life was one of tragedy and severe poverty. Bessie's parents died when she was a young girl, and her oldest sister assumed the awesome responsibility of trying to keep the family together. Times were brutally harsh for the Smith children in Chattanooga at the turn of the century.

Bessie's desire to earn a loftier place in life came her way around 1912, when her older brother returned home as part of the Moses Stokes touring company, which featured the most famous female blues singer of that era, Gertrude Rainey. Ma Rainey, as she was better known, was Bessie's idol.

Smith, seizing the opportunity, joined the Moses Stokes company, leaving the memories of her impoverished childhood behind. She had gained valuable performance experience, singing for a number of years in the streets of Chattanooga to help out the family finances. When it came time for her to leave home and make her mark on the world, she was ready. Smith remained with the company until 1921.

The early 1920s were an exciting time because of the rapid progress and optimistic mood the entire country was experiencing. The Roaring Twenties was a time of economic prosperity, fast-paced lifestyles, and good music. One of the formidable forces behind the memorable music of that period was Bessie Smith.

After leaving the Moses Stokes Company, Smith knocked around for a while in other companies, then moved to Philadelphia. There, she met Jack Gee, who was her first great love. Also in Philadelphia she was "discovered," and her dream of a successful recording career began to take shape.

She was signed by Columbia Records and went to New York to make albums. On February 15, 1923, Bessie Smith cut two songs, "Gulf Coast Blues" and "Down Hearted Blues." Hundreds of thousands of her records were sold, surpassing all other blues singer at the time, including Ma Rainey. A few months later she married Jack Gee in a ceremony in Philadelphia.

From 1923 to 1929, Bessie Smith recorded some 160 sides for Columbia Records. These were Smith's salad days. Some of the songs released during this period include "Tain't Nobody's Business if I Do," a bawdy song that demonstrated her independent spirit. Other well-known hits included "Mama's Got the Blues" and "Poor Man's Blues," both written with her black audience in mind.

The album *Nobody's Blues But Mine*, which covers the period between 1925–1927, contained the classics "Alexander's Ragtime Band" and "After You've Gone," as well as "Back Water Blues" and "Preachin' the Blues." On the album *Any Woman Blues* the hits "Sam Jones Blues" and "My Sweetie Went Away" are found, as well as duets with rival Clara Smith on "Far Away Blues" and "I'm Going Back to My Used to Be."

Undoubtedly one of the greatest musical collaborations of the twentieth century occurred when Smith teamed up with Louis Armstrong. They were the two biggest musical stars of the 1920s, and they engaged in a musical duel that left listeners breathless. Some of the songs they performed together included a legendary rendition of "St. Louis Blues," "Reckless Blues," "You've Been a Good Old Wagon," and "Cold in Hand Blues."

Smith toured the country and, like Ma Rainey, had her own revue. The large troupe would invade a site, turn the place upside down, entertain the crowds, leave them begging for more, and then pick up stakes and do it all over again in the next town. Smith's playing engagements were a far cry from today's megamillion-dollar concert tours, but she drew thousands of people to her shows. In her prime, Smith made $2,000 a week, which was a fantastic amount of money in those days. She was in high demand and found work in revues like the Harlem Frolics, the Midnight Steppers, and the two-reel movie *St. Louis Blues*.

Despite her incredible success, things were never easy for Bessie; her life was complicated. Her marriage to Jack began to fall apart because of her constant touring. Smith's outrageous behavior didn't help matters, and the two drifted apart. Gee (no angel himself) was guilty of unsanctified behavior, which eventually led to a separation and finally a divorce. To deal with the pressure, Bessie turned to drinking. Smith, who was a head-strong woman, lashed out at those around her when she was hurt, angry, or depressed. Her behavior was sometimes erratic.

But no matter how turbulent her life became, Bessie remained the public's darling. She provided an inspiration to the black people who came to her show in droves. She was their empress, the greatest blues singer in the world. In the era before the media became a link between the famous and the common people, Bessie was her own marketing manager. In concert, she was able to touch everyone in a magical way, which no one before or since has been able to duplicate.

The year 1929 will always be remembered for the stock market crash, but it also marked the end of the first great blues era. The two events were closely linked together. At this point Smith's career took a downward turn from which she never fully recovered.

The year 1929 also marked the introduction of sound pictures. The need for live shows to entice the people into the theaters was no longer needed, and her career suffered another severe blow. Despite the decline of her popularity, Smith, with the accompaniment of pianist James P. Jouhnson, recorded the classic "Nobody Knows You When You're Down and Out," which became an anthem for millions of people during the Great Depression.

In an effort to prolong her singing career, Smith embarked on a Broadway career. Though Bessie's debut was a strong one, the play itself was labeled a disaster and cost her a future in acting. When Columbia dropped her in 1931, it seemed to be the end of Bessie's career as a blues singer. But although her life was artistically in serious decline, her love life exploded with the appearance of the romantic, swashbuckling figure of Richard Morgan, who won Bessie's heart.

Morgan was a sharp-dressing, smooth-talking businessman who walked into Bessie's life at one of her most desperate moments. Although acquainted with each other since the mid–1920s, they had remained just good friends until the time seemed ripe. Morgan and Smith fell in love and became devoted to one another.

Smith recorded again in 1933, but her records did not sell like they had at the height of her fame. The record industry, which had been practically wiped out by the Great Depression, took its toll on the careers of many of the blues singers from the 1920s. But Smith, who always maintained a stubborn streak, refused to let her blues career die.

She had often recorded against a jazz background and in the late 1930s repeated the process. She released a few titles, including "Do Your Duty," "Gimme a Pigfoot," "Take Me for a Buggy Ride," and "Down in the Dumps," backed by the swing-era talents of instrumentalists Frankie Newton, Jack Teagarden, Benny Goodman, and Chu Berry. Other hits included "Weeping Willow Blues" with cornetist Joe Smith and "Empty Bed Blues" with trombonist Charlie Green. Joe Smith, Green, Fletcher Henderson on piano and Coleman Hawkins on tenor later backed Smith up on "Cake Walkin' Babies" and "Yellow Dog Blues."

Because of her free spirit and ability to accept life's curveballs, Smith proved that she could roll with the punches. Instead of wallowing in the blues, her recordings with the swing bands became some of her best work. Her career seemed to be back on track; with the prospect of recording with Lionel Hampton (Richard Morgan's nephew) it seemed as if good times had returned.

Unfortunately, Smith never completed her comeback. On September 26, 1937, Morgan and Smith were traveling in their Packard when, in an effort to avoid a truck, Morgan crashed. Bessie suffered life-threatening injuries and died later that morning. She was only forty-three years old.

Bessie Smith was the first superstar of the blues. She sold millions of records, and her concerts were important events as people lined up for hours in hopes of getting a ticket. Bessie became a household name—not just among the black population, but throughout the country. It was a remarkable feat considering she was relegated to a narrow race market and that her only media outlet was the radio, which was also segregated.

Smith was the greatest female blues singer in history. Her trademark singing style was based on her impeccable timing, pure emotions, and an uncanny ability to shift from a straight to swing feel with relative ease. She sang like others played the guitar. She could bend, slur, dip, and glide a note. She possessed a unique sense of rhythm and was able to change keys instantly. Though not an educated woman, Smith understood the nuances of words and used this skill to create subtle tension, emphasizing certain syllables, which transformed the entire meaning of a line into something fresh and exciting. The depth and breadth of her singing talent is unquestionable, but she was also an intelligent student of music who understood the essential secrets of blues textures.

Smith's contribution to the blues exceeds her recorded output. She was an innovator of the highest order. She took the blues from the tent shows and vaudeville circuits to the northern concert halls. She proved that the blues could sell very well if given the chance. She opened the doors for many of the blues singers, both female and male, who followed the wide trail she blazed. Bessie Smith gave the blues their most majestic expression.

Bessie was a complete stage performer who was also part actress. She teased and engaged the audience, drawing them into her special world; she made them an integral part of every performance. She displayed all of her emotional sides on stage, providing the audience with a montage of personalities. She appeared on stage wearing flowing scarves, jeweled hats, long feathers, and fabulous furs.

It is almost beyond the scope of one's imagination to realize the impact Bessie Smith would have had on the jazz sound of the late 1930s and early 1940s if she would have had the chance to follow that career path. If she had lived a little longer she would have undoubtedly become one of the great rhythm and blues singers of the 1950s.

The memory of Bessie Smith has continued for six decades since her death. In 1976, Vic Dickenson released the album *Vic Dickenson Plays Bessie Smith*, which includes a marvelously relaxed "Nobody Knows You When You're Down and Out."

Despite the recognition she received and her many triumphs, rumors abounded about the turbulent life she lived. She drank heavily and supposedly had many affairs with musicians while still married to her first husband. Some sordid accounts of her life painted the portrait of a poor country girl who was a loner and disillusioned and drank to drive her troubles away. It is commonly believed that if the tabloids had been prominent in Bessie's era as they are presently, the rags would have feasted on her like they do on many of today's celebrities.

But all the bad rumors are part of the Bessie Smith legend in the same manner that they are part of the Robert Johnson story. Whether Bessie Smith drank too much, had numerous gentlemen callers, or possessed a vicious temper does not take away from the essential contribution she made to the blues. Many of the rumors are suspect, and many efforts have been made to clear away the untruths in a number of books that have appeared after her death. Unfortunately, no matter how the bits and pieces of her life are put together a clear portrait of her can never be truly complete. Noted blues scholar Chris Albertson wrote an excellent book simply entitled *Bessie* that did much to dispel the nasty rumors that plagued Smith's name since her death.

Bessie Smith was inducted into the Blues Foundation Hall of Fame in 1980 and the Rock and Roll Hall of Fame in 1989. Smith, like Robert Johnson, lived and died for her art. Every female blues singer that has appeared after her can trace a direct link to her. One of the best examples of the powerful influence Bessie Smith had on future generations is rock-blues queen Janis Joplin. Joplin ardently claimed that her favorite singer was Bessie Smith. In 1970, shortly before her own tragic death, Joplin, in partnership with an other unknown patron, split the cost of a headstone in honor of Bessie Smith. The inscription of the tombstone read "The Greatest Blues Singer in the World Will Never Stop Singing." The tribute demonstrates that Bessie Smith was not just any woman who sang the blues, she was and forever will be known as the one and only empress of the blues.

Discography

The Complete Recordings of Bessie Smith Vol. 1, Columbia C2K-47091.
The Complete Recordings of Bessie Smith Vol. 2, Columbia C2K 47471.
The Complete Recordings of Bessie Smith Vol. 3, Columbia C2K 47474.
The Complete Recordings of Bessie Smith Vol. 4, Columbia C2K 52838.
The World's Greatest Blues Singer, Columbia GP 33.
Bessie's Blues: Bessie Smith 1923–1924. Philips (E) BBL 7513.
The Bessie Smith Story Volume 1, Columbia CL 855.
The Bessie Smith Story Volume 2, Columbia CL 855.
The Bessie Smith Story Volume 3, Columbia CL 855.
The Bessie Smith Story Volume 4, Columbia CL 855.

IDA COX (1896–1967)

Raisin' Cain

The seeds of the black women's liberation movement were planted during the classic blues era. For the first time in their history, black women were able to escape the harsh economic restrictions that had been imposed on them. This new independent spirit was a characteristic shared by many of the female blues stars of the day, including Bessie Smith, Sippie Wallace, Victoria Spivey, Alberta Hunter, Trixie Smith, and Lucille Bogan. There was another classic blues singer who was also not above raising a little cain of her own. Her name was Ida Cox.

Ida Cox was born Ida Prather in Taccoa, Georgia, on February 26, 1896. The daughter of poor sharecroppers, her early life was not much different than that of millions of other young black children growing up in the old South at the turn of the century. She faced a future of desperate poverty and limited educational and employment opportunities. However, little Ida possessed a special key that enabled her to escape a certain grim future: She was born to sing the blues.

Like so many other blues singers, Ida got her start singing as part of a church choir. She joined the African Methodist Choir at a young age and developed a strong interest in gospel music. It was obvious that from the very beginning she visualized herself as an entertainer singing for the people.

She left home in her early teens and worked the southern tent and vaudeville circuit. Her first professional job was with F. S. Wolcott's Rabbit Foot Minstrel Revue, where she made her first appearance at the tender age of fourteen. When not singing, she earned her living as a sharp-witted comedienne, gaining valuable stage experience.

She eventually left to work with Jelly Roll Morton for a brief time before securing a recording contract with Paramount, a label that she shared with her idol, Ma Rainey. In fact, Ida's first recording preceded Rainey's by just a few short months—certainly a feather in her cap. Paramount was an important blues label and is credited with recording many blues pioneers, including Ma Rainey, Blind Lemon Jefferson, Blind Blake, Charley Patton, and Eddie "Son" House.

From 1923 to 1929, Cox recorded almost eighty sides for Paramount, Broadway, and Silverstone companies, often using a variety of pseudonyms with common last names like Smith, perhaps to take advantage of the popularity of Bessie Smith. Her singing style leaned more toward vaudeville than pure blues. But the fiery spirit she injected into the delivery of the songs, coupled with the universal appeal of her lyrics, has kept her material fresh even seventy years after its initial release.

The first sides Cox recorded for Paramount (in June 1923) included "Any Woman Blues," "'Bama Bound Blues," and "Lovin' Is the Thing I'm

Wild About." On this first recording session, her sole musical accompaniment was provided by Lovie Austin on piano.[1] Austin was also instrumental in ensuring a high level of quality on all the sides that Cox recorded, which earned her pioneer credentials as a record producer.

Despite Austin's deft touch around the recording studio, the real star was Ida herself. With only Austin's piano as musical accompaniment, Cox's pure talent and professional edge was vibrant throughout her recordings. It was clearly evident from the very start that Ida possessed the vocal talents necessary to be a successful recording artist.

On her second session (in December 1923) Cox recorded "Bear-Mash Blues," a song that she co-wrote with Jesse Crump, her new piano accompanist and eventually her husband (in 1927). Also contributing their talents in that second session were Jimmy O'Bryant on clarinet, Tommy Lardnier on cornet, and, on a few sides, Lovie Austin again. The above musicians became known as the Blues Seranaders, Austin's group that also occasionally moonlighted as Ida's band. On different songs additional musicians were brought in for special sessions. Over her career, Cox worked with many of the biggest names in jazz, which clearly indicates their great respect for her.

In the late 1920s Cox formed her own traveling show called Raisin' Cain, which she managed to keep afloat well into the next decade despite the hard economic times. After the demise of the company she traveled with the Darktown Scandals Troupe. Cox also appeared at Carnegie Hall in John Hammond's "From Spirituals to Swing" concerts. Her unforgettable version of "Four Day Creep," on which she was backed by the immense talents of Dicky Wells on trombone, James P. Johnson on piano, Lester Young on tenor saxophone, and Buck Clayton on trumpet, was a highlight of the concert series and was recorded for posterity.

From this point on to the end of her career, Cox recorded strictly with a jazz background. She had a profound influence on the popular music of the day. She worked with the immortal Charlie Christian just a few years before his tragic death.

---

[1]*Lovie Austin was born Cora Calhoun on September 19, 1887, in Chattanooga, Tennessee, birthplace of the great Bessie Smith. Austin, who obtained a college education—a rarity for black women at the time—was instrumental in the careers of some of the biggest female blues stars of the day, including Ida Cox, Ma Rainey, Ethel Waters, and Alberta Hunter. Austin paid her early dues playing vaudeville shows before she became a session musician for Paramount Records. She was a polished jazz/blues pianist as well as a noted band leader, composer, and arranger. After the end of the first golden age of the blues, Austin settled in Chicago, where she taught piano. She died there in 1972.*

Although the careers of other classic female blues singers had expired, Cox continued to perform well into the 1940s, until she suffered a debilitating stroke in 1945 that forced her to retire. She moved to Knoxville, Tennessee, and the music world lost a true gem.

In 1961, after a fifteen-year absence, Cox made a recording comeback. She was backed by an elite group of jazz musicians that included Coleman Hawkins, Roy Eldridge, Jo Jones, and Sammy Price. The result was a satisfying album entitled *Blues for Rampart Street*. Although Cox was in her mid-sixties, the powerful voice that had been so dominant for twenty years was evident on such tracks as "Mama Goes Where Papa Goes," "Hard Time Blues," and one of her signature pieces, "Wild Women Don't Have the Blues."

She retired a few years later and returned to Knoxville. On November 10, 1967, the music world was in mourning on the news of her death. She was seventy-one years old.

Ida Cox became a huge star and remained one for a long time. She was also an important pioneer who blazed a trail that many other blues singers followed. Her contributions to the blues are many, and her influence on future generations is extremely important.

Armed with an independent spirit, Ida Cox was one of the first female blues singers who wasn't afraid to express her opinion. Many of her songs possessed a decidedly unique black female point of view. The black female protest voice, which was rather faint at the turn of the century, emerged and gained strength in the 1920s with bold singers like Ida Cox leading the way.

Cox was also one of the few female blues singers to write her own songs, which enabled her to express a purely liberated female viewpoint that became her trademark. In many ways, she blazed the path for future performers with a strong female perspective like Aretha Franklin, Helen Reddy, and rocker Pat Benatar, to name only a few.

In the classic "Wild Women Don't Have the Blues," Cox writes/sings candidly about sexual freedom. For a black woman to even bring up this subject in public in the 1920s required great courage. Ida was a strong-willed black woman struggling in a white man's world, but she was never afraid to speak out. This intense passion to voice her own sentiments on a variety of subjects gave her music a sharpened edge that separated her from the records of the other blues queens of the 1920s.

Cox also wrote songs about the plight of her own people. "Pink Slip Blues" is a bold statement about unemployment. The work opportunities for blacks in 1920 were severely limited, and Cox was not afraid to let the rest of the world know about it. The universal appeal of her lyrics not only made sense in the 1920s, but is also relevant to the plight of today's less fortunate.

Her song "Last Mile Blues" deals with the controversial issue of capital punishment from a liberated woman's perspective. Lynchings were a common threat for blacks, and hundreds took place. To this day, the debate over capital punishment rages on, making "Last Mile Blues" a unique and universal statement by a black female singer from a different era.

Another side of Cox's songwriting ability was her eerie graveyard songs. "Graveyard Dream Blues," "New Graveyard Dream Blues," "Coffin Blues," "Bone Orchard Blues," and "Cemetery Blues" all deal with a macabre issue. But death and grieving are part of everyone's life. Once again, Cox created songs that worked on a universal level, transcending the hardened boundaries of race, creed, or color.

Other songs that Cox recorded include "Worried in Mind Blues" and "Blues Ain't Nothin' Else But!" Both are classic examples of her incredible talent. All of her songs clearly indicate that she had a unique passion for the blues; they were as much a part of her as she was a part of them.

The appeal of Ida Cox goes beyond her lyrics. She was in many ways the complete female blues singer of that era. She did not possess the rugged voice of Ma Rainey or Bessie Smith, but she was able to weave her own magic that held audiences spellbound. Cox had a special delivery all of her own that enabled her to give her songs the unique treatment they deserved.

Ida Cox was also a very astute businesswoman. She was able to continue singing during the Great Depression, when many of the female classic blues singers were forced to stop. With her excellent business mind, she organized her own troupe, which lasted for a decade. Once again she was breaking barriers. Virtually no black females owned and managed their own businesses back in the 1920s and 1930s.

Competition was stiff because of the large number of talented female blues singers during the 1920s, so Cox was fully aware that the special lyrical quality of her songs and immense talent constituted only part of her act. A stylish lady, she embellished her stage presence with an extensive wardrobe. She presented to the audience a total package of talent, beauty, sophistication, and charm. Cox had a particular influence on Koko Taylor, Etta James, Tina Turner, and Whitney Houston, who have also tried to project themselves as complete female entertainers to win over the audience.

Ida Cox sang the blues in a way that no one had ever done before her—and that no has been able to do since. Her contributions to the blues as a classic singer are just part of her personal appeal. Her spirited attitude and ability to express her feelings made her a unique performer. She was a pioneer, an example to black women of the time and future generations. Her independence, universal lyrics, and outstanding talent made her one of the true blues queens of the golden era. Ida Cox was a lady who was never afraid to raise a little cain.

Discography

Ida Cox, Collector's Classics CC 56.
Wild Women Don't Have the Blues, Rosetta 1304.
Blues For Rampart Street, Riverside 1758.
Ida Cox Vol. 1 (1923), Fountain.
Ida Cox Vol. 2 (1924–1925), Fountain.
Ida Cox Vol. 3 (1925–1926), Fountain.
Ida Cox Vol. 4 (1927–1929), Fountain.
Ida Cox, Blues Ain't Nothin' Else But, Milestone.
Ida Cox, Hard Time Blues, Fontana.
Ida Cox and Bertha Chippie Hill, Queen-Disc Q-048.

SIPPIE WALLACE (1898–1986)

Special Delivery Blues

The essential magic of the blues exists in the individual interpretation of each singer. Although styles are often copied, no two blues singers sound exactly the same. During the 1920s, the golden age of the classic female blues singers, each blues queen had her own distinct sound. Although some possessed a cosmopolitan sophistication in their vocal phrasing, others demonstrated a more rough, rural approach. Among the many styles that were prominent during that period, one female singer gained fame with her brand of very special blues. Her name was Sippie Wallace.

Sippie Wallace was born Beulah Thomas on November 1, 1898, in Houston, Texas. At the time, Houston was developing a blues identity that blossomed over the years and continues strong to this day. Wallace's first introduction to music came via the church, where she learned the rudiments of singing and playing the piano. Blessed with older brothers who had an active interest in music, Wallace was exposed to a wide variety of styles including blues, country, and spiritual.

Wallace began to perform at an early age with her brother Hersal Thomas. They played street corners for spare change; here, Wallace learned about performing in front of a different kind of audience than she was normally exposed to. The time she spent singing proved invaluable experience for her later blues career. But she possessed higher ambitions than playing street corners and in the church choir the rest of her life. This raw determination and strong spirit provided her with the necessary confidence to leave home and seek her fame and fortune.

With her gritty, powerful voice it didn't take long for Wallace to make a name for herself on the Texas club circuit. She also appeared in many of the various tent shows, where she was known for her gutsy blues. Although she eagerly chased stardom with a genuine perseverance, she was forced to climb the ladder of success one painful step at a time.

In 1915, believing that greater opportunities were available in New Orleans, Sippie moved there with Hersal. There she met Matt Wallace, her future husband, whom she married in 1917 when she was nineteen years old. Though New Orleans proved to be a thriving blues community and good for her career, in 1923, she moved to Chicago to be with her brothers.

In the Windy City, Wallace wasted no time in establishing her reputation as a determined and talented female blues singer who could strike a fire into the hearts of her audience. Her hard work and dedication was soon rewarded when she signed a contract with Okeh Records. From 1923 to 1927, Wallace was one of the most frequently recorded female blues singers in the country.

The success of the first two songs, "Shorty George" and "Up the Country Blues," enabled Wallace to cut more sides for Okeh. She was backed by Louis Armstrong on the song "Special Delivery Blues." The song "Bedroom Blues" was composed by her two brothers. The erotic "I'm a Mighty Tight Woman" became her show stopper. There are two different recordings; the first version of the song featured Natty Dominique on cornet, Johnny Dodds on clarinet, and Honore Dultrey on trombone. She also recorded "Oriental Man," "Brown Bottom Bess," and "Lady Love" in 1927.

During her golden period, Wallace recorded over forty sides for Okeh Records. Many of the songs were written by Wallace herself or were the result of a collaboration between Sippie and her two brothers. But amid the joyous triumphs there were also some heavy personal losses. Hersal died from food poisoning in 1926 before he was twenty years old. His death was an unfortunate foreshadowing of the tragedy that would eventually shatter Wallace's happy life.

In many ways the first golden age of the blues is similar to that of the first generation of rock and rollers of the 1950s. But, though individual problems ended the rock period, the Great Depression practically wiped out the recording industry and brought an abrupt end to the classic blues period of the 1920s. Sadly, Wallace was one of the blues singers whose career was destroyed by depression following the stock market crash.

In 1929, Wallace relocated to one of the original blues meccas, Detroit. However, by then her blues career was just a memory. She had been a sparkling success and for a short time span—one of the best female blues singers on the circuit. Her blues career may have been over, but Wallace still had a strong voice and used it to do God's work.

After the death of her husband and her brother George in 1936, Wallace sought salvation as a way to cope with the deaths of the two closest people in her life. For three decades she was the singer and piano player for the Leland Baptist Church in Detroit. The blues had lost one of their most prized female singers, but the Baptist church had gained a devoted and talented woman.

Wallace's blues career was silent throughout the late 1930s, all of the 1940s and 1950s, and part of the 1960s. In 1966, at the golden age of sixty-eight, Sippie Wallace attempted the hardest act in show biz: a comeback. At the strong urging of her longtime friend, Victoria Spivey, Wallace was coaxed into recording and performing again.

Her timing could not have been better. She returned to the stage at the height of the great blues boom of the 1960s. She performed at blues and folk festivals throughout the country and became the darling of the new audiences. With Victoria Spivey, Wallace recorded an album called *Sippie Wallace and Victoria Spivey*, issued on Spivey Records in 1970. The album was made up of old blues standards that Wallace and Spivey had made famous in another time.

Wallace continued to record and received excellent support from old-time blues friends Roosevelt Sykes and Little Brother Montgomery on her next effort. The standout cut on her album *Sippie Wallace Sings the Blues* was "Women Be Wise, Don't Advertise Your Man."

Although the late 1960s proved productive for Wallace, the next decade was not her best. Sippie, in her seventies, a ripe old age for a blues queen, was slowed by a mild stroke. But her Texas spirit would not let her give up all she had worked for, and she resumed the second phase of her career.

Always an inspiration to the young blues fans, beginning in the late 1970s, Bonnie Raitt appeared in Wallace's life. A huge fan, Raitt used her connections in the music business to ensure that Wallace was not left by the wayside. The two combined to produced the fine album *Sippie*, which was a real winner.

Although failing health prevented Wallace from being as active as she wanted to be in the following years, she continued her blues career. On November 1, 1986, Sippie Wallace sang her last blues note. She was eighty-eight years old.

Wallace was a blues star in two very different musical eras. She definitely stands out among the collection of female blues singers of the 1920s for many different reasons. It is difficult to measure the magnitude of her star during her best days. Although she never challenged Bessie Smith for title of empress of the blues, Sippie was certainly the equal of fellow Texas blues singer Victoria Spivey. Had her career not been cut short in the 1930s there is a good chance she would have achieved greater popularity.

However, there is no doubt that Wallace commanded great respect from some of the leading musicians of her time. Louis Armstrong, Johnny Dodds, Sidney Bechet, and Clarence Williams are just some of the big names who backed her on the songs she recorded in the 1920s.

Wallace holds a special place as a blues influence. She was one of the most beloved female blues singers in history, and she magically touched Bonnie Raitt. It is rumored that Raitt decided to pursue a blues career after she heard the album *Sippie Wallace Sings the Blues*. It certainly must have been a huge thrill for Raitt when she performed on Wallace's album in 1982. The bond between Wallace and Raitt helped bridge the gap between two generations of blues queens.

In the galaxy of classic female blues singers of the 1920s, Wallace holds her own special place for the contributions she made. She fits somewhere along the line between Bessie Smith and Ida Cox. Although she was a bawdy singer in the rough-cut image of Bessie Smith, Wallace was a pure Texan. She delivered raucous, brash, and sharp-edged blues with risqué lyrics and powerful assertion. She didn't possess the cosmopolitan sophistication of her close friend Victoria Spivey or Ida Cox. Wallace never moved far away from her Texas roots and carried the Lone Star State flag as proudly as any other Texan blues artist.

Although she has not yet been elected to the Blues Foundation Hall of Fame, Sippie Wallace was in an honor program all her own. The blues are built on emotion, and every singer brings to each song his or her own personal intensity. As an individual singer, Wallace interpreted the music in her own unique way. She stamped her individual touch on the songs that made her famous. Sippie Wallace made the world a nicer place to live with her "special delivery" blues.

Discography

Sippie Wallace 1924–1927, Blues Document BD 2093.
Sippie Wallace 1923–1929, Blues Document Blp 593.
Women Be Wise, Alligator AL 4810.
Victoria Spivey and Sippie Wallace, Spivey.

VICTORIA SPIVEY (1906–1976)

Moanin' the Blues

During the 1920s dozens of female blues singers worked the grinding circuit of speakeasies and other less-than-desirable venues all over Texas and other Southern states in the hopes of someday becoming a big star. Many of these women never broke out of the local bar circuit and eventually faded from the scene. Through a combination of determination, fate, and superior talent one of those Texas blues singers graduated from the rough grind by moanin' the blues. Her name was Victoria Spivey.

Victoria Spivey was born on October 15, 1906, in Houston. A product

of the Texas blues tradition, she began her career singing in the church
choir like many of her contemporaries. But her vocal talents were not to
be confined within the sacred walls of the church. By her late teens she
was singing in the most undesirable places; however, performing in these
small, sordid venues allowed Spivey to pay her dues as a blues singer.

Her major break came in 1926 when she was signed by the Okeh
label. Her first release was "Black Snake Blues." The song was not a huge
hit, and Spivey was unable to earn a living solely from her singing, so she
was forced to find other means of employment. For a couple of years she
worked as a staff songwriter for a music company in Missouri. Though
she didn't compose any classics, the experience she gained enabled her to
sharpen her songwriting skills. Many of the female blues singers of this
era relied on other sources for material to record, but pioneers like Spivey
and Ida Cox changed this process.

Spivey returned to the Houston area, but soon realized that she
needed a different venue. Because she loved to dance and act and was partial to the opportunities available in a large metropolitan area, she moved
to New York City and made it her home base. In the following years, the
Big Apple became the center of her universe. Her proximity to Broadway enabled her to land a role in the all-black movie musical *Hallelujah!*
She also appeared in the musical Hellzappoppin' Revue as well as many
other shows.

Throughout the 1930s, as the careers of many of the classic female
blues singers of the 1920s had dried up, Spivey continued to make records
for Victor, Vocalion, Decca, and Okeh. Because she was situated in New
York, she was able to perform one-night engagements that not only paid
well but also kept her name fresh in blues circles. Her occasional partner
for these single-concert appearances in New York and other East coast
cities was dancer Billy Adams. She also led a red-hot jazz band through
the Midwest, which only increased her popularity.

Spivey, an original and talented singer, spent much of the 1930s and
1940s singing for the big bands that were all the rage. She made appearances with Duke Ellington, Count Basie, Louis Armstrong, Benny Goodman, and many of the noted jazz band leaders of the era. Although she
had not turned her back on the blues entirely, the jazz gigs paid the rent
quite nicely.

After World War II, Spivey turned to a more traditional style of
blues. However, because of changing times she was now a rhythm and
blues singer. She continued her recording career, but her strength remained

in live performances. New York City had dozens of clubs featuring jazz-blues that were tailored for Spivey's particular singing talents.

When the musical tastes of the country began to change at the beginning of the 1950s, the venues that she had worked in the last fifteen years began to dry up. She became discouraged at the direction her career had taken; when she was unable to make a decent living as she had done in the past, she turned her back on the blues world and went to sing in the church.

In the early 1960s Spivey returned just as the folk-blues revival was gaining steam. A gutsy lady who had survived many lean times including the Great Depression, Spivey possessed a good business sense and created her own record label. In the following years, many famous blues singers recorded for the label, including Muddy Waters. But mostly, her company was responsible for recording many of the classic female singers of yesteryear, including Sippie Wallace and Lucille Hegamin.

Throughout the 1960s and 1970s Spivey continued to perform and record. She appeared in folk and blues festivals all over the country and toured Europe on a number of occasions. Though she didn't regain the popularity she had enjoyed during the 1920s, she remained an active blues singer who was always able to satisfy an audience.

By the early 1970s, Spivey had slowed down considerably and only recorded and performed sporadically. On October 3, 1976, twelve days shy of her seventieth birthday, Spivey died in New York City.

Victoria Spivey was a blues star for almost forty years; in the female blues hierarchy only Bessie Smith and Ida Cox hold a higher position. Her particular style of moaning the blues influenced an entire generation of soul and pop singers. She possessed a fierce, independent Texas spirit and was one of the few blues singers ever to form her own label. Her business acumen was so sharp that it enabled her to carry on after the careers of many of the blues queens of the 1920s fell by the wayside after the collapse of the recording industry at the end of the decade.

Because so many blues singers experienced severe poverty during their childhood and lacked a formal education, they were often easy targets for greedy promoters, record producers, and managers who stole from them. Even some of the greatest bluesmen, like Muddy Waters, B. B. King, T-Bone Walker, and Lonnie Johnson, were cheated out of royalties that were due to them. Victoria Spivey is one of the few blues singers whose strong business sense ensured that she would not be defrauded from the money that rightfully belonged to her.

Seventy years after making her initial recordings, Spivey's name remains vibrant in the blues community. She provided the world with such classic songs as "TB Blues," which dealt with the seriousness of turberculosis, a common disease among poor blacks in the early twentieth century. The universal appeal of her lyrics appeared in songs like "Dope Head Blues," which deals with the dangers of hard drugs and serves as a warning message to all succeeding generations.[1]

Other classic songs that Spivey gave to the world include "Detroit Moan," "Arkansas Road Blues," "How Do You Do It That Way?," "Don't Trust Nobody Blues," "Dreaming of You," "The Alligator Pond Went Dry," "Murder in the First Degree," and "Give It to Him Gertrude," to name only a few. Because of her expressive vocal style, Spivey was able to give each song a unique stamp.

One of the greatest entertainment weapons that the female blues singers possessed was sex appeal. Although performances were not as liberated as they are today, the blues women of the 1920s flirted and enticed their audience. Spivey was an attractive, classy lady, tall, with a well-formed body and a pretty face. There was a trace of sexuality about her performance that hinted at something more, and she used this edge to grab the audience's attention and burn images into their minds with her seductive, moaning blues wails.

Forty years later, Janis Joplin, the rock-blues queen of the hippie generation, projected a seductive pose. She could look used and tired, then downright alluring the next minute. Many of the most modern pop and soul singers, like Aretha Franklin, Whitney Houston, Diana Ross and the Supremes, Martha and the Vandellas, Etta James, Koko Taylor, and the luscious Tina Turner, carried on the tradition first began by Spivey and other blues singers of that golden era.

Spivey not only included subtle seduction in her performances but some of her songs were also rather suggestive. The self-penned song "Organ Grinder Blues," which was rather risqué for the times, became a terrific show stopper.

Perhaps the most important part of Spivey's musical success was in her special delivery. In the vast spectrum of female blues singers Spivey

---

[1]"Dope Head Blues" was a forerunner to many rock songs with a drug theme including J. J. Cale's "Cocaine," Lynyrd Skynyrd's "Oh, That Smell" and "The Needle and the Spoon," Neil Young's "The Needle and the Damage Done," and Jefferson Airplane's "White Rabbit." But though some of these songs might glorify drug use, Spivey's song was strictly an anti-drug anthem.

was at the opposite end of the scale occupied by Ma Rainey, Bessie Smith, Willie Mae Thornton, Koko Taylor, and other heavy belters. Spivey's delivery was softer, more calculated, and with rounded edges. She was an urban singer who spun her own blues sound by combining her Texas roots with the citified blues.

Although she lacked the talent of Bessie Smith or Ida Cox, Spivey delivered effective blues. She recorded with many of blues stars, including Lonnie Johnson, Little Brother Montgomery, and Sonny Greer. On her signature song, "Moanin' the Blues," she was supported by jazzmen Red Allen on trumpet, Albert Nicholas on clarinet, Charlie Holmes on tenor saxophone, J. C. Higginbotham on trombone, Louis Russell on piano, Will Johnson on guitar, and Pops Foster on string bass. On some of her other songs she was backed by the immortal Louis Armstrong.

Victoria Spivey belongs in the same special category of blues singers whose voices were instantly recognizable. The high falsetto of Skip James, the classic phrasings of Ida Cox, the sandpaper vocals of Charley Patton and Eddie "Son" House, the deceptive voice of Blind Willie McTell, and the mountain holler of Big Joe Turner are all noted blues styles. With her skillful ability to moan the blues Spivey joins the elite company mentioned above.

Spivey remains one of the most treasured female blues singers. As a competent songwriter, savvy businesswoman, and noted singer, Spivey deserves a special place in the female section of the blues Hall of Fame. Her solid contributions to the music enabled other female blues singers to establish careers of their own. Although there may have been singers with more talent who gained greater fame, no one could moan the blues like Victoria Spivey. Her spirit lives on forever.

Discography

Victoria Spivey, 1926–1931, Document 590.
Victoria Spivey, Spivey Records Lp-2001.

WILLIE MAE THORNTON
(1926–1984)

Hound Dog Blues

The inspiration for the rock and roll craze of the 1950s was the blues and rhythm and blues. All of the successful acts of the first generation of rockers borrowed heavily (and in many instances stole outright) from the original creators. Although some of the rockers became rich on old blues and R&B standards, the pioneers of the music often remained poor. In 1956, while Elvis Presley had the entire nation rocking to the song "Hound Dog," the original singer of the song remained in relative obscurity, which gave this great female singer a case of the Hound Dog Blues. Her name was Willie Mae Thornton.

Willie Mae Thornton was born in Montgomery, Alabama, on December 11, 1926. She was one of seven children, and her life was not much different than all the other poor black children living in the South trying to make the best of the Depression years. Her activities were centered around the church and, like many of her contemporaries, Thornton first started singing at an early age in the choir. But Willie Mae's singing career was not destined to be strictly regulated to gospel music. In her teens, the blues came calling, and she could not resist their sweet temptation.

When she was in her mid-teens, Willie Mae left home to pursue a career as a blues singer. She joined the Hot Harlem Revue, which was based in Georgia. She paid her dues for the next seven years in the revue and earned a reputation as one of the finest young female blues singers in the country. After the heavy grind of tough years on the road, she decided to lay down some roots and chose Houston as her new home.

Thornton quickly found work in the bars and clubs in and around the Houston area and built up a solid reputation. In 1951 things finally started to happen for her. Her big break came when she was spotted by Johnny Otis, who brought her on his show. Her power-packed performances did not go unnoticed, and she was finally rewarded with a recording contract from Peacock-Duke Records, based in Houston and owned by the legendary promoter Don Robey, the man who gave Gatemouth Brown his big chance.

One of the first songs Thornton recorded was "Hound Dog Blues," written by Jerry Leiber and Mike Stoller. The song was a smash hit, and despite recording other material, she was linked to "Hound Dog Blues" for eternity. Unfortunately, the version many people are familiar with is the one Elvis Presley cut a few years later. A comparison of the two is interesting because Thornton's delivery has a distinct blues slant, whereas Presley's is pure rock and roll.

Elvis's interpretation of the song became a million-copy seller, but it is quiet evident when comparing the two that "Big Mama" Willie Mae Thornton was an extremely talented and mighty singer who could hold her own against any vocalist, including the king of rock and roll. Unfortunately for music fans everywhere, Thornton and Presley never collaborated on a version of "Hound Dog Blues." The two singers playing off one another's vibrant and powerful vocal talents would have been absolutely breathtaking!

Thornton continued to record for Peacock until 1957, when after much success in the studio and on stage Willie Mae's career began a steady decline. Always the traveling blues singer, Thornton packed her bags and moved to the West Coast in the San Francisco Bay area. She found plenty of work performing at the many blues clubs in the city.

A change in Thornton's fortunes began in the mid–1960s with the fusion between rock and blues. Thornton, a dynamic rhythm and blues singer, possessed such a strong voice that she could handle almost any kind of material. Her appearances at many jazz and rock festivals in the 1960s exposed her to white audiences for the first time. Because she could shake the rafters as well as any rock singer on the circuit, Thornton became the darling of the rock-blues crowd. It also didn't hurt that Janis Joplin, the rock-blues queen of 1960s, included one of Thornton's most powerful songs, "Ball and Chain," in her repertoire. Also, the praise lavished on Big Mama by Joplin only increased the former's popularity with a crowd too young to remember when "Hound Dog Blues" became a nationwide hit.

Of the many rock festivals at which Thornton sang, the one that truly energized her career was the Sky River Rock Festival and Lighter Than Air Fair in Sultan, Washington, on Labor Day weekend 1968. Willie Mae arrived at the concert without a band, but convinced James Cotton and his blues aggregation to jam with her on stage. With the band playing behind her, Willie Mae blew the audience away. At one point during her two-hour blistering rendition of the blues, a naked fellow joined her on stage and danced with the Big Mama. It was a moment of pure magic and endeared her even more to the rock and roll crowd. Despite the fact that the line-up featured such popular bands as the Grateful Dead, Santana, legendary bluesman Muddy Waters, and James Cotton, it was Willie Mae who stole the show and captured the imagination of the crowd that weekend. She returned to appear in the Second Annual Sky River Rock Festival and also made her presence felt at the Denver Pop Festival, which she opened dressed in Texas garb belting the blues in fine fashion.

This newfound popularity with the rock and roll generation enabled her to tour in Europe, where she knocked out audiences with her electrifying performances. Thornton became as popular in Europe as she was in her own country. The international fame she enjoyed was special because very few female blues singers at that time had ever enjoyed success across the Atlantic. Many of the classic blues singers of the 1920s never even had the opportunity to tour outside of the continental United States.

Back in America, Willie Mae often toured with veteran Chicago bluesmen who had the utmost respect for her incredible talent. She began recording once again and released *Big Mama Thornton in Europe* and *Big Mama Thornton with the Chicago Blues Band*, a line-up that included the likes of Muddy Waters, James Cotton, and Otis Spann.

With the decline of the blues boom in the 1970s, Thornton saw her popularity slip a bit; however, she remained prominent on the blues scene for the remainder of the decade and into the 1980s. She continued to record and performed at various blues festivals, guaranteeing the crowd a show of pure power. Despite her advancing age, Thornton was still able to provide the audience with their money's worth.

Thornton was the original earth mother, a woman who never weighed under 200 pounds. The stress on her heart eventually proved too much; on July 25, 1984, "Big Mama" Willie Mae Thornton died of a massive heart attack in Los Angeles. It seemed that she had been singing the blues since the beginning of time, but Thornton was only fifty-eight years old at the time of her death.

Willie Mae Thornton was a blues star of a special magnitude in a way that no one could ever copy. Although she scored a few hits early in her career and recorded some good albums during the latter part of her career, she never sold records in the same large quantities as those who covered her songs. Despite her lack of commercial success, Willie Mae was always an exciting live act. On stage, she was a striking physical presence who sported a grin, cocky and self-assured. Her performances were a known and sellable commodity; she was always the complete professional and knew how to work a crowd as well any other singer on the circuit.

In the constellation of blues stars, "Big Mama" Thornton holds a special position. She was a bawdy blues singer who belted the blues out in a style that reminded people of Bessie Smith; however, Willie Mae was an individual who left her personal mark on the blues. Ma Rainey was a blues pioneer and earned the title "Mother of the Blues" and Bessie Smith was named "Empress of the Blues," but Thornton will forever be known as the "Heart of the Blues." Thornton lived for the blues and the spirit of the blues lived in her.

As one of the most important women blues singers of the twentieth century, Thornton was a bridge that linked the blues of the 1920s to the modern style. Her style was harsh and coarse—she was a true shouter with the grit of a bulldog.

She was in many ways the female blues counterpart to Big Joe Turner. The blues shouter from Kansas City, Missouri, was a mountain of a man who gave his songs the energy of an atomic blast. Thornton, likewise, injected so much energy into her songs that it seemed as if the world was being decimated into a billion pieces. Both Thornton and Turner sang from their hearts and in their voices one could hear the influences of the old field hollers.

Willie Mae's diverse style influenced a number of singers. Her ability to reproduce the chants of the field shouters doing hard labor (which is the essential source of the blues in America) sets her apart from other modern singers. She was able to use her physical attributes as well as her incredible vocal talents to provide the audience with a complete, dynamic package. There was an earthy essence to her singing that was uniquely her own. Her forceful, hard-rock delivery paved the way for future female rockers as Janis Joplin, Pat Benatar, and Bonnie Raitt.

But there is more to the blues legend that is Willie Mae Thornton. With her every performance, she enhanced the reputation of the blues. She proved over and over again that the blues was not just a sad, plaintive music, but one that represented the entire spectrum of the human condition. Through a combination of her toothy smile and sheer love of blues music, Thornton will best be remembered for her delivery and phrasing of the type of blues that left people happy and satisfied.

Although not blessed with striking beauty, Thornton demonstrated that one did not have to be beautiful to sing the blues well. Her career was built on substance instead of flash and is the reason why her career lasted for more than forty years. The gusto she injected into every song, whether live or on record, became her calling card.

Despite her unique talent and solid popularity, Thornton never received the credit she deserved. She achieved a unique cult status comparable to that of Elmore James (who was regarded as a one-riff, Robert Johnson imposter who didn't deserve as much attention as he was given). In some blues circles, Thornton was judged as a Bessie Smith imitator who had to scream the blues to cover up a lack of talent. Both James and Thornton attained a strong cult following after their deaths and have been recognized for their special contributions to the blues.

"Big Mama" Willie Mae Thornton was inducted into the Blues Foundation Hall of Fame in 1984, the year of her death. In any conversation involving the great blues women, her name must be included. It is unfair to think of her as simply the original singer of the song that Elvis turned into gold. But her contributions to the blues go beyond a rendition of one song. Thornton gave the blues a toughness, a spirited independence that influenced all those who realized she was something very special. Considered mainly a rugged blues mama, Thornton was also a gutsy rock and roll singer. To accord uniquely gifted singers like Willie Mae Thornton less credit than they deserve is to shortchange the blues and the entire realm of popular music of the past century. Although she never collected her just financial rewards, Thornton was a trouper for her entire career and brought joy to millions of people with her unique talent. Willie Mae Thornton never let the old Hound Dog Blues affect her love for the music.

Discography

Ball 'n' Chain, Arhoolie 1039.
Big Mama Thornton with the Chicago Blues Band, Arhoolie 1032.
The Original Hound Dog, Ace 940.
Hound Dog: The Duke-Peacock Recordings, MCA-Duke-Peacock MCAD 10668.
Willie Mae Thornton: She Back, Backbeat BLP 68.
Sassy Mama, Vanguard VSD 79354.

Koko Taylor (1935–)

I Got What It Takes

The pursuit of a successful blues career is equivalent to rolling a pair of blank dice. There are no formulas for success; talent alone does not ensure fame. Perseverance is a definite asset, but perhaps the essential element is a genuine dedication to following one's heart. The blues flow from the heart, and if one believes one has what it takes, then just maybe, if all the elements fall into the right place, one will become a blues queen like Koko Taylor.

Koko Taylor was born Cora Walton on September 28, 1935, in Memphis, Tennessee. The daughter of a sharecropper, she shared the same hardships that were common in the lives of other black children growing up poor in America during the Great Depression and the War years. But Cora had dreams and a special drive. She was convinced that she possessed something special that would allow her escape from a life of poverty.

Cora's first musical exposure was gospel, a background she shares with countless other blues singers. She had the distinct advantage of being born in the first generation of blues singers able to benefit from the recordings of the classic female blues singers. Ma Rainey, Bessie Smith, Ida Cox, Victoria Spivey, Sippie Wallace, Trixie Smith, and others were around (on records) to help shape Cora's developing blues sound. By her teens, her musical tastes had changed from gospel to the blues. She began singing in small, smoke-filled clubs around Memphis; although it was a far cry from performing at Carnegie Hall she knew that she had to pay her dues.

Despite a thriving blues atmosphere in Memphis, Taylor felt that her opportunities were limited, so she moved up North to Chicago, the mecca of the urban blues scene. She moved to the Windy City for obvious reasons—she was determined to make a name for herself in the town Muddy Waters was making famous. Armed with a strong spirit and her own special talent, she arrived in Chicago with her future husband, Robert Taylor, in 1953.

Despite being present during the golden age of Chicago blues, Taylor's career did not take off right away. For the first five years, Koko (her adopted blues name) paid her dues by doing domestic work during the day to make ends meet and singing on her spare time. On the weekends, she and her husband scoured establishments like the 700 Club and Sylvio's, carefully observing the famous names in Chicago blues performing live. In the beginning, Taylor melted in the background, just eager to watch and pick up important performance tips.

Eventually she found work in the smaller clubs and quickly gained a solid reputation as a lady who could really belt out a blues song. She was accepted by the veteran Chicago bluesmen and began to sit in with Muddy Waters, Howlin' Wolf, Little Walter, and others on a regular basis. In the dark, noisy clubs of Chicago's South Side, Koko Taylor earned her blues badge and a reputation as one gutsy lady. Yet, despite establishing solid credentials as a true blues queen, fame was unattainable until she caught her big break.

Although she had performed with many of the stars on the Chess label, it took Willie Dixon's sharp eye for talent to realize that Koko possessed a remarkable quality. He signed her to the Chess label and gave her one of his own compositions, "Wang Dang Doodle." Together, Dixon and Taylor made the song a million-dollar seller in 1966. Despite an extensive repertoire that includes many hits, "Wang Dang Doodle" remains Koko Taylor's signature tune.

Taylor's musical relationship with Dixon spawned two albums, *Basic Soul* and *Koko Taylor*, both positive steps in her attempt to become the new Blues Queen on the scene. Some of the songs she provided the world at this time included "Love You Like a Woman," "I Love a Lover Like You," "Don't Mess With the Messer," "Don't Care Who Knows," "I'm a Little Mixed Up," "Nitty Gritty," "Twenty-Nine Ways," and "You Made Me." On many of these cuts she was backed by Buddy Guy and Johnny Shines on guitar, Willie Horton on harmonica, and Sunnyland Slim on piano.

Her sphere of influence spread with appearances at the Montreux Jazz Festival and other such musical events throughout the United States. She became a fixture at these blues festivals and quickly built a reputation as a dynamic live performer. While the rock generation was hailing Janis Joplin as the great new rock-blues queen, everyone in blues circles knew that Koko Taylor already had a lock on that position.

Taylor decided to expand her horizons and accepted a part in the film *The Blues Are Alive and Well in Chicago*. The role did not lead to an acting career, but it did bring her to the attention of Bruce Iglauer of Alligator Records. In one of the wisest moves Iglauer ever made, he signed Taylor to a recording contract in 1974. At this point the Koko Taylor fame train truly began its unstoppable run.

Taylor formed her own band, Blues Machine, and toured constantly, criss-crossing the country. She became a staple at blues clubs and festivals all over America as well as internationally. It wasn't long before the awards came her way by the truckload. She is credited with having won more W. C. Handy awards than anyone else in the field. Her strong presence kept the blues torch lit through the late 1970s when the genre was pushed aside amid the onslaught of disco and punk rock. But Taylor was always able to find an appreciative audience and kept her career strong while other blues acts fell on hard times.

The blues revival of the 1980s, which featured such prominent acts as Stevie Ray Vaughan, Albert Collins, Albert King, and George Thorogood, must also include Koko Taylor. Taylor had been churning out hard-driving Chicago-style blues for twenty years, and in many of her appearances at blues festivals across the country it wasn't uncommon for her to steal the show with her personal brand of blues. She was, unquestionably by this time, the leading female blues singer in the world.

By the end of the 1980s, Taylor's name had become synonymous with the blues. No blues festival was complete without her unmistakable and powerful presence. Not only did Taylor sing better than any other female blues singer on the circuit but she also provided blues fans with the same kind of total package of glamour, stage presence, talent, and incredible music as the classic blues women of the 1920s.

By 1989, Taylor's star was so bright that it earned her a guest spot at the inaugural party for President George Bush. But not all was rosy for Taylor that year. While on the road, she almost lost her life in a car accident. She had to take considerable time off from performing to mend her broken bones.

As if the previous year wasn't enough excitement, 1990 provided Taylor with even more moments of triumph and tragedy. She made a splashing appearance in the movie *Wild at Heart*. She also found the time to record the album *Jump for Joy*, a critical and commercial success. She also lost her husband, Robert "Pops" Taylor. His death was devastating because the pair had been married for thirty-seven years, and he had served as her road manager. Taylor not only lost her strongest business associate but her lifelong companion and soulmate.

She rebounded from the tragic loss and resumed her sparkling career, making numerous appearances in every corner of the country. In the 1990s, with blues fever still burning brightly from the previous decade, a new generation discovered Koko Taylor. Her continued popularity proves that a good thing only gets better with time. She continues to perform and record on a steady basis as the undisputed reigning blues queen.

Koko Taylor is a blues superstar. Her albums are consistent best-sellers, and her performances are important blues events. Her longevity alone makes her something special—she has been singing the blues for over forty years. She possesses a dynamic stage persona that is warm and friendly, sexy and enthralling, fierce and determined.

As a veteran blues performer, Taylor, along with B. B. King and John Lee Hooker, is one of the ambassadors of the blues. She has always carried the blues torch proudly through the lean as well as the boom years. Her dedication is outstanding, and she is a true inspiration to all other female blues singers who are just beginning their careers.

Taylor's trademark is her rich, gritty voice, tailored after her idols, Bessie Smith and Willie Mae Thornton. Although she doesn't possess the unique talent of Smith or the complete power of Thornton, Koko's exciting delivery of blues, soul, and R & B material has earned her the reputation of a solid performer. Her voice is controlled, but hints at dangerous possibilities, which gives her music a dark and exciting edge. Koko does not whine or pamper the blues, she belts them out with an unmatched authority that is instantly recognizable.

She has forged a name for herself not only in the blues world but also on the international scene by proving she can expertly handle any type of material. Her album *Jump for Joy* marked a slight change in direction from the traditional, hard-edged blues flavor that has become her trademark to a more contemporary sound. But no matter what the musical style, Koko Taylor always delivers the goods professionally and with class.

Though she is definitely one of the modern blues singers, her talent is so overwhelming that she could easily be mistaken as one of the classic female blues singers of the 1920s. Taylor borrowed much from the blues queens of the first golden age. She adopted Ida Cox's classic sensibility, Victoria Spivey's stylish flavor, Bessie Smith's girlish enthusiasm, Ma Rainey's warmth, and Willie Mae Thornton's love of the blues, shaping the bits and pieces into her own personal style.

Her remarkable contribution to the blues puts her in the prestigious company of other women singers, including Ma Rainey, Bessie Smith, Ida

Cox, Sippie Wallace, Victoria Spivey, Willie Mae Thornton, Etta James, Sarah Vaughan, Dinah Washington, Lucille Bogan, and Ruth Brown. (Only Etta James from the above mentioned group shares with Taylor the honor of being one of the architects of the rocking, amplified Chicago blues school.)

Koko Taylor was elected into the Blues Foundation Hall of Fame in 1997. She has yet to be inducted into the Rock and Roll Hall of Fame. That she is the supreme queen of the blues is no coincidence. From the very beginning of her professional career she proved that she was something special and has retained that fire throughout her whole career. There have been hundreds of blues singers who started their careers at the same time she did, but none had the stamina that Koko possessed. Koko Taylor has conquered all the obstacles that have stood in her way by repeating her personal mantra: "I Got What It Takes."

Discography

I Got What It Takes, Alligator AL 4706.
The Earthshaker!, Alligator AL 4711.
From the Heart of a Woman, Alligator AL 4724.
Queen of the Blues, Alligator AL 4740.
Live from Chicago: An Audience with the Queen, Alligator AL 4754.
Jump for Joy, Alligator AL 4784.
What It Takes/The Chess Years, MCA-Chess CHD 9328.
Koko Taylor 1968, Chess 1832.
Koko Taylor 1972, Chess 9263.
South Side Lady, Evidence 26007.
South Side Baby, Black & Blue 33505.
Force of Nature, Alligator AL 4817

ETTA JAMES (1938–   )

The Messenger's Voice

The strong link between the classic blues generation and the postwar female singers is a vital reason why the music has retained its vibrancy.

The singers of the 1920s were guiding lights for those who appeared later, ready to assume the blues torch. One particular modern blues queen listened carefully to the golden works of Bessie Smith, Ida Cox, Ma Rainey, Billie Holiday, and Victoria Spivey and has carried the messenger's voice inside her heart for the length of her blues career. She is Etta James.

Etta James was born Jamesetta Hawkins on January 25, 1938, in Los Angeles, California. The Southern states—Georgia, North and South Carolina, Tennessee, Florida, Arkansas, Texas, and in particular Louisiana and Mississippi—represent the birthplace of a large majority of blues singers. Only a handful of blues artists can claim a birth certificate from a different region of the country or another part of the world. However, although Etta was thousands of miles away from the true heartbeat of the blues, because of the record player she was able to receive a solid blues education.

Although her geographical location was different, like hundreds of other singers before her she first started singing in the church choir. She progressed from there to singing in clubs in and around the Los Angeles area as a teenager. Although the city of angels was not particularly famous for churning out blues singers it was Etta's home base in the formative years of her musical career.

She caught her big break in 1955 when she met Johnny Otis, who was so impressed with her vocal talents that he decided to work with the then unknown Jamesetta Hawkins. Ever the creative soul, she adopted her stage name by transposing the letters from her birth name: Jamesetta became Etta James.

James and Otis teamed up together to write the song "Roll with Me, Henry," which was her first taste of commercial success. The song was a humorous jab at Hank Ballard's string of earlier hits "Work with Me Annie" and "Annie Had a Baby." Since "Roll with Me, Henry" was a suggestive title that hinted at risqué lyrics that could have discouraged radio play, the song's title was changed to "Wallflower," and it topped the rhythm and blues charts at number two.

Etta went on to record other hits, such as "Good Rockin' Daddy" and "Most of All" during the 1950s. She was a regular and very popular member of the Johnny Otis show. By the end of the 1950s she was hailed as one of the finest rhythm and blues singers in the business. James, who had recorded her hits on Modern Records, switched to the Chess subsidiary label Argo starting in 1960.

On her new label James hit gold with "All I Could Do Was Cry" and "My Dearest Darling." Her new solo career was put on hold temporarily while she worked with Harvey Fuqua and the Moonglows. They had a hit single together, "If I Can't Have You," which proved that Etta James could handle any kind of material.

The first part of the 1960s were good for Etta. Aside from providing backing vocals on Chuck Berry's "Around and Around" and "Back in the U.S.A.," she scored a number of hit singles, including "At Last," "Just in Me," "Something's Got a Hold on Me," "Stop the Wedding," and "Pushover." Although she was not a pure blues singer in the same sense as a Bessie Smith, Etta incorporated many blues ideas into her songs. By 1963, she was as firmly established in the music business as any other female blues/rhythm and blues/pop singer. She was on the verge of superstardom.

But from the end of 1963 to 1967, Etta James lived a life of seclusion due in part to an alleged heroin problem. As a result, her career took a severe nosedive as she struggled to overcome an addiction that threatened her very existence. By the time she was ready to resume another phase of her recording career in 1967 she had lost four prime years to heroin.

But James rebounded nicely with her album *Tell Mama*. Aside from the title track, the album included the songs "I'd Rather Go Blind," "Watch Dog," "The Love of My Man," "I'm Gonna Take What He's Got," "It Hurts Me so Much," "Just a Little Bit," and others. The album produced a couple of hits—"Tell Mama" and "I'd Rather Go Blind." The latter topped the charts at number twenty-three. Sadly, it seemed as if James had not completely kicked her addiction because at the beginning of the 1970s she had once again succumbed to drug dependency. When she finally admitted that her destructive habit would eventually kill her, she checked herself in a rehab center. After intense therapy, she emerged two years later ready to take on the world again.

In 1973 she began the long journey back to respectability. Her album *Etta James* included the songs "Sail Away," "Leave Your Hat On," and "God's Song." The album sparked some interest, but a complete comeback was a painfully slow process. In an effort to make up for lost time she worked diligently to restore the damage caused by her substance abuse problem. She performed in small nightclubs and continued recording for Chess Records, but wasn't able to score a hit like she had done so easily in the past. Only through raw determination and hard work over a long period of time was James was able to assure concert promoters and record executives that she was clean for good and could be counted on to work in a professional manner.

Her skillful use of the media helped Etta regain her position as one of the top blues queens. An appearance in a bar scene on the television show *Insiders* was good for her career. The inclusion of her song "Wallflower" in Steven Spielberg's multimillion-dollar box office hit *Back to the Future* was a positive step forward. Another of her songs, "The Blues Don't Leave," was part of the soundtrack for the movie *Heartbreakers*.

In 1977, she recorded the album *Deep in the Night*, which contained the Eagles' "Take it to the Limit," Alice Cooper's "Only Women Bleed," Hank Williams's "Lovesick Blues," and Kiki Dee's "Sugar on the Floor." Although the album did not garner the sales she hoped it would, it accelerated her effort to regain her old popularity.

After five years of solid touring in small venues, Etta James had proven to those in the music business that she was once again a bankable artist. She began to appear at blues festivals all over the United States and other countries. She became a force in the world of the blues to the delight of many of her old and new fans.

In 1978, James opened for the Rolling Stones on their Some Girls tour. Her supporting role played a vital part in a booming career that had once been declared over. With every performance thereafter she only solidified her renewed career. Six years later, James sang at the opening ceremonies of the 1984 Olympic Games in Los Angeles. The Olympics, one of the major television events of the summer, exposed her to a large audience from all over the world. In 1986, she appeared in Taylor Hackford's *Hail! Hail! Rock and Roll!* singing a duet with Chuck Berry in honor of his sixtieth birthday. She also recorded with blues master B. B. King.

Though James made a strong comeback on the stage, her recording career never regained its former strength. It wasn't until 1990, with the release of *Stickin' to My Guns* on Island Records, that her career comeback was complete. Although the album was not pure blues and contained more of a funk sound, it was a critical and financial success.

In 1992, James recorded *The Right Time* on Elektra, and it was a smash hit. The album contained the haunting ballads "Evening of Love," You've Got Me," and "Nighttime Is the Right Time" and featured guest appearances by Steve Winwood and Jim Capaldi. It was recorded at the Muscle Shoals studio in Alabama, which gave the album a funky, yet laid-back sound.

Now that she has overcome her drug dependency, James has reclaimed her spot as one of the top blues queens. She published her autobiography, co-written with David Ritz, in 1994. Her concerts are sold out on a regular basis, and her records are critical and commercial successes.

Etta James is a blues star. She has proven her mettle time and again in the past forty years. If she had not fallen prey to heroin, there is a good chance she would have become one of the best-selling female blues singers in history. Her talent is undeniable, and she has always been able to make a hit record.

Etta James links the past to the present. Although she is a contemporary singer, shades of Sippie Wallace and Bessie Smith are detectable in her style. She ranks as one of the best rhythm and blues singers in the last forty years, and she has extended the parameters of her sound to include soul, funk, and pop. James has cleverly kept up with the times without sacrificing her style by combining new ideas with her old sound.

Her vocal style is a contrast of differences. Her phrasing is subtle, carefully planned, and eloquent, and the feeling she puts in a song is pure energy, like a swirling hurricane. She doesn't fake the blues—she sings with the hurt of someone who has known the hardest of times.

Her vocal style is patterned after her two biggest idols, Dinah Washington and the immortal Billie Holiday. From Holiday she learned about finesse and feeling, and from Washington pronunciation and precision. She combined all of these elements with her sheer power and flair for entertainment to arrive at her own sound.

Etta James has been part of three distinct musical eras. She was one of the great pioneers of rock and roll. Although considered a top rhythm and blues singer, she was one of the main links between old blues and the new rock beat. In the 1960s, she became one of the best soul singers in the business. She ranks with Otis Redding and Wilson Pickett as one of the most important interpreters of this kind of funkier blues. Today, she continues to belt out rhythm and blues hits with the power of someone half her age and has become a contemporary singer.

She has a very impressive résumé. She shares with Koko Taylor the distinction of being great blues singers who recorded with the famous Chess label. Both James and Taylor contributed extensively to the Chicago blues sound. Although neither recorded for Chess during the 1950s, they were a big part of the label's sound in the 1960s.

Etta James is a feisty, headstrong female who has always lived on the edge. She is a complicated character, susceptible to long periods of isolation and outbursts. But there is no denying her genuine talent and heart. Her career has not been without controversy, but she has always been able to deliver the goods when it counted. Through it all she remains one of the most recognizable voices in the blues today. Her powerful, electric style has inspired a new generation of young female blues singers.

In 1993, James was inducted into the Rock and Roll Hall of Fame, which only emphasizes her versatility. In the last forty years James has had her hand in every major musical direction except disco and rap. She has been a soul spirit, a rock and roll queen, a rhythm and blues gem, a pop princess, and a funky mama. But her style is deeply rooted in the blues, and she has been able to stretch the genre until it sounded different without losing its authenticity.

Discography

At Last, MCA-Chess CHC 9266.

Second Time Around, MCA-Chess CHD 9287.

Etta James Rocks the House, MCA-Chess CH 9184.

Tell Mama, MCA-Chess CHD 9269.

Her Greatest Sides, Vol. 1, MCA-Chess CH 9110.

The Sweetest Peaches: The Chess Years, Vol. 1 (1960–1966), MCA-Chess CHD 9280.

The Sweetest Peaches: The Chess Years, Vol. 2 (1967–1975), MCA-Chess CHD 9281.

Etta James, Chess CH 50042.

Etta James, Cadet 4013.

Come a Little Closer, Chess 60029.

Twist with Etta James, Crown CLP 5250.

The Essential Etta James, Chess.

PART FIVE

Blues Outside the Delta

A large majority of blues singers hail from Mississippi. However, many southern states and the United Kingdom have also been prime breeding grounds for blues singers. The diversity of singing styles reflects the particular regions.

Lonnie Johnson and Professor Longhair were born in Louisiana; Blind Willie McTell was from Georgia; Pete Johnson and Big Joe Turner both hailed from Missouri; Roosevelt Sykes was born in Arkansas; Blind Boy Fuller and Sonny Terry called North Carolina home; Brownie McGhee was a native of Tennessee; and John Mayall, the only non-American featured in this book, was born in England. These singers represent the following blues styles: country-blues, New Orleans, regional down-home Atlanta, boogie-woogie and jump, piano, Virginia-Piedmont, East Coast, and British blues, respectively.

This section may appear to be merely a collection of individual blues singers who don't fit into one of the other four categories, but it is exactly the opposite. Every one of the blues singers featured in this section was an important pioneer to his respective style.

Lonnie Johnson was a vital link between the country-blues and citified blues. Blind Willie McTell was the dean of the Atlanta blues in the same way that Professor Longhair was the dean of New Orleans blues. Pete Johnson was a boogie-woogie king, and Big Joe Turner was an original Kansas City blue devil. Roosevelt Sykes was a pioneer of prewar blues piano. Blind Boy Fuller was a leading exponent of the Virginia-Piedmont school of blues. Sonny Terry and Brownie McGhee were also practitioners of the Piedmont blues style and used its best elements to create the East Coast blues school. John Mayall remains a staunch British supporter of the blues and has provided a finishing school for many of the best young talents found in England in the last thirty years.

The singers discussed in this section represent different musical styles and different eras. Although they may not always have received a lot of recognition, their contributions to the blues are just as important as those of their fellow musicians from the Delta, Chicago, and Texas.

LONNIE JOHNSON (1894–1970)

Mr. Johnson's Blues

The country-blues, the guitar-driven music of the poor Southern black folk that emerged in the late nineteenth century, encompasses many different regional styles, including Delta, Piedmont, Tennessee, Memphis, Atlanta, early Chicago, ragtime, and folk. The acoustically flavored down-home blues flourished in the hands of the pioneer masters who delivered the music to the international stage. One of the most celebrated country-blues guitarists attained immense fame by playing his own particular brand of blues. His name was Lonnie Johnson.

Alonzo "Lonnie" Johnson was born in New Orleans on February 8, 1894, into a musical family. His father often formed a string ensemble to play in front of visitors; with thirteen children, he was provided a healthy talent pool. The experience Lonnie gained from playing in the family's band gave him advantages that would one day prove beneficial to his career. Before Lonnie chose the guitar as his instrument of choice, he learned how to play the violin, piano, and bass.

As a youngster, Lonnie and his brother James played at the city cafés for whatever change people threw their way. When the United States entered World War I, Lonnie left to play music for the boys overseas. On his return from Europe he discovered that his family had been nearly wiped out by the influenza epidemic. Devastated by the tragedy, he moved with his brother James—who had miraculously survived the deadly plague—to St. Louis.

After the war, the musical tastes of the country began to change drastically. The many formative elements of jazz, which had filled the streets during Mardi Gras, were consolidated. Suddenly, there was a new epidemic sweeping the land—jazz. However, with this fever there was money to be made.

The creation of jazz was an outgrowth of the blues. In its infancy, jazz lived in the shadows of the blues, but eventually found its own identity and exploded onto the scene. More than any other music, jazz fit the tempo of the Roaring Twenties. The music was hot, fast-paced, and demanded excellent musical skills, which Lonnie Johnson possessed in great abundance.

Lonnie would be instrumental in helping shape the sound of the new music, but to deliver his ideas to the public he needed to record his songs. He entered a blues contest that promised a recording contract with sponsor Okeh Records as first prize. The competition was fierce; after a marathon eight-week run, a winner was finally declared—Lonnie Johnson.

Soon after his victory, he was ushered into the recording studio and cut his first two songs, "Mr. Johnson's Blues" and "Falling Rain Blues." The executives of Okeh Records quickly realized that Lonnie was a valuable discovery. Not only could he sing and write a catchy tune but he was also more than a capable performer on several instruments. Overnight, he became well known through musical circles; because of his virtuoso talents, he was able to record with jazz giants Louis Armstrong and Duke Ellington. Recordings such as the Armstrong Hot Five's "I'm Not Rough" and "Hotter Than That" and Ellington's "The Mouche" and "Hot and Bothered" bear the distinct Johnson guitar touch.

He continued to record between 1927 and 1929 at a dizzying pace. Because was a proficient singer, songwriter, and musician, he was comfortable with and more than able to handle any type of musical style. His versatility is one of his trademarks that sets him apart from many other blues singers of the era.

Some of Johnson's greatest efforts of this period are his duets with guitarist Eddie Lang. The pair was sensational and may have been one of the first racially mixed bands in musical history. They recorded such swinging favorites as "Bullfrog Moan," "A Handful of Riffs," "Two Tone Stomp," and the excellent "Guitar Blues."

The Roaring Twenties came to a crashing end, and the Great Depression was a miserable time for many out-of-work musicians, including Johnson. Because of the decline in people's ability to afford records, the recording industry suffered outright. Lonnie, who only knew the life of a musician, was unable to continue his music career. He took a job in a factory to avoid starvation and did not record any songs between 1932 and 1938.

In 1939, as the Great Depression came to end, Johnson began phase two of his illustrious blues career. A new recording contract with Decca and a new hit—"He's a Jelly Roll Baker"—quickly propelled Johnson back into the spotlight. But the musical scene had changed since his heyday in the late 1920s. His new songs were no longer called blues, but rhythm and blues.

Other songs he recorded during this period include "Man Killing Blues," "Hard Times Ain't Gone Nowhere," "Flood Water Blues," "Swing out Rhythm," "Something Fishy," "I'm Nuts Over You," "Friendless and Blue," "Devil's Got the Blues," "New Falling Rain Blues," and "Mr. Johnson's Swing." Many of these songs featured the Honeydripper, Roosevelt Sykes, on piano.

At the beginning of the decade new markets were opening up for musicians, and Lonnie took full advantage of the opportunities. The burgeoning pop scene promised the best financial rewards, and Johnson scored a couple of hits with "Tomorrow Night" and "Pleasing You." His popularity in America enabled him to travel overseas, where he could increase his fan base on an international level.

Lonnie Johnson arrived in England in 1952 amid a blues craze. The genuine brilliance of a true American bluesman was exactly what the British craved, and Johnson did not disappoint his blues-starved audiences. His appearance at London's Royal Festival Hall earned rave reviews. His hot run in Great Britain, however, was shortlived as the skiffle fad swept England and left him on the outside looking in.

On his return to America from the 1952 British tour, Lonnie hoped to resurrect his fading career. But, with the advent of rock and roll, he was swept away and relegated to music's land of the forgotten artists. He moved briefly to Cincinnati, then Philadelphia, where he worked different jobs including as a chef and a janitor in a hotel. It seemed the end of the road for the sad-looking blues-jazz king of the 1920s who had electrified audiences with his dazzling artistry.

But once again, the change in the public's musical tastes intervened to save Lonnie's career. In the years between the demise of the first generation of rock and rollers and the British invasion, folk music was all the rage. White college students began a nationwide search for the country-blues singers who had dominated the music scene in the 1920s and 1930s. It was only a matter of time before someone discovered Lonnie Johnson, who was quietly working as a janitor at the Benjamin Franklin Hotel in Philadelphia.

With admirable courage and a sense of having something to prove, Johnson was ready to embark on phase three of his long and distinguished career. His comeback engagement was at the Playboy Club in Chicago, where he earned close to $400 a week, a princely sum for a musician who had been mopping floors not so long ago. His triumphant month-long stay at the prime venue in the Windy City sparked renewed interest in his music.

He became an in-demand performer in America where he appeared at folk festivals and in Europe, where he toured extensively to enthusiastic reviews. Despite the obvious triumphs, the folk music fad was over all too quickly. With the advent of the British invasion led by the Beatles, everyone turned their attention again to rock music, and Johnson was swept away from the spotlight.

Arguably, if he had been a younger man, Johnson could have made a serious impact on rock. But he was tired and spent, and the career of one of the most brilliant musicians of the twentieth century was over. He moved to Toronto in the late 1960s and lived out the rest of his life there. In 1970, due to a stroke and a prior serious accident, Johnson died on June 16. He was seventy-six years old.

Although his star blazed brightly on three different occasions, Lonnie Johnson never became a superstar in the true sense of the word; however, his vast contributions to the blues affected the development of the music in immeasurable ways. Without doubt, Johnson was a country-blues pioneer whose only true equal was Blind Lemon Jefferson. As an innovator, Johnson held a stately position. He was a man who suffered his share of tragedies, but also enjoyed his share of triumphs. His resilience was remarkable.

Because of the rich diversity of Johnson's music—which was recorded over a forty-year period and includes blues, jazz, pop, and folk—it is sometimes difficult for contemporary blues fans to connect with the man and his guitar-driven sound. To truly appreciate and understand the chameleon talents of Lonnie Johnson one must give considerable and equal attention to the three phases of his career.

During his first period of stardom Johnson recorded about 130 sides. Although he was one of the great blues pioneers of the era, he also made enormous contributions to jazz. Lonnie Johnson is one of only a handful of musicians who were instrumental in the early development of both musical forms. He was able to fuse the two musical styles while keeping their individual sounds distinct. In many ways, Johnson was as important to the blues as he was to jazz.

In the 1940s and early 1950s Lonnie proved that he could be a successful pop artist and became one of the best-selling rhythm and blues singers of the era. His incredible versatility enabled him to make a comeback when other blues singers of the 1920s and 1930s remained in obscurity. Under contract with King Records, the Lonnie Johnson who sang the rhythm and blues songs was far removed from the man who had recorded with Louis Armstrong and Duke Ellington twenty years earlier. Some of the songs Johnson made famous during the second phase of his career include "Move Over," "Hot and Bothered," "Misty Morning," "Playing with the Strings," "Stompin' 'em Along Slow," "Away Down the Alley," and "Blues, Blues in G," recorded with the Tiny Bradshaw Band in 1951.

Johnson's shortest time in the spotlight was the last phase of his career. He came full circle and returned to the country-blues, which he had started playing as a young man. More than any other time in his career, Johnson's third phase of popularity represents a desire to make a bundle of money before the opportunity was taken away again. He had learned from previous negative experiences.

Despite starring in three different musical eras, it is a fact that Johnson has never received full credit for his guitar skills. He is credited with introducing the flat pick to urban blues guitarists. His use of vibrato and his jazz-flavored style set the stage for what was to come later. Johnson leaned heavily on the major pentatonic and mixolydian scales, creating a bittersweet sound that became his trademark.

Johnson possessed a gentle sophistication, an urban sensibility, and a deep knowledge of the guitar that certainly had no precedent. His unique brand of jazz-tinged blues with assured technical prowess affected Big Bill Broonzy, the warm, expressive bluesman who was essential in linking the raw country sound with the more polished city blues. Much of Johnson's work also made a lasting impact on B. B. King, who in turn has been the source of inspiration for nearly every blues-rock guitarist of the postwar era. Johnson not only made an impact on B. B. King but also on Charlie Christian, arguably the greatest of the jazz guitarists. Johnson's smooth, melodic jazz lines can be heard in the styles of Charlie Christian and Django Reinhardt; Christian in turn was a special influence on rocker Chuck Berry.

A partial list of the people Lonnie Johnson worked with during the three phases of his remarkable career includes Duke Ellington, Louis Armstrong, Victoria Spivey, Spencer Williams, Eddie Lang, Elmo Scooter, Charlie Creath, Clara Smith, Bertha Chippie Hill, Martha Raye, Bessie Smith, Jimmy Dodds, Pete Seeger, and Joan Baez. Although he recorded some 200 of his own songs during his long and varied career, he can also be heard through the music of many distinguished musical greats of the twentieth century.

Johnson's legend goes beyond just his music. He embraced the lifestyle of a bluesman wholeheartedly with his fancy clothes and numerous lady friends. He lived for the moment and did not worry about what the next day might bring. He possessed a special talent that remained unappreciated for long periods of time, but one that he could summon from its slumbers on a moment's notice.

In 1990, Lonnie Johnson was inducted into the Blues Foundation Hall of Fame. It was a fitting honor for a man who worked hard to expand the parameters of the blues to appeal to a larger audience. Though many words can be used to describe the musical career of Lonnie Johnson, the most appropriate is *survival*. He knew hard times as well as good times, and through it all he managed to provide the world with his own brand of Mr. Johnson's blues.

Discography

Steppin' on the Blues, Columbia CK 46221.
Blues by Lonnie Johnson, Original Blues Classics 502.
Lonnie Johnson, 1926–1940, Blues Documents 2064.
Losing Game, Prestige-Bluesville OBCCD 543-2.
The Complete Folkways Recordings, Smithsonian-Folkways SF 40067.
Lonnie Johnson, Bluebird B 8779.
Lonnie Johnson, Okeh 8775.
Blues & Ballads, Bluesville 531.
Idle Hours, Bluesville 518.
Blues by Lonnie Johnson, Bluesville 502.
Complete Recorded Works (1925–32) Volume 1, Document 5069.
Complete Recorded Works (1937–1940), Document 5070.
The Blues of Lonnie Johnson: 1937–38, Swaggie S 1225.

BLIND WILLIE MCTELL (1901–1959)

Dean of Atlanta Blues

The down-home Atlanta blues, which are primarily guitar-driven, were created from a cross-pollination of musical influences including rag, Piedmont, country, and Delta grit. Although classified as Piedmont blues, the practitioners of the regional Atlanta style developed their own distinct sound, which encompassed elements of other blues traditions. Barbecue Bob, Curley Weaver, and Buddy Moss were important first-generation exponents of Atlanta blues. But like other regional down-home styles, the Atlanta school had its own dean, leader, and champion. His name was Blind Willie McTell.

McTell was born on May 5, 1901, in Thompson, Georgia. Very little is known of his early years—for instance, whether he was actually born blind or lost his sight at a later age. Despite his obvious physical challenge, McTell did not allow it to hamper his ambitions to become a blues master.

He attended a number of special schools to learn how to read Braille, aware that this skill would help him during his lifetime. He also received instruction on how to play the guitar from his mother. McTell listened well, practiced hard, and dreamed of the life of a bluesman.

After his mother's death, McTell packed his bags and headed out on the road, hoboing throughout Georgia and other southern regions, playing fish fries and rent parties. He hooked up with the other Atlanta bluesmen Buddy Moss, Barbecue Bob, and Curley Weaver and roamed all over Georgia before settling in Atlanta. While Charley Patton, Eddie "Son" House, and Willie Brown were playing their grinding Delta blues, McTell and his cohorts were creating the regional Atlanta blues sound.

Because McTell was a first-generation recording artist, it is difficult to determine who helped shape his unique guitar and vocal style. Certainly the time he spent performing at medicine shows and carnivals throughout the Virginia Piedmont region had a profound influence on his development as a blues singer. Obviously McTell based his sound on a variety of sources—he was capable of playing more than just blues. His varied repertoire consisted of ballads, pop songs, folk, and rag numbers.

By his mid-twenties, McTell had established a reputation around Atlanta as the city's most important blues singer. Because of his local fame he was given the opportunity to record some of his material for the Victor and Columbia labels. From 1927 to 1932, McTell recorded on a continual basis, mainly for Columbia, but he also cut sides for other companies under several pseudonyms.

Although he was the acknowledged champion of the Atlanta regional blues sound and possessed a fluid guitar style and striking vocals, McTell was never a big commercial success. He never became a country-blues star of the same magnitude of other down-home blues vanguards, most notably, Delta king Charley Patton and Texas blues proponent Blind Lemon Jefferson.

Although his songs might not have made him a star, the sides McTell cut were pure quality and are the supreme reason why his compositions still sound fresh some seventy years after their initial recording. He made little money from his studio material, so McTell was forced to play street corners in Atlanta with close friend Curley Weaver for the spare change passersby threw into their tin cup.[1]

By 1933, the record industry, which was suffering greatly from the ill effects of the Great Depression, dropped many artists from their rosters. McTell had been a prolific recording blues singer for five years, but he would not be given another chance to make records until 1935. These later sessions took place in Chicago and didn't bring him any more recognition than his early ones. It was another five years before McTell recorded again, this time for the Library of Congress under the watchful eye of John Lomax, the self-appointed guardian of American blues.[2]

From 1941 to 1945, the years of World War II, McTell maintained

[1]*Any biographical discussion of McTell is not complete without exploring his special musical connection with fellow Atlanta bluesman Curley Weaver. Weaver was born James Weaver on March 25, 1906, in Covington, Georgia. Brought up in the country, he arrived in Atlanta while still in his teens, determined to make a name for himself in the city's blues scene. A quality guitar player who accompanied McTell in the recording studio on a number of occasions, Weaver also recorded with other Atlanta bluesmen Barbecue Bob and Buddy Moss. Weaver, along with McTell, was at various times part of the Georgia Cotton Pickers and Georgia Browns, two loosely formed bands that consisted of the city's leading blues lights. Aside from the local minor hit "No No Blues," Weaver wasn't much more of a commercial success than McTell. McTell and Curley recorded together for the Regal label in 1949. By the time of his death in 1962, Weaver was completely blind and had returned to his rural home town of Covington. His influence on McTell was extremely important.*

[2]*In many ways Lomax was a true pioneer, a visionary who realized how extremely important it was to record the first-generation blues singers for posterity. The realm of music he recorded is a genuine history book of early-twentieth-century America.*

his blues career through street performances in Atlanta, often accompanied by Curley Weaver, Buddy Moss, and Barbecue Bob. All four were
born within five years of each other, but McTell recorded much more than
the other three, which clearly illustrates that he possessed an edge in talent over his contemporary Atlanta bluesmen.

It wasn't until 1949 that McTell recorded again, this time for Atlantic
and Regal Records. He also recorded in the mid–1950s for Prestige-Bluesville.
Unfortunately, none of these sessions produced the big hit that he needed
to continue his blues career, and he slowly faded from the blues scene.

On August 19, 1959, Blind Willie McTell passed away in Mil-
lidgeville, Georgia. He was fifty-eight years old.

Blind Willie McTell was a regional blues superstar. He was to the
Atlanta blues what Charley Patton was to the Delta blues and Blind
Lemon Jefferson was to the Texas blues. He was recognized as the father
of Atlanta blues; however, on a national level he was barely known at all.
Nevertheless, McTell was a true pioneer whose unique musical skills
enabled him to shape the future course of not only Atlanta blues also but
the entire southeastern region musical scene.

McTell was a skillful finger-picking guitarist whose fluid motion,
intriguing vocals, and songwriting ability with a regional flavor enabled
him to expand on the prominent rag-blues sound of the Virginia Piedmont region. He not only played the blues but also included pop, ballads,
and folk into his style. The guitar-driven Atlanta blues that he created
along with Curley Weaver, Buddy Moss, and Barbecue Bob was the music
of a proud people.

McTell was a guitar innovator of the highest order. He brought a
thorough knowledge and consistency to the twelve-string guitar sound
that gave the instrument a lively edge that no one else was ever able to
copy. Like Leadbelly and Robert Jr. Lockwood, who both played the
twelve-string, McTell was able to absorb many influences and incorporate them into his playing, which gave him a broader sound.

There were also elements of rock and roll in his guitar style. Not only
did McTell pave the way for future Atlanta bluesmen but he was also one
of the fathers of Southern rock, the man who blazed the initial trail for
southern-fried boogie bands like the Allman Brothers, Lynyrd Skynyrd,
Molly Hatchet, .38 Special, the Marshall Tucker Band, and other groups
that emerged in the late 1960s and early 1970s. The Allman Brothers even
recorded McTell's "Statesboro Blues," making it the centerpiece of their
live shows.

·

A blues singer who never truly received the credit he deserved because of his lack of commercial success, McTell remains one of the most creative of the first-generation bluesman. He gave the world a wealth of songs that immortalized the daily life of not only the southeastern region of the country but particularly his native Georgia.

Some of the gems McTell recorded include "Mama, 'Tain't Long 'for' Day" and "Three Women Blues," as well as "Broken Down Engine Blues" and "Stomp Down Rider." However, he will forever be known for such state-flavored songs as "Georgia Rag," "Atlanta Strut," and his masterpiece, "Statesboro Blues." Statesboro, a town in Georgia located near the South Carolina border, is mainly a farming community with limited industry. McTell put the tiny town of Statesboro on the musical map.

Other songs that McTell gave the blues world include "Love Changing Blues," "Travelin' Blues," "Drive Away Blues," "Writin' Paper Blues," "Southern Can Is Mine," "Ticket Agent Blues," "Dying Crapshooter's Blues," "King Edward Blues," "Stole Rider Blues," "Mr. McTell Got the Blues (takes 1 and 2)," "Dark Night Blues" "Come Around to My House Mama," "Razor Ball," and "Scary Day Blues." He was a prolific songwriter and one of America's greatest storytellers.

Much attention has been devoted to the modern blues artists, but one should never forget pioneers like Blind Willie McTell. The Atlanta blues never acquired much attention, despite the efforts of McTell, and later the Allman Brothers, but the regional down-home music is the essential story of the blues.

McTell was inducted into the Blues Foundation Hall of Fame in 1981. This is a fitting honor for a man whose musical contributions have influenced three generations of blues and rock singers. Blind Willie McTell was an original singer who deserves respect not only on a regional level but also as a national blues treasure. Though he never became a commercial success, there is no doubt that Blind Willie McTell remains the dean of the Atlanta blues school.

Discography

The Early Years (1927–1933), Yazoo CD 1005.
Blind Willie McTell—Complete Recorded Works, Vol. 1 (1927–31), Document DOCD 5006 (import).
Blind Willie McTell—Complete Recorded Works, Vol. 2 (1931–33), Document DOCD 5007 (import).

Blind Willie McTell—Complete Recorded Works, Vol. 3 (1933–35), Document DOCD 5008 (import).
Blind Willie McTell (1927–1935), Yazoo 1037.
Complete Library of Congress Recordings, RST BDCD 6001.
Pig 'n' Whistle Red, Biograph BCD 126 ADD.
Blind Willie McTell: Last Sessions, Prestige-Bluesville.
Blind Willie McTell: Statesboro Blues, Victor Vi V38001.
Blind Willie McTell: The Post-War Years 1949–1950, Regal.
Blind Willie McTell: The Victor Recordings 1927–1934, Victor Records.

PETE JOHNSON (1904–1967)

A Boogie-Woogie King

The piano blues encompasses a wide variety of styles including ragtime, barrelhouse, West Coast jazz, the rollicking rhythms of the Chicago sound, and boogie-woogie. Some of the seminal figures in blues history were pianists who made enormous musical contributions with their dexterous touch. In the early part of the century the country experienced a boogie-woogie craze. Although enormously popular, the boogie-woogie fad didn't last very long. In the late 1930s and early 40s, there was a second boogie-woogie fever that spread throughout the country like a raging fire out of control. One of the kings of this boogie-woogie rebirth was Pete Johnson.

Johnson was born on March 25, 1904, in Kansas City, Missouri. The early details of his life are somewhat sketchy, but it is known for certain that he spent part of his youth in an orphanage. Desperate to find an escape from the hardships and loneliness he experienced as a child, Johnson discovered the world of the blues. Music became his beacon of hope as he worked earnestly to uncover the subtle secrets that would enable him to succeed in his chosen profession.

Johnson began his musical career as a drummer, and for six years he performed at parties and in clubs around his hometown. But he grew tired of the drums and developed an interest in playing the piano, which seemed much more exciting. During his tenure on the drum chair, he carefully observed the intricate sense of timing and rhythm that pianists required to create their magic. After diligently practicing and seeking the direction of a variety of pianists, Johnson became proficient enough to find work playing house parties and selective clubs in the 1920s.

One magical evening at the Sunset Cafe, a large man with a round, friendly face arrived to perform his set. He was a blues shouter who went by the descriptive name of Big Joe Turner. Johnson was mesmerized by the electrifying performance that Turner gave that night and approached him with a certain amount of curiosity. Pete and Big Joe became partners and performed together at the Sunset Club and other hot spots in Kansas City. Johnson was a hard-driving piano player and perfectly complimented Turner's powerful vocal delivery. They weren't trying to incite another boogie-woogie craze, but that was exactly what Johnson and Turner ended up doing some three years later.

In 1938, John Hammond was scouring the country in search of blues acts to appear in his Spirituals to Swing concerts. He found Johnson and Turner performing at the Sunset Club and immediately signed them up. The pair traveled to New York and were instant hits at the event. They were also featured guests on the "Benny Goodman Camel Caravan Radio Show."

While in New York Johnson met two other pianists who were instrumental in fueling the boogie-woogie craze of the late 1930s and early 1940s. Albert Ammons and Meade "Lux" Lewis soon joined Johnson to form the Boogie-Woogie Trio.

Because of their immense contributions to the music of that era and the blues in general, it would be unfair to just skip over the names of Ammons and Lewis without providing a short biographical sketch. Albert Ammons was born on September 23, 1907, in Chicago, Illinois. He was ten years old when he started to play the piano and soon he became an important player in the Chicago blues scene. In 1929 he joined the Boogie Woogie Stomp Band, which also included trumpeter Gary Kelly, bassist Isreal Crosby, and drummer Jimmy Haskins. He also played briefly with the Count Basie Band. Ammons was also part of François Moseley's Louisiana Stompers and later, in 1931, played with William Barber and His Headquarters, as a second pianist.

Eventually Ammons made his way to New York to take part in the Spirituals to Swing Concerts. Seemingly overnight, he was caught in the boogie-woogie surge along with Johnson, Turner, and Lewis. By the mid–1940s the boogie-woogie fire had been extinguished, and Ammons performed more often with the noted jazz musicians of the era including Harry James and Benny Goodman, and he eventually joined Lionel Hampton's band in 1949. Ammons died the same year, on December 5, at the age of forty-two.

During his early days in the Windy City while driving a taxi cab, Ammons befriended Meade "Lux" Lewis. Lewis was born on September 4, 1905, in Chicago. He learned how to play the piano at an early age and was deeply influenced by the piano exploits of Jimmy Yancey and Pine Top Smith. By his early teens Lewis was playing at various clubs in Chicago, and in 1927 he scored a hit with his "Honky Tonk Train Blues," a song he recorded for Paramount.

Ammons and Lewis became quick friends, sharing a love of good music and good times. Lewis was invited to participate in the Spirituals to Swing Concert in New York, and it was there that he and Ammons hooked up with Johnson.

The trio recorded together at the Cafe Society, a swanky Manhattan club, until 1941 when the boogie-woogie craze was quickly fading out. Lewis moved back to Chicago, where he worked with Joe Sullivan for a time at Eddie Condon's Club from 1946 to 1947. Later on, he relocated in Los Angeles, where he did some recording and played local clubs. On June 7, 1964, long after the interest in boogie-woogie had subsided, Lewis died in an automobile accident in Minneapolis. He was fifty-eight years old.

The brief time that Johnson, Ammons, and Lewis spent together is an important chapter in blues history. It was an era of good times, good friends, and good music. The three men delighted audiences with their potent, hard-pounding, rock-your-baby blues.

Once interest in boogie-woogie was over, Lewis left New York, but Johnson and Ammons stayed behind and often recorded as a duo. But, by the late 1940s Johnson's career had taken a sharp turn downward. In a desperate effort to revive his career, he appeared in the film *Boogie Woogie Dream* near the end of the decade. He also recorded with Hot Lips Page, Budd Johnson, and Clyde Berhardt, providing the world with such blues classics as "Dive Bomber," "Zero Hour," "Rock it Boogie," and "Rock 'n' Roll Boogie."

In 1950, Johnson moved to Buffalo, New York, and continued his career playing at various clubs around the city. In 1952, Johnson took part (with Art Tatum and Eroll Garner) in Piano Parade. It was also that year that Johnson suffered a career-threatening accident when he lost part of his little finger while changing a tire. (In an eerie coincidence, Albert Ammons had earlier lost the same fingertip as Johnson in a separate accident.)

In 1954, Johnson was mostly out of the music business and was employed as a janitor, though he still played an occasional gig. In 1955, he was included in a session with Jimmy Rushing, one of the great blues shouters of the 1930s. The session helped Johnson rejuvenate his name, if only for a fleeting moment. In 1956, a more promising project saw him reunited with his old partner, Big Joe Turner. The session resulted in the album "Boss of the Blues," which was a critical and financial success. Unfortunately, it was one of Johnson's last musical highlights.

In 1958, Johnson had the opportunity to tour Europe with Turner, and the duo proved that they were still a mighty blues force. Although their musical reputation in the United States had faded considerably, their exposure in Europe brought them a legion of new fans. After his appearance at the Newport Jazz Festival Johnson disappeared from the musical scene.

It wasn't until 1967 that Johnson resurfaced to play Carnegie Hall as part of Joe Turner's Cafe Society All-Stars, and, although the reunion brought together old friends and memories, it was apparent that Johnson was gravely ill. On March 23, 1967, Pete Johnson died in Buffalo. He was two days shy of his sixty-third birthday.

For more than a decade Pete Johnson was a blues star. Along with his friends and bandmates, Albert Ammons and Meade "Lux" Lewis, he wrote an unforgettable chapter in blues history. While the boogie-woogie craze seemed like a fad, it was one of the foundations on which rock and roll was built on.

Johnson was an innovator who took the best elements of the first boogie-woogie craze and improved on the initial blueprint. He was a polished pianist whose dizzying abilities added a new dimension to the pianists' handbook. A highly technical musician in his own right, Johnson developed riffs and licks that found their way in the repertoire of many pianists who were later credited with creating the initial rock and roll sound.

Boogie-woogie piano players were astute virtuosos who hammered out repetitive bass figures with their left hands keeping eight beats to the bar while playing rhythmic chords with their right hand. The boogie-woogie sound is best defined as a combination of walking bottom base notes coupled with intricate solos. Boogie-woogie pianists were creative individuals who often improvised instantly and simultaneously played percussion, bass, and melody.

The boogie-woogie kings of the 1930s and 1940s were the forefathers of rock and roll piano. Along with Big Joe Turner and the early Delta bluesmen they must be credited with inventing the highly publicized offshoot of the blues long before Bill Haley and the Comets received credit for formulating the "new" music. Rock and roll was created in the smoke-filled bars of the black ghettos where bluesmen like Pete Johnson worked out the basic rhythms, which eventually evolved into the century's most popular music. The music of the first generation of rock and rollers is drenched with the trappings of boogie-woogie. Elvis Presley, Chuck Berry, Jerry Lee Lewis, Fats Domino, and Little Richard incorporated large chunks of the boogie-woogie sound into their music.

Johnson's influence on other rock keyboard/pianists is deep. Ray Manzarek of the Doors played in the boogie-woogie style, providing bass lines and intricate jazzy solos. Canned Heat was a great boogie-woogie band. Other bands, such as ZZ Top, the Allman Brothers, Lynyrd Skynyrd, and the entire realm of Southern rock owes a great debt to the boogie-woogie piano kings for their rollicking rhythms and highly technical musical ability.

Pete Johnson is also famous for introducing songs that became true classics into the blues repertoire. His signature tune, "Roll 'em Pete," often performed with Big Joe Turner, is instantly recognizable and is a case study for any aspiring blues pianist. He also contributed "Barrelhouse Boogie" and "You Don't Know My Mind." Johnson, in collaboration with Big Joe wrote the driving blues favorite "Cherry Red."

Other songs that are part of the Johnson catalog include "Shuffle Boogie," "Lone Star Boogie," "B & O Blues," "How Long, How Long," "Pete's Blues," "Let 'em Jump," "Pete's Blues No. 2," "Boogie Woogie," "66 Stomp," "Hollywood Boogie," "Yancey Street Blues," and "Central Avenue Drag." Each of these numbers remains as a testimony to his incredible musical ability and powerful blues vision.

Although the boogie-woogie kings didn't receive their proper credit for their major contributions to rock and roll, they did gain the respect of the jazz world. The collaboration between Johnson and the jazz greats includes a recorded performance with Harry James. Ammons and Lewis also recorded with some of the biggest names in jazz.

The boogie-woogie kings of the 1930s and 1940s created a cult following and greatly influenced modern music. In the hierarchy of pianists, Johnson ranks among the most technically accomplished. Although boogie-woogie was considered "nasty" and "radical" by the purists, the style earned a special place in blues history. Boogie-woogie not only formed the basic sound of rock and roll but also infiltrated jazz, pop, and soul.

Pete Johnson was one of the most influential figures in blues history. He played a large part in the career success of Big Joe Turner. Johnson teamed up with Ammons and Lewis to create a piano treasure that has been plundered and pillaged by two generations of musicians. But most important, during one of the most inspired eras in blues history, Pete Johnson was a boogie-woogie king whose piano will never be silenced.

Discography

Pete Johnson, 1938–1947, Document 535.
Central Avenue Boogie, Delmark DD 656.
Tell Me Pretty Baby (with Joe Turner), Arhoolie CD 333.
Pete Johnson: Master of the Blues & Boogie-Woogie, 1904–1967, Vol. 1, Oldie Blues OB 2805.
Pete Johnson: Master of the Blues & Boogie-Woogie, 1904–1967, Vol. 2, Oldie Blues OB 2806.
Pete Johnson, Blue Note.
Jumpin' with Pete Johnson, Riverside.

ROOSEVELT SYKES (1906–1984)

The Honeydripper Blues

Even in a field packed with varied styles and outstanding sylists, some blues pianists created sounds so unique that they earned their own distinctive nicknames. One of the greatest of the pre–World War II piano players used his gifted hands and musical genius to create his own "Honeydripper" blues. His name was Roosevelt Sykes.

Sykes was born on January 31, 1906, in Elmar, Arkansas. Although born in the Wonder State, Sykes was raised in St. Louis, where at an early age he was taken by gospel music. He learned how to play the organ and sang in the church choir. His ambitions, however, stretched far beyond a career as a gospel singer; by his late teens he was ready to strike out on his own, armed with his polished piano skills and burning desire to become a bluesman.

He moved back to Arkansas and immediately immersed himself in Helena's thriving musical scene. Because the piano was not a mobile instrument like the guitar, harmonica, saxophone, or violin, Sykes was forced to make the established rounds of the barrelhouse piano blues circuit, which consisted mostly of juke joints. Sykes teamed up with Lee Green, and the pair often worked together, rocking the roadhouses with their brand of firewagon blues.

By the late 1920s Sykes had tired of the Arkansas blues scene and craved a change. He decided to return to the place of his upbringing, St. Louis, which he made his permanent home for the next ten years. The City of Arches remained his base while Sykes toured throughout the country, but he adopted Chicago and Memphis as his two favorite cities. At this point in his career Sykes established his performance credentials by playing numerous one-night shows and sometimes longer engagements. Soon his name was prominent in the three key blues markets of St. Louis, Chicago, and Memphis.

But, what he truly needed was a hit song to further solidify and expand his burgeoning reputation as one of the finest and most furious piano players in the country. He achieved that in 1929 when he recorded a slick, fast-paced, dynamic version of "Forty-Four Blues," released by Okeh records. The song became the popular single that Sykes had hoped it would be and his career blossomed as a result.

The 1930s were a dark period in the careers of many blues musicians because of the harsh economic times, but Sykes thrived in St. Louis. He was a favorite solo artist as well as a highly in demand session man and accompanist. The piano, even though it didn't surpass the guitar in popularity, became a staple in the barrelhouses, honky-tonks, and speakeasies of the prewar period. Sykes was one of the prime blues pianists who challenged the guitar for the spotlight.

Throughout the decade, Sykes could usually be found in one of the city's blues clubs entertaining the crowd playing "Forty-Four Blues," "Jivin' the Jive," or "Trouble and Whiskey." Sometimes he performed with other noted St. Louis pianists like Jimmy Oden and the interchanging solos and hot rhythm licks made the audience jump, scream, and beg for more. With his ability to make people move to the hypnotic sounds he created with his magical hands Sykes had unlocked one of the essential keys to the enduring popularity of the blues—he understood how to entertain the people.

He also continued his recording career in an era when the music business had been practically wiped out. Although he recorded mostly for small labels and used pseudonyms for some reason, Sykes retained a name for himself in the music business. Because he was such a versatile piano player he was always in demand to appear on records cut by other blues artists.

While Robert Johnson, Charley Patton, Son House, Big Joe Williams, and Skip James were busy spreading the lowdown Mississippi Delta sound; while Blind Willie McTell was busy establishing the appeal of regional Atlanta blues; while Big Bill Broonzy, Tampa Red, Big Maceo, Albert Ammons, Meade "Lux" Lewis, and others were working Chicago's South Side blues venues; and while Big Joe Turner and Pete Johnson were shouting and rolling out the blues in Kansas City; not far away, Sykes was creating his unique blues sound in St. Louis. In 1941, after a decade as the reigning king of St. Louis blues pianists, Sykes took his remarkable talent to Chicago, where he often jammed with Memphis Minnie, Tampa Red, Big Maceo, Big Bill Broonzy, and Sonny Boy Williamson I. He also continued his solo career and cut sides with the Bluebird and Bullet labels. Sykes, who had long ago established his reputation as an incredible arranger and session man, added his considerable talents to the records of others, such as the Jump Jackson Band.

In 1946, in an unprecedented move, Sykes formed his own band and called it the Honeydrippers. The source of the name is either attributed to the sweet blues the band created or Sykes's personal appeal with the opposite sex. The band began to tour the South after the war and gained much respect for their brand of driving Midwest blues.

After some ten years on the road Sykes returned to Chicago, but found that the musical climate had changed while he had been gone. The hard-edged, nasty sound of Muddy Waters and the electric blues school had taken over the Windy City. Roosevelt, always sensible, realized that there would be little work for him in Chicago, so he moved to one of his old haunts, New Orleans.

Because Sykes already boasted a very impressive résumé he had very little difficulty becoming a fixture in the Creole City's musical scene, where work was plentiful. Sykes quickly added New Orleans to the list of American cities that he had conquered with his impressive piano ability. New Orleans had always been a musical hotbed of excitement and welcomed Sykes with open arms.

Throughout the 1950s and 1960s, Sykes was a mainstay on the New Orleans blues circuit, with occasional side trips to his old stomping grounds in St. Louis. He also frequently played long engagements in Memphis, another city which had always been good to him. Despite the constant moving, he always managed to record his songs for lesser-known labels such as Prestige-Bluesville as well as the bigger companies like Decca, Crown, and Delmark. He was able to constantly shift from one strategic blues city to another without destroying his recording career either as a solo artist, with his band, or as an accompanist—a fact that only emphasizes how much of a dominating force he was in the blues world.

Sykes had continued to play the blues even when their popularity was not at a high level, so it was only fair compensation that he benefit from the blues boom of the 1960s. Sykes was one of the many bluesmen who toured Europe, winning over a new legion of fans who received an excellent taste of what Helena, St. Louis, Chicago, and Memphis had been enjoying for years. In his native country, Sykes was a major drawing card and appeared at numerous blues and folk festivals.

The blues drought of the 1970s did little to slow Sykes down despite his advanced age and increasing health problems. He toured constantly and recorded at a consistent pace. Arguably, by the early 1980s, he had lost some of his previous luster. His infrequent live appearances became events. Despite his noticeable absence from the touring circuit, he remained to the very end a respected musician in blues circles.

On July 17, 1984, Roosevelt Sykes passed away in New Orleans, Louisiana. He was seventy-eight years old.

Sykes was a blues star of understated magnitude. Although he always seemed at the edge of superstardom, he could never find a way to cross that fine line. He didn't gain the attention that other blues musicians attracted, yet few ever had the continued and uninterrupted success that he enjoyed for nearly sixty years. He was a dedicated and professional individual whose stamina was truly incredible.

Roosevelt's longevity was certainly one of his major advantages. In a business where careers are broken more quickly than a guitar string,

Sykes played the blues for seven decades. Certainly his career was much longer than such blues legends as Robert Johnson, Sonny Boy Williamson I, Elmore James, Otis Spann, Magic Sam, Blind Lemon Jefferson, Freddie King, Stevie Ray Vaughan, and Bessie Smith. Many of the aforementioned blues artists have attained a loftier position in their brief careers, so it appears that the man responsible for the honeydripper blues has been shortchanged.

Sykes was instrumental in the success of four different blues cities. He was a vital part of the Arkansas blues scene in 1920s, St. Louis in the 1930s, Chicago in the 1940s, and New Orleans in the 1950s and thereafter. Throughout his career he recorded as a soloist, accompanist and band leader.

Because of his incredible versatility, it is nearly impossible to associate Sykes with one particular piano blues style. He was capable of playing ragtime, boogie-woogie, the rocking rhythms of the Chicago sound, barrel house and jazz-tinged blues with equal ease. But he possessed a unique touch that elevated him above many of his contemporaries. He was more than just a competent blues pianist, he was someone special who took the art of piano blues to heights it had never reached before.

In the hierarchy of blues pianists, Sykes ranks with the fashionable Leroy Carr (the Delta key pounder), Sunnyland Slim, and early boogie-woogie kings Speckled Red, Walter Davis, and Blind John Davis. These men helped define the pre–World War II blues sound. In many ways Sykes stands above these musicians. Although Carr was very successful, he died at a young age. Walter Davis, Blind John Davis, and Speckled Red were all fine pianists, but none had very long careers. Only Sunnyland Slim can be said to have enjoyed the same longevity as Sykes, but even he never attained the same level of popularity as the Honeydripper.

As a pianist in the pre–World War II era Sykes was a huge influence on the modern blues piano players. All the boogie-woogie kings—Pete Johnson, Albert Ammons and Meade "Lux" Lewis—borrowed heavily from Sykes. They incorporated his use of intricate chord patterns and thumping bass notes—two essential ingredients in boogie-woogie—into their own style. Otis Spann, who starred in the Muddy Waters Band, adopted Sykes's versatility. Sykes also influenced modern blues pianists like Eddie Jones and Henry Boyd. Big Maceo Merriweather learned from Sykes when the two performed together in Chicago in the early 1940s.

During his distinguished career he recorded many great songs, including "You so Dumb," "No Good Woman Blues," "Hard Luck Man

Blues," "Don't Put the Lights Out," "All my Money Gone Blues," "My Life's Blues," "Low as a Toad," "Mellow Seven," "Don't Push Me Around," "Peeping Tom," "Boogie Honky Tonk," "Booze Blues," and "Time Wasted on You." This partial list is only a small part of his entire catalog, but it represents a good selection of the songs he spun into gold.

Roosevelt Sykes was a large, brooding man whose natty attire was part of his image. He was a keen ambassador and always represented the blues with class and dignity. A man who was able to adapt to any style, he was also responsible for passing the torch from one generation to the next. His status as one of the pioneers of prewar blues and his many contributions during the modern era make him a special entry in blues history.

Discography

The Country Blues Piano Ace, Yazoo 1033.
The Honeydripper, 1929–1941 Blues, Document 2013.
The Honeydripper, Vol. 2, 1936–1951, Blues Documents 2088.
Roosevelt Sykes and His Original Honeydrippers, Oldie Blues OL-2818.
In Europe, Delmark 616.
Raining in my Heart, Delmark 642.
Goldmine, Delmark DD 616.
West Helena Blues (The Post-War Years, Vol. 2, 1945–1957), Wolf WBJ 005.
Roosevelt Sykes Sings the Blues, Crown CLP 5237.
Roosevelt Sykes, Bluesbird 34-0721.
Hard Drivin' Blues, Delmark DS 607.
Roosevelt Sykes Blues, Folkways 3027.
Roosevelt Sykes: The Honeydripper, Prestige 7722.

BLIND BOY FULLER (1907–1941)

Rattlesnakin' Daddy Blues

With pockets of black populations scattered throughout the Southern states, different styles of blues emerged each with its own group of devoted practitioners. Although the Mississippi Delta and Texas sounds have garnered more attention, the Virginia-Piedmont style produced an interesting group of blues singers. Blind Blake, Sonny Terry, Brownie McGhee, and the Reverend Gary Davis were all serious students of the Piedmont school. However, the group's leader, the man who gave the style instant recognition, was known as the "Rattlesnakin' Daddy." His name was Blind Boy Fuller.

Fuller was born Fulton Allen on July 10, 1907, in Wadesboro, North Carolina. Although he learned how to play the guitar at an early age, he did not initially settle on a musical career. Before he went blind, he drove cars for a living and worked at other menial jobs around North Carolina. Once he lost his eyesight, however, he became Blind Boy Fuller and turned to the blues to make a living.

Fuller began his blues career playing on street corners and in front of tobacco houses earning spare change. He preferred a steel-built guitar that enabled him to produce a loud, rough sound like the growl of a junk-yard dog. Armed with a thick, hard voice, Fuller was a complete blues-man; he struggled earnestly to build his career, but met with only frustration. It wasn't until a chance meeting with James Baxter Long that Fuller's career began to take shape.

J. B. Long had the right connections, and once he assumed the role of Fuller's manager and producer, Blind Boy's career took off. Long was an honest manager—a rarity in the music business. He was also very pro-tective of his act. His reputation around blues circles was as a hard-nosed, practical man who was not particularly congenial. Long was interested in making money and though he didn't necessarily use Fuller, he was smart enough to realize that when his main client made money, so did J. B. Whatever his faults might have been, Long played an integral part in Fuller's rise from obscure street musician to important recording artist.

In 1935, Fuller cut his first sides for the American Record Company in New York. The partnership between Fuller and ARC was one of the most musically productive combinations of the Depression era. While many blues singers were out of work and numerous record companies went bankrupt, Fuller and ARC were producing records at a steady pace. The affiliation lasted until Fuller's death. From 1935 to 1940, Blind Boy recorded over 130 songs, making him one of the most prolific blues artists of the period.

Fuller's success in the studio was the result of a combination of fac-tors. Certainly the patient and steady guiding hand of J. B. Long was an important element. Long was not interested in an elaborate production and used the bare minimum number of musicians. This was possible because Fuller sounded like an entire band by himself.

Blind Boy Fuller was one of the most accomplished blues singers in history, and his talent has never been properly acknowledged. He was an excellent musician as well as a clever songwriter capable of producing a very marketable tune. In the studio, he was often accompanied by the Reverend Blind Gary Davis on second guitar and Bull City Red on energetic washboard. Fuller also recorded with blues harmonica master Sonny Terry.

But more than any other single factor in Fuller's success was his incredible versatility as a bluesman. His supreme guitar skills allowed him to record more than just straight blues. His rich repertoire included rag, pop songs, Piedmont-style blues, and old-fashioned, down-home North Carolina country-blues.

Although Fuller was often a solo artist and used a skeleton group in the studio, in 1934, he made his most important blues connection with the celebrated harp player Sonny Terry. The two met one Saturday afternoon in Wadesboro when they were both playing on the same street corner for spare change. They joined forces and played a few songs that day and discovered that their styles meshed well together. At the end of the day, Fuller returned to Durham, where he lived with his wife, and left an open invitation for Sonny to look him up if the latter was ever in Durham.

A few weeks later, Sonny arrived at Fuller's and the two formed a loose partnership. Terry ended up living with Fuller, and on weekends the duo roamed up and down Highway 70 playing their blues in the tobacco towns like Burlington, Greensboro, and Winston-Salem. During the week they played fish fries and house parties around Durham.

They also recorded a number of songs together, including "Bye Bye Baby Blues," "Pistol Slapper Blues," "Georgia Ham Mama," "Long Time Trucker," "Jivin' Big Bill Blues," "I'm a Stranger Here," "I Feel Like Shoutin'," "Three Ball Blues," "Bus Rider Blues," and many others. Sometimes they were accompanied by Bull City Red in the studio. Later on, near the end of his recording career, Fuller often used the pseudonym Brother George and His Sanctified Singers.

While still a young man Fuller developed kidney problems. During surgery, he lost consciousness and never woke up. He died on February 13, 1941. He was only thirty-three years old.

Blind Boy Fuller became a huge regional star. In Durham, he was an important man, almost a household name. His fame, however, did not really spread past the borders of North Carolina despite his distinction of being one of the most recorded blues artists of the late 1930s. If his career had not been cut down in its prime, Fuller would have become a more important figure in blues history.

Yet, despite his brief career, he managed to leave an indelible mark as one of the genre's most original characters. Blind Boy Fuller was a gambler, a rambler, and a jealous man. He almost always carried a gun for protection and wasn't shy about using it. He was a roamer who knew the streets and back alleys of North Carolina better than a person with perfect eyesight. He made numerous contributions to the blues. Though Fuller recorded songs in different styles he is best remembered as a keen student of the Virginia-Piedmont blues style.

The Virginia-Piedmont blues style was a southeast coast school whose boundaries consisted of the states of Florida, Georgia, Virginia, and North and South Carolina. The Piedmont is the foothill region of the United States which lies between the Atlantic coastal plain and the Appalachian mountains. The region begins somewhere in the New England states and stretches down to North Carolina where the plain widens. The Virginia-Piedmont blues school was a more loosely formed group than the circle of Mississippi Delta bluesmen or the electric Chicago blues group, but still became a force to be reckoned with. Besides Fuller, the Virginia-Piedmont School produced noted bluesmen such as Blind Blake,[1] Reverend Gary Davis, Sonny Terry, Brownie McGhee, and Bull City Red.

Blind Boy Fuller was an important influence on a number of blues singers from North Carolina. He steadied the blues outlook of Sonny Terry as well as Brownie McGhee. He was also helped out Rev. Gary Davis and Bull City Red. If Fuller had toured more outside his native state, he might have assumed a greater role in the blues scene of the south Atlantic region.

[1]*One of the major influences on Fuller was the first-generation bluesman known as Blind Blake. Born Arthur Phelps around the year 1890, little is known of the singer who called himself Blind Blake and sometimes Blind Arthur. He is believed to have been from the Jacksonville, Florida, area and may have even been from the exotic Georgia sea islands. Although the information on his personal life is vague, one fact is undisputed: In the late 1920s and early 1930s Blind Blake became one of the most important recording artists. He shares this honor with Blind Lemon Jefferson and Lonnie Johnson. Because of Blind Blake's success other country-blues artists were sought out by record companies. More than any other bluesman, Blind Blake was the foremost torchbearer of the Virginia-Piedmont blues style, which was based on an intricate finger-picking scheme. Blake was inducted into the Blues Foundation Hall of Fame in 1990.*

Fuller also shares with Blind Willie McTell the distinction of being a regional champion. McTell, the dean of Atlanta blues, is the most famous name in Georgia blues history. Fuller, despite stiff competition from Sonny Terry, remains the greatest figure in North Carolina blues history. He became the father of North Carolina blues. This uncontested title is a fitting tribute to a man who despite obvious physical obstacles became one of the leading lights in the blues at a time when the genre was suffering a lull in popularity.

Blind Boy Fuller is a classic example of the forgotten blues recording stars of the period between the 1920s and the 1940s. A man who was instrumental in shaping the musical direction of popular music after the war, Fuller's blues career lasted about ten years. Yet in that short span of time he was able to provide the world with a great blend of blues styles and an impressive recording catalog.

Aside from the aforementioned titles, Fuller also gave the world "Truckin' my Blues Away," "Winter Blues," "Homesick and Lonesome Blues," "You Can Never Tell," "Mannie," "Jivin' Woman Blues," "Funny Feeling Blues," "I Crave my Pigmeat," "Meat Shakin' Women," "Walking my Troubles Away," "Painful Hearted Man," "Corine What Make You Treat Me So?," "Sweet Honey Hole," and "Weeping Blues" to name but a few. The depth and breadth of his catalog is truly astonishing considering his relatively brief recording career.

Fuller was also one of many blues singers who were instrumental in the development of rock and roll. His dynamite swinging song "I'm a Rattlesnakin' Daddy," with its accessible lyrics, catchy rhythm, and a terrific walking bass, provided crucial elements used by early rockers. If he had lived longer, Fuller might have become one of the greatest of the early rockers. He possessed a strong voice, a rocking guitar sound, an imaginative songwriting spark, and a feel for the kind of songs that made people dance.

A man who deserves to be inducted into the Foundation Blues Hall of Fame, Blind Boy Fuller was an original bluesman whose success was formidable considering the thinness of the times. He was a force in the lives of many young bluesmen in the 1930s, especially Sonny Terry, who later enjoyed a successful career with partner Brownie McGhee. Blind Boy Fuller will probably be best remembered as the vastly talented, North Carolina blues guitarist who gave the world his rattlesnakin' daddy blues.

Discography

Truckin' my Blues Away, Yazoo 1060
East Coast Piedmont Style, Columbia CK 46777.
Blind Boy Fuller, Vol. 1 (1935–36), Document 5091.
Blind Boy Fuller, Vol. 2 (1937), Document 5092.
Blind Boy Fuller, Vol. 3 (1937), Document 5093.
Blind Boy Fuller, Vol. 4 (1937–38), Document 5094.
Blind Boy Fuller, Vol. 5 (1938–39), Document 5095.
Blind Boy Fuller, Vol. 6 (1940), Document 5096.

BIG JOE TURNER (1911–1985)

Shoutin' the Blues

The very first blues singers were the field workers who were attempting to alleviate the heavy burden of working in the cotton fields. Yet this primitive vocal style is one of the prime roots of blues singing, especially the raucous, extrovert styles of the blues shouters who came into prominence during the 1930s. The blues shouters served as an early blueprint for the later emergence of the entire screaming generation of rock singers. The leading exponent of the shouting blues style was a man whose emotional intensity gave his music a sharp-edged, roadhouse sound. His name was Big Joe Turner.

Joseph Vernon Turner was born in Kansas City, Missouri, on May 18, 1911. Like countless other black children of his generation, his first musical exposure was the gospel he heard in church. He sang in the choir, which provided his initial training ground. Turner took all the basics that he had learned singing in the choir and used them to perform on street corners, earning spare change to help out the family finances.

Although music was in his blood, he did not begin to forge his career until he was in his early twenties. Before he earned his living as a singer, Turner drove a junk wagon, selling old items that he found in the dump and repaired himself. Once he secured his first professional singing job at age twenty-one, he felt that better times were ahead.

Although he had begun his professional singing career, Turner was forced to work as a bartender at the Sunset Cafe to help support his family after his father's death. One fateful night when Turner was tending the bar a young boogie-woogie pianist walked into the nightclub; his name was Pete Johnson. On hearing his expertise on the piano, Turner (who also tickled the ivory keys) forged an immediate musical friendship with the talented Johnson that endured for the next forty years. They became known around Kansas City nightspots for their electrifying performances. While Johnson pounded out tough, boogie-woogie piano rhythms Turner shouted lyrics with the force of a hurricane.

In 1938, John Hammond attended one of their performances and quickly signed them up for his Spirituals to Swing concert. Johnson and Turner made the trip to New York and found additional work in the Big Apple. It was at this time that their rocking piano/vocal show was exposed to the nation and sparked a boogie-woogie craze that lasted into the next decade.

Despite a strong reputation as a live performer, it wasn't until the late 1930s that Turner was given the chance to record as a pianist playing in the boogie-woogie style. Some of his better-known songs of this era include "Roll 'em Pete," "Percy Brown," "Lucille," and the ever-popular "Cherry Red." "Cherry Red" and "Roll 'em Pete" were written in partnership with Johnson, as was the song "Wee Baby Blues." Their songwriting collaboration spawned many other blues classics.

The Kansas City blues that Johnson and Turner created during this period were considered citified. Meanwhile, in Chicago, a different kind of urban blues was being developed in the capable hands of Tampa Red, Big Bill Broonzy, Big Maceo, Sonny Boy Williamson, Albert Ammons, Meade "Lux" Lewis, Jazz Gillum, and Memphis Minnie.

Turner was such a versatile performer that he also recorded with some of the jazz greats of the era, including Count Basie, Eddie Lockjaw Davis, and Harry Edison on *The Bosses* album. He also recorded with Milt Jackson, Roy Eldridge, and Pee Wee Crayton on the song "Nobody in Mind." Turner also jammed with an all-star trumpet section comprised of Edison, Eldridge, Dizzy Gilespie, and Clark Terry, which produced the album *The Trumpet Kings Meet Joe Turner*. The record was a huge hit and proved that blues singers and jazz musicians could work well together.

Throughout his career Turner was an active performer. He was featured in the Duke Ellington revue *Jump for Joy in Hollywood* in 1941.

Though his work with Johnson is legendary, he also found time to play with the other boogie-woogie masters Meade Lewis and Albert Ammons. He toured with both Johnson and Ammons. Turner also worked with Joe Sullivan on the West coast in 1940 on the album *Cafe Society Swing & the Boogie Woogie*. Turner appeared on the Art Tatum sessions *Swing Combos: 1935–41*, as well as *Swing Street, Vol. 4*.

When boogie-woogie was replaced by rhythm and blues, Turner easily made the adjustment and became one of the most popular R&B artists of the late 1940s and early 1950s. With his dynamic vocal style, Big Joe became one of the first rock and roll stars long before the term was even coined. When R&B developed into rock and roll in the 1950s, the new music swept the country. What few people realized was that rhythm and blues artists like Turner had been playing rock and roll for years—the rhythmic structure of blues and boogie-woogie were the essential foundation of the initial rock and roll sounds.

By the end of the 1940s, Turner was one of the most respected blues singers; despite his popularity, like many other black artists of that era, he was confined to the narrow race market. If he had been exposed to white audiences he would have become a huge star, and the rock and roll craze might have begun a few years earlier.[1]

Turner continued to record and had several hits in the 1950s, including "Chains of Love," "Sweet Sixteen," "Honey Hush," "Chill Is On," "Don't You Cry," "Shake, Rattle and Roll," and "T.V. Mama," the latter recorded with Elmore James. His later hits included "Hide and Seek," "The Chicken and the Hawk," "Morning, Noon and Night," "Flip, Flop and Fly," and "Corinna, Corinna."

One of Turner's most satisfying projects of the decade was the 1956 *Boss of the Blues* album, which featured his longtime friend Pete Johnson, as well as alto saxophonist Pete Brown, Lawrence Brown, and Freddie Green. The collection of songs on the album defined the urban blues. Some of the highlights of the album include "Roll 'em Pete," "Cherry

---

[1]*It is unfair and unjust that many of the songs recorded by white singers (who made a fortune off them) were first written, recorded, and performed by black singers who received little or nothing for their efforts. Many of the first wave rock and rollers shamelessly plundered the R&B treasures of the black bluesmen. The songs "Hound Dog," first performed by Big Mama Willie Mae Thornton; "That's all Right, Mama," written by Arthur "Big Boy" Crudup; and "Shake, Rattle and Roll," written by Big Joe Turner were covered by Elvis Presley and Bill Haley and the Comets, respectively. While the white singers rocketed to fame and became rich, the original writers and singers of these songs were often left without any compensation.*

Red," "How Long Blues," "St. Louis Blues," "Wee Baby Blues," "Pennies from Heaven," and "You're Driving Me Crazy." The landmark album also contains a superlative example of Turner's piano skills on the song "Morning Glories.

Like other black artists Turner enjoyed considerable crossover success once the barriers of racial prejudice were finally broken down in the mid–1950s. He was an instant hit with the young white audiences. He appeared in the movie *Shake, Rattle and Roll* and was often part of rock and roll packages touring throughout the country. When the first great wave of rockers faded away because of death, imprisonment, and army service, Turner returned to the R&B circuit and teamed up with Pete Johnson again.

Turner toured Europe and performed at many festivals, regaining some of his earlier popularity. Despite suffering from arthritis and overall failing health, he continued to record on a steady basis. A compilation album, *The Best of Joe Turner*, was released in 1963. In 1971, he was part of a rock and roll revival series that was very successful and prompted Atlantic, his record company, to issue all of Turner's hits from the 1950s. The album was entitled *Joe Turner: His Greatest Recordings*. It is one of the many repackaged albums of his material.

In the 1970s Turner was a regular on the Johnny Otis show and continued to tour into the 1980s. He recorded the album *Blues Train* on Muse Records in 1983 and appeared in *The Last of the Blue Devils*, a 1980 documentary film that featured Kansas City jazz of yesteryear. Despite his active musical career, health problems continued to plague Turner in the late 1970s and into the 1980s. At one point, his arthritis was so bad that he recorded albums while in an arm chair. Turner was still an active performer when on November 24, 1985, he passed away in Inglewood, California, from a heart attack. He was seventy-four years old.

Big Joe Turner was a major blues star who shined brightly for over five decades. He took part in three major musical movements of the century: the boogie-woogie craze of the late 1930s and early 1940s, the rhythm and blues boom of the 1940s and early 1960s, and the emergence of rock and roll in the mid–1950s. An important innovator as well as a major influence on two generations of blues and rock singers, Turner earned a prominent place in blues annals.

Big Joe Turner was an innovative singer. Many seminal blues figures established their credibility with a particular musical instrument, but Turner did it with his voice. His shouting blues influenced some of the most famous singers of the past fifty years, including Bill Haley, Elvis, Little Richard, Mick Jagger, Jim Morrison, and an entire galaxy of competent hard-rock vocalists. He also influenced blues singers B. B. King, Buddy Guy, Otis Rush, Magic Sam, and Robert Cray.

If Big Joe would have been born in the early 1940s—like a majority of the rock warriors of the 1960s and 1970s including Led Zeppelin, the Rolling Stones, the Beatles, the Who, and the Doors—he would have made a greater impact on rock music with incalculable consequences. Although he may not have been able to muster the same sex appeal as Elvis or Jim Morrison, Turner certainly possessed the vocal prowess to become a great rock singer. Under the right circumstances, he also might have challenged Robert Plant for his hard rock–blues throne.

Not only did Big Joe Turner made enormous contributions as a vocalist and occasional piano player, he was also a talented individual capable of penning hit songs. Throughout his career, from his days with Pete Johnson and as a popular rhythm and blues singer, he provided the world with a large catalog of classic songs. Aside from the aforementioned songs, there was also "SK Blues," "It's a Low Down Dirty Shame," "Hollywood Bed," "Rebecca," and "Sun Risin' Blues," to name only a few. His greatest hit, "Shake, Rattle and Roll," was later covered by Bill Haley and the Comets and propelled them into the pages of rock history. Although some critics have pointed to "Shake, Rattle and Roll" as the beginning of rock and roll, true blues scholars know otherwise.

In 1983, Big Joe Turner was inducted into the Blues Foundation Hall of Fame. Four years later he became a member of the Rock and Roll Hall of Fame. While the cover versions of his songs outsold his original efforts Turner had a huge influence on blues and rock. As the most famous blues shouter, Big Joe Turner was able to shake, rattle, and roll into a permanent place in blues history.

Discography

Greatest Hits, Atlantic 81752.
The Rhythm & Blues Years, Atlantic 781752-2.
Jumpin' the Blues, Arhoolie 2004.
The Boss of the Blues, Atlantic 8812.
I've Been to Kansas City, Vol. 1, MCA 42351.
Singing the Blues, Mobile Fidelity MFCD 780.
Tell Me Pretty Baby, Arhoolie 333.

Texas Style, Evidence ECD 26013-2.
His Greatest Recordings, Atlantic SD 33-376.
The Best of Joe Turner, Atlantic SD 1844.
Joe Turner Sings K. C. Jazz, Atlantic 1234.
Big Joe Rides Again, Atlantic 1332.
Joe Turner and Jimmie Nelson Crown, CST 383.
I Don't Dig It, Juke Box Hit (618).
Memorial Album—Rhythm & Blues, Atlantic 81667.
Big Bad & Blue: The Big Joe Turner Anthology, Rhino.
Jumpin' with Joe: The Complete Aladdin and Imperial Recordings, EMI
     Records Group.
Early Big Joe, MCA 1325.
Joe Turner, Early Big Joe (1940–44), MCA.
Joe Turner Sings the Blues Vols. 1 & 2, Savoy/CBS Realm.
Joe Turner, Nobody in Mind, Pablo.
Joe Turner, In the Evening, Pablo.

═══════

SONNY TERRY (1911–1986) AND
BROWNIE MCGHEE (1915–1996)

East Coast Blues Duo

The blues have been performed by solo artists, small combos, full bands, and in elaborate jazz settings. However, one of the most productive arrangements in blues history has been the duo. In the late 1920s and early 1930s, guitarist Scrapper Blackwell and pianist Leroy Carr became partners and, despite their brief time together, made a lasting impression. The dynamic team of Pete Johnson and Big Joe Turner became a formidable twosome in the late 1930s and early 1940s. During the beginning of World War II a new blues team emerged from North Carolina. Eventually they resettled in New York City and reinvented the East coast blues sound. They were Sonny Terry and Brownie McGhee.

Sonny Terry was born Saunders Terell on October 24, 1911, in

Greensboro, North Carolina. Brownie McGhee was born Walter Brownie McGhee on November 30, 1915, in Knoxville, Tennessee. Before they became the most famous duo in blues history, they led quite separate lives.

Sonny Terry grew up poor, like most other black children in the shadow of the Roaring Twenties. Sonny learned the basics of the harmonica from his father when he was eight years old and developed his own individual style after long hours of hard practice. Although not born blind, Terry lost sight in one eye when he was eleven years old, and lost sight in the other five years later. Eventually, Terry struck out on his own and ended up in Wadesboro, North Carolina. He played at the tobacco warehouses and on the street corners, picking up spare change. He also joined a medicine show for a while, but quit when he discovered he was being shortchanged.

One Saturday afternoon in 1934, Sonny was playing his harmonica on the street when a guitar player liked what he heard. The guitarist's name was Blind Boy Fuller. They played together that day and when Terry moved to Durham they became partners. The time Sonny spent with Fuller paved the way for his later association with McGhee.

Fuller and Terry recorded together, and as a result of these recordings Sonny was invited to play at John Hammond's Spirituals to Swing concert in 1938. After his triumphant appearance at Carnegie Hall, Sonny returned to Durham and resumed his life as a street performer. He also worked at a blind factory to receive his pension check.

Occasionally, Fuller and Terry played the tobacco warehouses all over North Carolina. A couple of years later Fuller died, ending the partnership. At this time Terry decided to team up with Brownie McGhee.

McGhee had experienced the same hard times that Terry did as a child. He learned to play the guitar at an early age and by his late teens was traveling through the South in tent shows and playing roadhouses, juke joints, and house parties. After hoboing throughout the South McGhee finally made his way to Durham and befriended Blind Boy Fuller. Through Fuller's manager, J. B. Long, McGhee was able to record his own songs, which included a cover version of Fuller's "Step It up and Go." After Fuller's death, McGhee recorded a tribute to his good friend and mentor, "The Death of Blind Boy Fuller." For a time, McGhee was called Blind Boy Fuller #2.

When he first met up with Terry, McGhee was sleeping in cars and playing the streets for spare change. Because of Fuller's sudden death, there was an opening on the bill in a concert in Washington, D.C. McGhee was asked to fill the vacant spot, and he did so, performing a couple of songs with Terry. When they returned to Durham they decided to become blues partners.

Although Sonny Terry was a clever and talented harmonica player who could enthrall crowds as a solo artist, the addition of McGhee's smooth vocals and Piedmont-influenced guitar style greatly enhanced his sound. One of their first concerts together occurred in New York City, where they befriended the disgruntled songster Leadbelly, who was instrumental in forging their acceptance to the white folk-blues audiences of Greenwich Village and other points on the cosmopolitan music scene. Along with Pete Seeger, Woody Guthrie, and Leadbelly, Terry and McGhee established the foundation of the folk-blues revival that exploded in the late 1950s and early 1960s.

Eventually, Terry and McGhee left the South and moved to New York, where they ended up living with Leadbelly for some time. The pair, along with Leadbelly, Pete Seeger, Woodie Guthrie, and Josh White, gathered on Mondays and had a down-home blues jam. They called their impromptu songfests Blue Monday. Unfortunately, there are no recordings that exist of these six American musical legends jamming on Blue Monday.

For the next thirty-five years New York City was the home base for Terry and McGhee. Both were engaged in various personal projects, but they never moved permanently away from the fold that was the McGhee-Terry partnership. They recorded together for numerous labels under a variety of pseudonyms, but there was no mistaking the dynamic interplay of Sonny's harmonica and Brownie's guitar. When not in the studio, McGhee was busy operating his Brownie McGhee's School of Blues in Harlem, while Terry was accompanying Leadbelly, Guthrie, and Seeger in the recording studio and on stage.

Although music was their prime interest, Terry and McGhee were always looking for ways to expand the boundaries of their careers. Since they were based in New York City—with Broadway an integral part of the Big Apple's art community—it was only a matter of time before the two tried their hands at acting. They appeared in a production of Tennessee Williams's *Cat on a Hot Tin Roof*, as well as Langston Hughes's *Simply Heaven*. Prior to that, Terry had appeared in *Finian's Rainbow* in 1946.

Much later in their respective careers the two graduated from the stage onto the big screen. Terry appeared in Steven Spielberg's *The Color*

Purple in 1986 as himself, and McGhee made his movie debut in Alan Parker's *Angel Heart*, also playing himself. In addition, Terry, along with Ry Cooder, provided the eerie background music to the blues cult movie *Crossroads*. Terry and McGhee even appeared on television, further extending their names to an even wider audience.

But music was their first love, and they played numerous concerts to liberal white audiences. It is interesting that during the period of segregation in American history, when a baseball player like Jackie Robinson faced all kinds of racial attacks, two black men from the rural South were playing authentic African American down-home blues to enthusiastic white audiences. In this sense, Terry and McGhee were early crusaders of the black civil rights movement long before the explosive events of the late 1950s and 1960s.

During the 1950s, the pair began performing outside of New York City, giving people across the country a taste of their unique brand of blues, which the Big Apple had been enjoying for a decade. The duo recorded proficiently and, supported by their constant touring, created a national market for themselves.

While Terry and McGhee had patiently been planting the seeds of the folk-blues revival of the early 1960s, they had continued to play the blues at small venues. Seemingly overnight, their brand of blues became highly in demand, and the pair reaped the benefits of those dues-paying years. Terry and McGhee, the longtime darlings of the white folk music scene in New York, were accepted throughout the country as early pioneers and champions of the original folk-blues movement.

While the 1940s and 1950s had been good to them, the 1960s were the golden years of Sonny Terry and Brownie McGhee. The pair played the Newport Folk Festival to loud cheers and became standard performers at several other major blues gatherings throughout the entire country. They toured Australia and India—virgin territory for American blues singers. They also toured Europe as part of a folk-blues package.

At the start of the 1970s the special friendship between Terry and McGhee, which had existed for more than thirty years, began to unravel. By the mid–1970s, their unique musical partnership, which had delighted audiences in many different corners of the globe, was officially over. They both continued to record and perform as solo artists, but the old fire was gone. Although they were terrific individual performers, Terry needed McGhee's strong vocals and fluid guitar style to compliment his earthy blues harmonica whoopings.

Terry recorded an album with Johnny Winter and Willie Dixon for Alligator Records called *Whoopin'*. Sonny saw his career slip away from him in the late 1970s and early 1980s due to health problems. After Terry's death in New York City on March 12, 1986 at the age of seventy-four, McGhee retired from the blues world. He died in Oakland, on February 16, 1996.

Sonny Terry and Brownie McGhee were blues stars for more than thirty years. Their spontaneous style was infectious and became one of the most identifiable sounds in blues music. Not only did the duo make a strong impact on the blues but they also skillfully used television, the big screen, and Broadway to promote their careers. However, the heart of their professional life was the blues. The essence of their sound existed in the individual styles of both men and their ability to blend them together.

Terry could express any kind of human emotion on the harmonica—grief, elation, hope, and anger—which enabled him to connect with the audience on a very personal level. He also possessed a convincing vocal style that complimented his harmonica ability. Though his vocal talents did not match the electrifying quality of his harmonica work, Terry was still an effective singer.

McGhee was a student of the Blind Willie McTell–Blind Boy Fuller–Blind Blake–East Coast blues guitar school that featured an impressive picking scheme and expressive fluidity. McGhee did much to carry on the tradition of the Piedmont blues style, but he was capable of playing any style. He also possessed a rich voice that became an integral part in the duo's overall sound.

They combined these abilities in interesting ways. They used a question and answer structure made famous by the field workers in the nineteenth century. They played off one another's musical skills with loud harmonica effects and drawn-out notes on the guitar. They sang in harmony and in solos. But without doubt, what made the Terry-McGhee duo work so well musically was their unselfish attitudes. They shared the spotlight as equals, alternating solos and creating a balance between harmonica and vocals and guitar and vocals.

Terry and McGhee have often been identified as exponents of the Virginia-Piedmont blues school; however, their music was a mélange of different styles. They mixed their respective North Carolina and Tennessee down-home regional blues with elements of Piedmont and folk to create the East Coast blues sound. Included in their repertoire were blues, swing, folk, rock, gospel, country, and work songs, covering an assortment of themes including travel, separation, fickle women, whiskey, and brief love affairs. Their songs also contained a playful, humorous element; Terry and McGhee made the blues fun. Their music contained an everyman quality, which was one of the main keys of its popularity.

The duo recorded more extensively during their prime than any country-blues pair, and they are famous for such songs as "Mountain Blues," "Fox Chases," "Shortnin' Bread," an intriguing version of "Skip to my Lou," "Back Country Blues," and the pair's most famous duet, "Walk On." They also recorded "Whoopin' the Blues," "Beer Garden Blues," "Hot Headed Women," "Telephone Blues," "Dirty Mistreater," "Harmonica Rhumba," "Four o'Clock Blues," "California Blues," "Jet Plane Blues," and many more.

Sonny Terry and Brown McGhee were also famous for their cover versions of numerous country-blues classics including Big Bill Broonzy's "Key to the Highway" and the classics "Freight Train Blues" and "Motherless Child." Whatever song the two interpreted, one could be assured that they were going to do something special with it.

Sonny Terry particularly was a master at giving Leadbelly's songs special treatment. Some of the Leadbelly classics they covered included "John Henry," "Rock Island Line," and "Keep Your Hands off Her," which Sonny recorded with Ledbetter himself.

The pair played cover versions of the great rural blues standards in a modern swing style, first for black audiences in Harlem, then for white students in Greenwich Village. This is a reflection of their dual influences on both white folk music and black country music. The pair popularized the traditional folk-blues with New York audiences in the 1960s that had an effect all over the country.

The pair were also champions of the East Coast blues, adding new dimensions to its sound and giving it the respect it deserved. Sonny Terry and Brownie McGhee were more than country-blues musicians. They gave the world beautiful, rich harmonies and left behind an impressive musical legacy. They were the ultimate East Coast blues duo.

Discography

Brownie McGhee & Sonny Terry, Smithsonian/Folkways SF 40011.
Sonny Terry and Brownie McGhee: Just a Closer Walk with Thee, Fantasy 541.
At the 2nd Fret, Bluesville 1058.
Brownie McGhee and Sonny Terry (At the 2nd Fret), Prestige 7203.

Sonny Terry & Brownie McGhee: Sonny Is King, Original Blues Classics
    OBC 521.
Sonny Terry & Brownie McGhee: Sonny's Story, Original Blues Classics
    OBC 503.
Sonny Terry & Brownie McGhee: Where the Blues Began, Fontana.
Whoopin' the Blues, Capitol.
Sonny Terry & Brownie McGhee: At Sugar Hill, Fantasy.
The Best of Sonny Terry & Brownie McGhee, Fantasy.
Sonny Terry & Brownie McGhee: A Long Way from Home, ABC-Blues Way.
Sonny Terry & Brownie McGhee: Blues from Everywhere, Folkways.
The Folkways Years, 1941–1963, Smithsonian/Folkways SF 40033.
The Folkways Years 1945–59, Smithsonian-Rounder 40034.

Sonny Terry

California Blues, Fantasy 24723.
Whoopin', Alligator AL 4734.
Sonny Terry, Collectibles 5307.
Sonny Terry's Washboard Band, Folkways.
Harmonica Blues, Folkways.
On the Road, Folkways.
Blind Boy Fuller with Sonny Terry and Bull City Red, Blues Classics.

Brownie McGhee

Brownie's Blues, Prestige-Bluesville OBCCD 505-2.
Climbin' Up, Savoy SJL 1137.
Brownie McGhee, 1944–45, Travelin' Man TMCD 04.
Brownie's Blues, Bluesville 506.
Complete Brownie McGhee, Columbia/Legacy.

====

PROFESSOR LONGHAIR (1918–1980)

New Orleans House Party

There are many famous blues scenes, but New Orleans, Louisiana,
has a special magic all its own. The Crescent City, a place of unusual

charm and great interest, has been a hotbed of musical activity for generations. It is the birthplace of many musical giants of the twentieth century, including Louis Armstrong, Sidney Bechet, Jelly Roll Morton, and Lonnie Johnson. The New Orleans blues sound is a mélange of Caribbean and rhumba rhythms, boogie-woogie, and the second-line strut of the Dixieland street parade music. For over sixty years one man kept the party going with his rollicking, rowdy piano playing. His name was Professor Longhair.

Professor Longhair was born Henry Roeland Byrd, in Bogalusa, Louisiana, on December 19, 1918, one of several children in a musical family. Byrd's father left the fold when little Henry was about six years old, and from that moment on the family was always scuffling to make ends meet. There wasn't a lot of money to go around to buy new instruments or even decent second hand ones. To grow up poor and black in the South in the 1920s had its many disadvantages, but was not without one slight advantage. Because he was forced to improvise and create music using instruments like comb-and-tissue-paper kazoos, the infamous single-string-built-on-a-wall guitar, a bucket and a stick, or a bottle and a stick instead of a real drum kit, Byrd learned to appreciated the delicate and subtle language of various rhythms.

One of little Henry's favorite activities as a young boy was to fall in on the "second line" with the passing marching band during a parade. As a background musician behind the more sophisticated first-line instruments, he was expected to provide a steady beat that fell against the main rhythm and to make a loud din. He rarely failed to deliver.

Although he played a dozen instruments while growing up, the guitar was his primary choice until he finally settled on the piano. Byrd's first piano was an old junker that he restored himself, and all of the rhythms that he had absorbed came flowing out of him with relative ease. But despite his proficiency on the piano he was a long way from a professional blues career.

Byrd, who had declared a love for music since a little boy, had paid some early dues, but in his late teens he truly began the long and serious apprenticeship in realizing his ambition of becoming a true blues singer. He started to frequent the roadhouses, lumber camps, and party houses that dotted the Southern landscape. His travels took him to Helena, Arkansas; Memphis, Tennessee; Houston, Texas; and various small towns surrounding his native New Orleans. He learned his craft as well as some of the toughest lessons of life through firsthand experience.

Although the guitar was the dominant blues instrument in the 1930s, the piano was quickly gaining ground. Guitarists had the huge advantage of being mobile with their instruments, whereas pianists were forced to play somewhere that had a piano. But the piano players got their revenge by drowning out their guitar-playing bandmates (until the invention of amplification).

Nevertheless, by the 1930s, blues piano had made a huge mark on the music. Jimmy Yancey, Pinetop Perkins, Leroy Carr, Jelly Roll Morton, and Clay Custer were some of the early great pianists. By the late 1930s, a whole new group of rocking-blues pianists happened on the scene, including Roosevelt Sykes, Sunnyland Slim, Pete Johnson, Albert Ammons, Meade "Lux" Lewis, Big Maceo Merriweather, and Henry Roeland Byrd who would be known as Professor Longhair.

It wasn't overnight success for Byrd. He remained a fixture on the southern barrelhouse circuit, rocking one back-of-the-town gin mill after another with intensity and vibrancy every night. It wasn't until 1949 that Professor Longhair began to record. By then he was firmly rooted in the New Orleans piano scene and was well known throughout the South.

'Fess, as he was affectionately called around New Orleans, first recorded with Star Talent in a New Orleans nightclub. The recording is rough and the sound quality not the best but the sessions featured one of Longhair's best-known songs, "Go to the Mardi Gras." The song has become a yearly tradition around festival time, and it isn't a real Mardi Gras party until the song is played.

Later on, 'Fess recorded for Mercury with his small combo. The songs were pure New Orleans blues grooves, and cuts such as "Boyd's Blues" and "Her Mind Is Gone" clearly indicate that Longhair was something special. However, aside from the obvious musical talent, another aspect present on the album became one of Professor Longhair's major trademarks. He was never afraid to laugh at himself or get silly with a lyric. His generally off-the-wall humor not only added a dimension to his music but also was a reflection of his true personality and self-marketing skills. He was aware that he was an entertainer and was required to play more than just slick, hard-driving piano songs.

Longhair next recorded for Atlantic Records in 1949. From these sessions (and a later one in 1953) came such songs as "Willie Mae" and "In the Night," as well as "Tipitana," further establishing his already strong musical credentials. Longhair was one of the hottest New Orleans blues pianists at the time, and he further endeared himself to the city's music fans. He was a hometown hero who had made New Orleans proud.

However, despite his success, including the hit "Bald Head" (on Mercury Records), Professor Longhair was forced to gig like crazy just to keep his head above water financially. His music was popular, but he never achieved the commercial breakthrough that he was seeking.

He switched to Ebb Records in the mid-1950s and provided the label with "No Buts No Maybes" and "Baby Let Me Hold Your Hand." Despite the quality of the music, neither song became a hit and Longhair remained locked in the New Orleans piano circuit, working to make ends meet much the same way he had as a child. He was forced to supplement the meager money he made playing the music he loved with an assortment of odd day jobs. For a time he supported himself as a full-time gambler.

His recording career, which was never prolific, continued through the 1960s and 1970s. In 1972, Longhair recorded *House Party New Orleans Style*, which included the songs "Thank You Pretty Baby," "Gonna Leave This Town," "Every Day I Have the Blues," and "Dr. Professor Longhair." The album, a comeback of sorts for 'Fess, was a very successful endeavor. This live effort that features his trademark driving Afro-Latin and boogie-woogie rhythms is a must at any rocking party.

In 1977, Longhair recorded *Rock and Roll Gumbo*, which featured the guitar and violin skills of Clarence "Gatemouth" Brown. Mostly a reworking of old New Orleans standards, including "Junco Partner" and "Rocking Pneumonia," the album was pure 'Fess.

In 1980, the album *Crawfish Fiesta* was released. It contained some of the most rollicking New Orleans piano ever recorded and also boasted a special appearance by Dr. John—who had grown up listening to 'Fess—on guitar.

Although it promised to bring Longhair some much-deserved recognition, he didn't live long enough to see it. On January 30, 1980, Henry Roeland Byrd, known to many as Professor Longhair or 'Fess, passed away in his sleep. He was seventy-one years old.

Professor Longhair never became a national or international star because he never toured outside his home state. But, in his native New Orleans, he became a nearly mythical figure. There is no denying that his personally eclectic style is the sound that became a launch pad for future New Orleans musicians. Though he was never able to make a comfortable living from his music alone, Professor Longhair was a proud flag bearer of not only the New Orleans blues style but also the entire piano genre.

The very essence of his sound was rhythm. He had the uncanny ability of mixing different beats—calypso, Latin, Cuban, boogie-woogie, and slow, swamp grooves to create something fresh, exciting, and a little zany. His understanding of rhythmic structures was second to none. He was able to create, on the spur of the moment, funky songs with a combination of thumping bass notes, intricate melodic passages, and a raw, untrained New Orleans voice.

In the long-standing tradition of piano blues Professor Longhair is an original. Because he was an apprentice to the barrelhouse piano blues he could rock with the hardest of them. A tall man with large, strong hands, Longhair could single-handedly bring an entire audience to its feet. He used the piano as a drum kit, kicking a rhythm sound out of it with his steel-tipped shoes. Longhair was also into cross-chording, a technique he perfected to get the notes he needed to make magic. This remarkable ability to translate the music he heard in his head to his capable hands made him important to the overall blues piano heritage.

But Longhair was more than a bronco-busting, barrelhouse, boogie-woogie stylist—he also possessed a more refined side. He had listened carefully to the slight tint that Jelly Roll Morton added to his piano playing, so he imitated what he heard. His uncanny ability to incorporate a variety of bass patterns and fuse them into something special is the secret to the Professor's appeal.

The boogie-woogie masters Pete Johnson, Albert Ammons, and Meade Lewis also understood the attractiveness of the Latin bass patterns and were able to slip them into their feverishly pounding bass. But Professor Longhair possessed a keener sense of rhythm than any of these boogie-woogie players and was able to separate his music from sounding like just another imitation of the boogie-woogie kings.

The influence of Professor Longhair on subsequent generations is very important. Though James Booker, Mac Rebennack, and Allen Tussaint may not be household names, Art Neville, Huey "Piano" Smith, and Fats Domino enjoyed more commercial success.[1]

Professor Longhair was a lanky, charming man with a wide, goofy

---

[1]*Fats Domino, inspired by the Professor, took the best elements of New Orleans piano and shaped them into a marketable product that earned him numerous gold records. In doing so, he not only became one of the dominant forces in the first generation of early rockers but he also ensured that Longhair's New Orleans piano tradition was carried on to a new and wider audience. A generation or so later, when Art Neville achieved success, he was also tipping his hat to Professor Longhair.*

grin. But behind that grin was the determination and heart of a true blues-man. He was a superb band leader and made the MidDrifs, Professor Longhair and the Four Hairs, Professor Longhair and His Shuffling Hungarians, and the Blues Jumpers household names.

Unfortunately, he never enjoyed great commercial success. His biggest hit, "Bald Head," reached number five on the rhythm and blues charts in 1950. Nevertheless, Longhair continued to play his unique New Orleans blues for all the world to hear. The one definitive characteristic that he possessed was the ability to not take himself too seriously. He created a party atmosphere with his driving blues instead of focusing on the melancholy side of the genre.

Professor Longhair remains one of the most famous citizens of New Orleans and rightly so. Along with Blind Willie McTell, Blind Lemon Jefferson, and Charley Patton, 'Fess was the greatest exponent of the music of his native region. On the eve of every Mardi Gras celebration the song "Go to the Mardi Gras" can be heard loud and clear through the streets of the city. Not only does it usher in the gala celebration, but it also pays tribute to the man who was always the life of the New Orleans house party.

Discography

New Orleans Piano, Atlantic 7225.
Rock and Roll Gumbo, Dancing Cat 3006.
Crawfish Fiesta, Alligator AL 4718.
Mardi Gras in New Orleans, Nighthawk 108.
House Party, Rounder 2057,
Fess: Professor Longhair Anthology, Rhino.
Houseparty New Orleans Style, Rounder.

JOHN MAYALL (1934–   )

The Blues Professor

Mentors have played a very important role in the development of the blues. The passing of precious blues secrets from one generation to the next is the essential ingredient that has guaranteed the genre's longevity as a major force in American and international music. One of the fathers of British blues who provided a training school for the cream of Britain's blues heroes and made a major contribution with his own recordings is known as the "Blues Professor." His name is John Mayall.

Mayall was born on November 29, 1933, in Manchester, England, into a musical family. His father, a jazz musician, possessed the greatest of all treasures for a youngster with a keen interest in music like John: a healthy record collection that included noted blues names like Muddy Waters, Little Walter, Sonny Boy Williamson II, Elmore James, Willie Dixon, and many other American artists. At an early age, Mayall developed a deep respect for jazz and blues.

Although he learned to play the guitar and ukulele, any thoughts of a musical career were held in check when he joined the British army for four years. After seeing action in Korea, Mayall returned to Manchester and enrolled in the local college, where he majored in art. At this time he began to turn toward a career in music.

He had an extensive background in the blues and jazz and was a capable musician, but Mayall was in his late twenties before he assumed the responsibilities of band leader. His group, the Powerhouse Four, played blues and jazz, although neither form of music was particularly popular in England at the time. Mayall never became discouraged, even though his music was not wholly accepted by the British public. He looked ahead, a remarkable quality that he has retained throughout his long and interesting career.

Despite his unique vision, Mayall was hard pressed to keep his band together, and personnel changes occurred on a regular basis. To pay the rent, Mayall worked during the day as a graphic designer, becoming one of the best at his trade in all of England. His talents did not go to waste once he became a musician—the evidence of his abilities can be found on various album covers.

The British blues boom of the early 1960s was ignited by three men. Alexis Korner and Cyril Davies opened up the Ealing Blues Club, which featured their band, Blues Incorporated. Here many of the future stars of British rock first got their start, including the Rolling Stones, Eric Clapton, members of Cream, and a host of others. Both Korner and Davies are important founders of the British blues movement, but neither had the profound impact of John Mayall.

Mayall managed to keep the Powerhouse Four together until 1963, when he changed the band's name to the Bluesbreakers. The group released a few albums, but did not develop a large following until 1965 when Mayall featured a blossoming blues guitarist named Eric Clapton, who had just left the popular British rhythm and blues group the Yardbirds. Because of Mayall's dedication and deep musical knowledge, the Bluesbreakers were always a good band despite constant changes in the lineup; with Clapton in the mix the Bluesbreakers became something quite special.

During his stint in the Bluesbreakers, Clapton attained his status as the ultimate British guitar hero. Mayall admired him so much that he gave his guitarist co-credit on the album, which was the first time that anyone had been given that honor. Despite being accorded star status on the album jacket, Clapton was only paid the standard fee. The record *Bluesbreakers—John Mayall with Eric Clapton* was released in 1966 and became an instant classic. After Clapton left the band (taking bandmate Jack Bruce to form Cream), Mayall and the Bluesbreakers regrouped.

Another skill that Mayall has displayed throughout his career is the ability to recruit the best new blues talent on the British blues scene. Mayall recruited John McVie, guitarist Peter Green and Aynsley Dunbar on drums. They recorded *A Hard Road*, which was a fine album and showcased Green's spectacular talents. In the liner notes on this album, Mayall declared he would never add horns to the Bluesbreakers sound.

Mayall's next project was an album with Paul Butterfield, an American blues enthusiast. Mayall also recorded a solo album entitled *The Blues Alone*. After the departure of Peter Green and John McVie to form Fleetwood Mac, Mayall, despite his earlier oath added two horn players, Chris Mercer and Rip Kent, to round out the band's sound. He also added an eighteen-year-old guitarist named Mick Taylor, one of the brightest blues lights in British music at the time. The sextet recorded *Crusade*, a tribute to American bluesmen whom Mayall felt were not getting the credit they deserved.

After a couple of live albums, Mayall formed a new band of Bluesbreakers that recorded the album *Bare Wires*. It contained material solely written by Mayall himself, instead of the Chicago-styled blues he had always so feverishly covered. The album, however, was not a great financial success.

After members of the *Bare Wires* crew left to form the group Colosseum, Mayall returned to a quartet format and recorded the album *Blues from Laurel Canyon*. But the band immediately broke up with the departure of Mick Taylor, who left to join the Rolling Stones after the tragic death of guitarist Brian Jones. Mayall had taught Taylor well, for the latter heavily influenced the Stones' sound for the next five years and is one of the main factors in the band's most successful period.

Mayall, ever the experimenter, formed a band in 1969 that had no drummer. The band included John Thompson and Johnny Almond, a noted bluesman who could play a dozen instruments including the saxophone, flute, vibroharp, organ, and guitar. The band recorded a live album, *The Turning Point*, at the Fillmore East that was more jazz than blues and marked a slight change of direction for Mayall. After recording *Empty Rooms* with essentially the same lineup that had played on the previous album and also included Larry Taylor of Canned Heat fame, Mayall broke up the band.

At the beginning of the 1970s Mayall started using American musicians for the first time and recorded the album *U.S.A. Reunion*, the title reflecting his current experimental tastes at the time. Mayall continued to record through the decade and featured a female vocalist, Dee McKinnie, which was a first for him. Because he had switched to ABC Records, Mayall aptly named his 1975 album, *New Year, New Band, New Company*. In the same year he recorded a solo album, *Notice to Appear*, in New Orleans.

Mayall continued to record into the 1980s, churning out such albums as *The Bottom Line* and *No More Interviews* on DJM Records. He continues even today to feature some of the best young blues talent in his various bands and often steps back to allow them to bask in the spotlight.

Mayall's last release was entitled *Blues for the Next Day* on the Silvertone label. The CD featured the songs "All Those Heroes" and "Hip Shakin' Strut," a Big Bill Broonzy tune, as well as "Dead City," based on Blind Lemon Jefferson's "Hangman's Blues." The song deals with the social injustice of being convicted of crimes of which one is innocent. The CD also contained a rousing version of "Sensation," the Freddie King instrumental chestnut.

Mayall continues to record and perform as a tireless champion of the blues.

John Mayall is a blues star, but in many cases has been surpassed by those who took a turn in his band. Even though he possesses a great deal of talent, his experimental flair prevented him from attaining superstar status. There is also the fact that Mayall never "sold out." Despite any shortcomings, he deserves credit as one of the major forces in British blues.

Although the phrase *British blues* suggests a geographical limitation, blues in Great Britain has developed its own distinct sound. British blues are a replication of American genres, but the English have been more than just imitators. They have immersed themselves emotionally into the music, which has allowed them to gain an understanding of the secrets of the blues.

One of the greatest contributions Mayall has made to the blues is the skillful use of his innovative talents to keep the blues flame alive. How many bluesman have ever formed a band without a drummer? Mayall was never afraid to experiment and bring new ideas to blues and rock music. Beyond anyone else in blues circles in the past thirty years Mayall has proven that a musician can expand the traditional parameters of blues music without losing the essential elements that make the genre so powerful.

Another of Mayall's major contribution to the blues has been the many roles he has assumed, including that of a singer, guitarist, organist, harmonica player, record producer, songwriter, and band leader. In some ways he is the background man of the British blues scene—England's answer to American blues giant Willie Dixon—although Mayall never wrote the gems that Dixon did. But more than anything else, Mayall has been an extraordinary teacher and provided many young blues scholars with the opportunity to hone their skills at his finishing school of the blues.

A partial list of Mayall alumni includes Eric Clapton and Jack Bruce who went on to form the band Cream; John McVie, Peter Green, and Mick Fleetwood who left Mayall's band to form Fleetwood Mac; Mick Taylor, who joined the Rolling Stones in 1969 and left five years later; Aynsley Dunbar, who played with the Jeff Beck Group, Frank Zappa, and Journey; and Larry Taylor who played with the blues band Canned Heat.

The fact that Mayall himself never scored a string of number-one hits or had a run of successfully commercial albums is not a discredit to his talent. His musicianship is undisputed, although songwriting has never truly been his forte. Aside from "Room to Move," no other song in the Mayall repertoire can be considered a hit song.

In a way, Mayall did achieve the commercial success that personally eluded him through the effort of those he trained. With every hit that Clapton, Bruce, McVie, Fleetwood, Green, Taylor, Flint, and the dozens of other Mayall-trained musicians scored they were paying tribute to their teacher. His influence on thirty years of British blues earned him the nickname "father of British blues."

John Mayall is one of the great ambassadors of the blues, a role he has assumed for the past forty years. Mayall has always believed in giving more than taking and his endless personal crusade to bring to light the importance of the old bluesmen who seemed forgotten in their homeland continues even today. Despite his constant experimentation, Mayall never forgot his roots and forever defended the rights of the exploited bluesmen.

Although he never enjoyed much commercial success and some of his innovations have been questioned, Mayall remains one of the most important figures in blues history on either side of the Atlantic. What he has not been able to give to the blues himself he has done through his students. This is why John Mayall bears the distinct title of professor of the blues.

Discography

Bluesbreakers—John Mayall with Eric Clapton, London 800 086-2.
London Blues: John Mayall, 1964–1969, Deram 844 302-2.
Room to Move: John Mayall, 1969–1974, Deram 314 517 291-2.
Best of John Mayall's Bluesbreakers, Polydor 2-3006.
Last of the British Blues, MCA 716.
Blues Breakers, London PS 492 80086-2.
John Mayall Plays John Mayall, London/Decca.
The Blues Alone, London/Ace of Clubs.
A Hard Road, London/Decca.
Crusade, London/Decca.
Diary of a Band, Vol. I, London/Decca.
Diary of a Band, Vol. II, London/Decca.
Bare Wires, London/Decca.
Blues from Laurel Canyon, London/Decca.
The Turning Point, Polydor.
Empty Rooms, Polydor.
USA Reunion, Polydor.
Memories, Polydor.
Back to the Roots, Polydor.
Jazz-Blues Fusion, Polydor.
Moving On, Polydor.
Ten Years Are Gone, Polydor.
The Latest Edition, Polydor.

New Year, New Band, New Company, Blue Thumb/ABC.
Notice to Appear, ABC.
A Banquet in Blues, ABC.
Blues for the Next Day, Silvertone.
Looking Back, London/Decca.
The World of John Mayall, Decca.
The World of John Mayall, Vol. II, Decca.
Down the Line, London.
Beyond the Turning Point, Polydor.
Thru the Years, London/Decca.

Appendix: Recordings by Three or More Blues Singers

Afro-American Spirituals, Work Songs and Ballads, Archives of Folk Song, Library of Congress, L 3.

American Folk Blues Festival 1962, Brunswick 009012.

Antoine's 10th Anniversary Anthology, Antoine's (includes Buddy Guy, Otis Rush, and Albert Collins).

Antoine's 10th Anniversary Anthology, Vol. 2, Antoine's (includes Buddy Guy, Otis Rush, and Albert Collins).

Atlantic Blues Special, Atlantic P-4589-A.

Atlantic 25th Anniversary: The Blues Years, Atlantic SD2-506.

Beauty of the Blues, CBS.

Best of Chicago Blues, Vanguard.

The Best of the Blues, Vol. 1, Imperial LP 9257.

The Blues: A Real Summit Meeting, Buddah 2BDS 5144.

Blues as Big as Texas, Vol. 1, CBS.

Blues at Newport (1959–64), Vanguards.

The Blues Came Down from Memphis, Charly CD 67.

Blues Deluxe: Recorded Live at the 1980 Chicago Blues Fest (includes Muddy Waters, Koko Taylor, Willie Dixon), Alligator.

Blues in the Mississippi Night (features Memphis Slim, Big Bill Broonzy, and Sonny Boy Williamson as told to and recorded by Alan Lomax; notes by Alan Lomax), Kyhadisi RCD 90155.

Blues Is Killin' Me—Chicago Blues, 1951–1953, Flyright FLYCD 28.

Blues Piano Chicago Plus, Atlantic SD 7221.

Blues Piano Orgy, Delmark 626.

The Blues Roll On (recorded in the field by Alan Lomax assisted by Shirley Collins), Atlantic SD 1352.

Blues Shout!, Pickwick 3173.

Blues Story, Midi 68005.

Blues Story, Vol. 2, Midi 60034.

The Blues Tradition (includes Big Bill Broonzy and William Brown), Milestone 2016.

The Blues, Vol. 10: The Great Vocalists, Joker 3592.

Bluesville, Volume 1 Folk Blues, ACE CDCH 247.

Bo Diddley/Muddy Waters/Little Walter: Super Blues, Checker LPS-3008.

Boogie Woogie Rarities, 1927–43, Milestone 2009.

A Bucket of Blues, Constellation CS-6.

Central Avenue Blues, Ace of Spades 1001.

Chicago Blues Anthology, Chess 2CH 60012.

Chicago Boss Guitars (includes Otis Rush, Buddy Guy, and Magic Sam), Flyright FLYD 18.

Classic Blues Vol. 1, Bluesway BLS 6061.

Classic Blues Vol. 2, Bluesway BLS 6062.

Classic R & B Hits, Vol. 2, Minit MLS 40009.

Coffeehouse Blues, Vee-Jay VJS 1138.

Combos Blues, Albatross 8474.

Country Blues Classics, Vol. 1, Blues Classics 3BC 5.

Country Blues Classics, Vol. 2, Blues Classics 3BC 6.

Country Blues Classics, Vol. 3, Blues Classics 3BC 7.

Delta Blues (includes Charles Patton, Son House, Elmore James), Route 339.

Dirt Blues, Minit MLS 40005.

18 King Size Rhythm and Blues Hits, Columbia CS 9467.

Golden Recordings from the Historical Vaults of Vee-Jay Records, ABC ABEX 785.

The Great Bluesmen, Vol. 1, Vanguard VSD 25.

The Great Bluesmen, Vol. 2, Vanguard VSD 26.

History of Rhythm and Blues Vol. 1, Atlantic SD 8161.

History of Rhythm & Blues Vol. 2, Atlantic SD 8162.

History of Rhythm & Blues Vol. 3, Atlantic SD 8163.

History of Rhythm & Blues Vol. 4, Atlantic SD 8164.

Masters of the Delta Blues: The Friends of Charlie Patton (featuring Son House, Tommy Johnson, Willie Brown, Kid Bailey, Bertha Lee, Ishman Bracey, Louise Johnson, and Bukka White), Yazoo 2002.

Jackson Blues 1928–1938, Yazoo L 1007.

The Jazz Guitar, Joker 76-6.

The Jazz Guitar Anthology, Vol. 1, Joker 4023.

Jazz Memories of the Blues, Capitol T-20642.

Lonesome Road Blues: Fifteen Years in the Mississippi Delta (1926–1941), Yazoo L 1038.

Memphis Blues, Kent K57 9002.

Memphis Masters, ACE 50.

Mississippi Blues (1927–1941), Yazoo L 1001.

Mississippi Bottom Blues (1926–1935), Manlish S 3802.

Mississippi Moaners (1927–1942), Yazoo L 1009.

Mississippi's Blues, Vol. 1 (1927–1942), Roots RL 302.

Mississippi's Blues, Vol. 2 (1927–1940), Roots RL 303.

Mississippi's Blues, Vol. 3 (1928–1942), Roots RL 304.

Oldies But Goodies Vols. 1–10 (Vol. 2), Original Sound SR 8850-60.

Original Boogie Woogie Piano Giants, Columbia KC 32708.

Original Rhythm & Blues Hits, RCA Camden Cal 740.

Portraits in Blues Vol. 1, Storyville 154.

R & B and Boogie Woogie, Vol. 2, Swing House SWH 30.

Really Chicago Blues (includes Johnny Shines, Otis Spann, and Walter Horton), Adelphi 1005.

Ride, Daddy, Ride!, Charly CD 272.

Rock and Roll Festival, Kent K57 544.

Rock 'n' Roll Forever, Vol. 1, Atlantic (1239).

Rock 'n' Roll Solid Gold, Vol. 1, Mercury (SR 61371).

Rock 'n' Roll Souls Vol. 1, ABC 9ABCX 1953.

Rock 'n' Roll Souls Vol. 2, ABC 9ABCX 1954.

Rock 'n' Roll Souls Vol. 3, ABC 9ABCX 1955.

Rock 'n' Roll Souls Vol. 4, ABC 9ABCX 1956.

Rock 'n' Roll Souls Vol. 5, ABC 9ABCX 1957.

Rock 'n' Roll Souls Vol. 6, ABC 9ABCX 1958.

Rock 'n' Roll Souls Vol. 7, ABC 9ABCX 1959.

Rock 'n' Roll Souls Vol. 8, ABC 9ABCX 1960.

Rock 'n' Roll Souls Vol. 9, ABC 94BCX 1961.

The Roots of Rock 'n' Roll, Savoy 2221.

Roots of the Blues, New World NW 232.

Sic 'em Dogs on Me (includes Bukka White, Charley Patton, Furry Lewis, John Hurt, Ishman Bracey), Herwin 201.

Son House, Willie Brown and Others: Walking Blues, Flyright 541.

The Sound of Harlem, Vol. 3 (includes "Crazy Blues" by Mamie Smith and Her Jazz Hounds, Bessie Smith, Alberta Hunter, Clara Smith, Victoria Spivey, Monette Moore, Gertrude Saunders, Edith Wilson, Lena Wilson, Ethel Waters, and Billie Holiday), Columbia C3L 33.

Stars of the Apollo Theater (includes Bessie Smith, Mamie Smith, Ida Cox, Big Maybelle, Sarah Vaughan, Ella Fitzgerald), Columbia KG 30788.

Story of Soul, Vol. 1, Capitol 154-85330.

Story of Soul, Vol. 2, Capitol 154-85331.

Story of Soul, Vol. 3, Capitol 154-85332.

Story of the Blues, Columbia C 20008.

Super Black Blues, BluesTime 29003.

Super Black Blues, Vol. 2, BluesTime 29009.

Super Blues, Checker LPS 3008.

Texas Blues, Kent KST 9005.

Texas Country Blues, Vol. 3, Roots RL-327.

Texas Guitar, Atlantic SD 7226.

Texas Guitar from Dallas to L.A., Atlantic SD 7226.

They Sang the Blues (includes Skip James, Furry Lewis, and Robert Wilkins), Historical Records 22.

This Is How It All Began, Specialty SPS 2117.

Underground Blues, Kent KST 535.

Urban Blues, Vol. 1, Imperial LM 94002.

Volumes of the Blues, Roulette 25207 25209-19; 25238-42.

Women of the Blues, RCA Victor LPV 534.

A World of Blues, Vol. 1, Imperial LP 9210.

Selected Bibliography

There have been hundreds of books about blues published. The following list does not include everything written, but presents a sparkling variety of blues books. The range includes biographies, autobiographies, surveys of black history, the blues and the church, blues as literature, blues texts, interviews, recordings in blues, and book-record studies.

Albertson, Chris. *Bessie* (New York: Stein and Day, 1972).

Ames, Russell. *The Story of American Folk Song* (New York: Grosset & Dunlap, 1955).

Asch, Moses, and Alan Lomax. *The Leadbelly Songbooks* (New York: Oak Publications, 1962).

Baker, Houston. *Blues Ideology and Afro-American Literature: A Vernacular Theory* (Chicago: University of Chicago Press, 1984).

Barlow, William. *Look Up at Down: The Emergence of Blues Culture* (Philadelphia: Temple University Press, 1989).

Bonds, Ray, ed. *The Harmony Illustrated Encyclopedia of Rock* (New York: Harmony Books, 1981).

Bradford, Perry. *Born with the Blues* (New York: Oak Publications, 1965).

Broonzy, William. *Big Bill's Blues* (As Told to Yannick Bruynoghe) (New York: Oak Publications, 1964).

Buerkle, Jack V., and Danny Burker. *Bourbon Street Black* (Oxford: Oxford University Press, 1973).

Case, Brian, and Stan Britt. *The Illustrated Encyclopedia of Jazz* (New York: Harmony Books, 1978).

Charters, Samuel. *The Bluesmen: The Story and the Music of the Men Who Made the Blues* (New York: Oak Publications, 1967).

_____. *The Country Blues* (New York: Rinehart, 1959).

_____. *The Legacy of the Blues* (New York: Da Capo Press, 1977).

_____. *The Poetry of the Blues* (New York: Oak Publications, 1963).

_____. *Sweet as the Showers of Rain: The Bluesmen*, vol. 2 (New York: Oak Publications, 1977).

Chase, Gilbert. *America's Music* (New York: McGraw-Hill, 1955).

Clifford, Mike. *The Illustrated Encyclopedia of Black Music* (New York: Harmony Books, 1984).

Cobb, James. *The Most Southern Place on Earth: The Mississippi Delta and the Roots of Regional Identity* (Oxford: Oxford University Press, 1992).

Colt, Stephen, and Gayle Wardlory. *King of the Delta Blues: The Life and Music of Charlie Patton* (Newton, N.J.: Rock Chapel Press, 1988).

Cone, James H. *The Spirituals and the Blues: An Interpretation* (New York: Seabury Press, 1972).

Cook, Bruce. *Listen to the Blues* (New York: Scribner's, 1973).

Dance, Helen Oakley. *Stormy Monday: The T-Bone Walker Story* (Baton Rouge: Louisiana State University Press, 1987).

Dixon, Robert, and John Goodrich. *Recording the Blues* (New York: Stein and Day, 1970).

Dixon, Robert M. W., and John Goodrich. *Blues and Gospel Records: 1920–1943* (St. Clair Shores, Mich.: Scholarly Press, 1982).

Evans, David. *Big Road Blues: Tradition and Creativity in the Folk Blues* (Berkeley: University of California Press, 1982).

Fahey, John. *Charley Patton* (London: Studio Vista, 1971).

Ferris, William. *Blues from the Delta* (New York: Da Capo Press, 1978).

Finn, Julio. *The Bluesmen* (New York: Quartet, 1980).

Floyd, Samuel A., Jr. *The Power of Black Music: Interpreting Its History from Africa to the United States* (Oxford: Oxford University Press, 1995).

Garoin, Richard M., and Edmond G. Addeo. *The Midnight Special* (New York: Bernard Geis Associates, 1971).

Garron, Paul. *Blues and the Poetic Spirit* (New York: Eddison Press, 1975).

Goble, Donald. *Brown Sugar: Eighty Years of America's Black Female Superstars* (New York: Harmony Books, 1980).

Greenberg, Alan. *Love in Vain: The Life and Legend of Robert Johnson* (New York: Doubleday, 1983).

Groom, Bob. *The Blues Revival* (London: Studio Vista, 1971).

Guralnick, Peter. *Feel Like Going Home* (New York: Outerbridge and Diensfry, 1971).

_____. *The Listener's Guide to the Blues* (New York: Facts On File, 1982).

Handy, W. C. *Father of the Blues: An Autobiography* (New York: Sidgwick and Jackson, 1957).

_____, ed. *Blues: An Anthology* (New York: Collier Books, 1972).

Harris, Sheldon. *Blues Who's Who* (New York: Arlington House, 1979).

Hart, Mary L., Brenda M. Eagles, and Lisa N. Howarth. *The Blues: A Bibliographical Guide* (New York: Garland Publishing, 1989).

Herzhaft, Gerard. *Encyclopedia of the Blues* (Fayetteville: University of Arkansas Press, 1992).

Hughes, Langston. *The Weary Blues* (New York: Knopf, 1947).

Jablonski, Edward. *Howard Arlen: Happy with the Blues* (New York: Doubleday, 1961).

Jones, Leroi. *Blues People: Negro Music in White America* (Westport, Conn.: MacGibbon and Kee, 1965).

Keil, Charles. *Urban Blues* (Chicago: University of Chicago Press, 1966).

King, B. B. (with David Ritz). *Blues All Around Me: The Autobiography of B. B. King* (New York: Avon Books, 1996).

Lang, Paul Henry, ed. *One Hundred Years of Music in America* (New York: G. Schirmer, 1961).

Leadbitter, Mike. *Delta Country Blues* (Boxhill-on-Sea, Eng.: Blues Unlimited, 1968).

_____, ed. *Nothing But the Blues: An Illustrated Documentary*. (London: Hanover Books, 1971).

_____, and Neil Shaver. *Blues Records 1943–1966* (London: Hanover Books, 1968).

Lee, George W. *Beale Street, Where the Blues Began* (New York: Robert O. Pallore, 1934).

Lomax, Alan. *The Land Where the Blues Began* (New York: Pantheon Books, 1993).

Lomax, John, and Alan Lomax. *The Leadbelly Legend* (New York: Folkways Publications, 1965).

Lovell, John, Jr. *Black Song: The Forge and the Flame* (New York: Macmillan, 1972).

McHee, Margeret, and Fred Chirenhall. *Beale, Black and Blues: Life and Music of Black America's Main Street* (New Orleans: Louisiana State University Press, 1981).

Mezzrow, Mezz, and Bernard Wolfe. *Really the Blues* (New York: Doubleday, 1972).

Middleton, Richard. *Pop Music and the Blues: A Study of the Relationship and Its Significance* (New York: Gallanez, 1972).

Mitchell, George. *Blow My Blues Away* (Baton Rouge: Louisiana State University Press, 1971).

Murray, Albert. *The Hero and the Blues* (Columbia: University of Missouri Press, 1973).

_____. *Stomping the Blues* (New York: McGraw-Hill, 1976).

Oakley, Giles. *The Devil's Music: A History of the Blues* (London: BBC Books, 1983).

Obrecht, Jax. *Blues Guitar: The Men Who Made the Music* (New York: Miller Freeman, 1993).

Oliver, Paul. *Aspects of the Blues Tradition* (New York: Oak Publications, 1970).

_____. *Bessie Smith* (New York: A. S. Barnes, 1971).

_____. *The Blackwell Guide to Blues Records* (New York: Blackwell Reference, 1989).

_____. *Conversation with the Blues* (New York: Horizon, 1965).

_____. *The Meaning of the Blues* (New York: Collier, 1963).

_____. *Screening the Blues* (London: Cassell, 1968).

_____. *The Story of the Blues* (Philadelphia: Chilton, 1969).

Olsson, Bengt. *Memphis Blues and Jug Bands* (London: Studio Vista, 1970).

Oster, Harry. *Living Country Blues* (New York: Viking, 1981).

Palmer, Robert. *Deep Blues* (New York: Macmillan, 1981).

_____. *Mother of the Blues: A Study of Ma Rainey* (Boston: University of Massachusetts Press, 1983).

Ramsey, Frederick, Jr. *Been Home and Gone* (New Brunswick, N.J.: Rutgers University Press, 1960).

Roberts, John Storm. *Black Music of Two Worlds* (Westport, Conn.: Praeger, 1972).

Rolling Stone Illustrated History of Rock 'n' Roll (New York: Rolling Stone Press/Random House, 1976).

Rooney, James. *Bossmen: Bill Monroe and Muddy Waters* (New York: Dial Press, 1971).

Rowe, Mike. *Chicago Breakdown* (New York: Eddison Press, 1973).

Rublowsky, John. *Black Music in America* (New York: Basic Books, 1971).

Russell, Tony. *Blacks, Whites and Blues* (New York: Stein and Day, 1970).

Sackheim, Eric, comp. *The Blues Line: A Collection of Blues Lyrics* (New York: G. Schirmer, 1975).

Sacre, Robert, ed. *The Voice of the Delta: Charlie Patton and the Mississippi Blues, Traditions Influences and Comparisons* (Liege, Bel.: Presses Universitaires Liege, 1985).

Santelli, Robert. *Big Book of the Blues* (New York: Penguin, 1983).

Scott, Frank, et al. *The Down Home Guide to the Blues* (Pennington, N.J.: A Capella, 1991).

Scroyer, Charles. *The Arrival of B. B. King: The Authorized Biography* (New York: Doubleday, 1980).

Shapiro, Nat, and Nat Hentoff. *Hear Me Talkin' to Ya* (New York: Rinehart, 1955).

Shaw, Arnold. *Black Popular Music in America* (New York: G. Schirmer, 1986).

_____. *Honkers and Shouters: The Golden Years of Rhythm and Blues* (New York: Macmillan, 1978).

Shirley, Kay, ed. *The Book of the Blues* (New York: Crown, 1963).

Silverman, Jerry. *The Blues* (New York: Chelsea House, 1994).

Southern, Eileen. *The Music of Black Americans* (New York: Norton, 1983).

Stambler, Irwin. *Encyclopedia of Pop, Rock and Soul* (New York: St. Martin's Press, 1994).

Stewart-Baxter, Derrick. *Ma Rainey and the Classic Blues Singers* (New York: Stein and Day, 1970).

Titon, Jeff Todd. *Down Home Blues, A Musical and Cultural Analysis* (Urbana-Champaign: University of Illinois Press, 1977).

Tosches, Nick. *Unsung Heroes of Rock 'n' Roll: The Birth of Rock 'n' Roll in the Dark and Wild Years Before Elvis* (New York: Scribner's, 1984).

Walton, Ortiz M. *Music: Black, White and Blue* (New York: William Morrow, 1972).

Welding, Pete, and Toby Byron, eds. *Bluesland: Portraits of Twelve Major American Blues Masters* (New York: Penguin, 1991).

Wilson, Al. *Son House*. Collectors Classics Series (Boxhill-on-Sea, Eng.: Blues Unlimited, 1966).

Index